THE LEGACY OF
EFUA SUTHERLAND:
Pan-African Cultural Activism

THE LEGACY OF EFUA SUTHERLAND:

Pan-African Cultural Activism

Editors

Anne V. Adams and Esi Sutherland-Addy

ayebia

An Adinkra symbol meaning
Ntesie Matemasie
A symbol of knowledge and wisdom

ARTS COUNCIL
ENGLAND

Copyright © 2007 Ayebia Clarke Publishing Limited
Copyright © 2007 Introduction by Anne V. Adams and Esi Sutherland-Addy.

The Legacy of Efua Sutherland: Pan-African Cultural Activism
Editors: Anne V. Adams and Esi Sutherland-Addy.

This edition published by Ayebia Clarke Limited
7 Syringa Walk
Banbury
OX16 1FR
Oxfordshire
UK

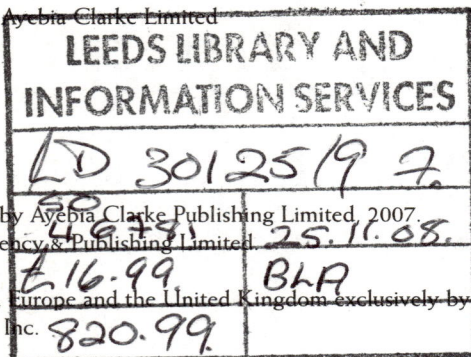

First published in the UK by Ayebia Clarke Publishing Limited, 2007.
Ayebia Clarke Literary Agency & Publishing Limited.

Distributed outside Africa, Europe and the United Kingdom exclusively by
Lynne Rienner Publishers, Inc.
1800 30th St., Ste. 314
Boulder, CO 80301
USA
www.rienner.com

Co-published in Ghana with the Centre for Intellectual Renewal
56 Ringway Estate, Osu, Accra, Ghana.
www.cir.com

British Library Cataloguing-in-Publication Data
A catalogue record of this book is available from the British Library.

Cover design by Amanda Carroll at Millipedia
Cover photographs courtesy of The Efua T. Sutherland Estate
Photographs © Willis E. Bell
Picture research by Amanda Carroll and Nana Ayebia Clarke

Typeset by FiSH Books, Enfield, Middlesex, UK.
Printed and bound in Great Britain by Mackays of Chatham, Chatham, Kent.

The publisher wishes to acknowledge the help of Arts Council Funding.

ISBN 978-0-9547023-1-1

Available from www.ayebia.co.uk or email info@ayebia.co.uk
Distributed in Africa, Europe & the UK by TURNAROUND at www.turnaround-uk.com

CONTENTS

Part III. Reminiscences And Tributes

ACKNOWLEDGEMENTS

The editors wish to thank all the contributors for the profound offerings they have so generously made to this volume. Your support and incredible patience have also served as a source of strength in what proved to be a lengthy period of gestation.

However, Nana Ayebia, our Publisher is the one who turned our aspirations into a definite reality by enthusiastically offering to be our Publisher. We salute her for her kind dedication and firm professionalism.

The Publisher would like to thank the following – without whose commitment and dedication this volume would not be where it is today: Bruce Clarke for his close reading and careful checking of the text, Kwadwo Osei-Nyame Jnr, for his unwavering encouragement and editorial work, Margaret Busby, OBE for her support and sterling work on the text and Index. Amanda Carroll – our designer for her usual flair and invaluable suggestions for the cover. To David and Kweku Clarke for their continuing support and guidance.

BIOGRAPHIES OF CONTRIBUTORS

ANNE V. ADAMS was a Professor of African/Diaspora Literatures at Kent State and Cornell Universities, in the United States, before retiring to assume the directorship of the W. E. B. Du Bois Memorial Centre for Pan-African Culture, in Ghana. During her academic career she had visiting appointments at universities in Congo-Brazzaville, Ghana, and Germany. She has served as President of the African Literature Association. Her research and publications focus on gender in African/Diaspora literatures (*Ngambika: Studies of Women in African Literature*, co-edited with Carole Boyce Davies) as well as Afro-German cultural studies, which include translations of works from German (*Showing Our Colours: Afro-German Women Speak Out* by Oguntoye, Opitz, Schultz; and *Blues in Black and White* by the Ghanaian-German May Ayim). She is consultant for the German publications of Toni Morrison's works.

AMA ATA AIDOO is a Ghanaian poet, playwright, short story writer, and novelist, as well as a university teacher, and consultant on education and gender issues. She is currently Visiting Professor at the Africana Studies Department, Brown University, USA, and the Executive Director of MBAASEM—an African women writers' foundation based in Accra, Ghana. In 2002, her play *Anowa* was listed as one of '100 Best Books Published in Africa in the 20th Century'. Ama Ata Aidoo's other published works include *Our Sister Killjoy* and *Changes* [novels], and *An Angry Letter in January* [poetry]. Prizes and awards Aidoo has received include three in 2005: Woman of Substance Award from the African Women's Development Fund; the Millennium Award for Literary Excellence from the Millennium Excellence Awards Foundation of Ghana, and was co-named for the Aidoo-Snyder Book Prize by the Women's Caucus of the African Literature Association. In 1999, the state of Ghana honoured her with The Companion of the Star of the Volta, and Mount Holyoke College awarded her an honorary doctoral degree in Humane Letters.

MAYA ANGELOU is hailed as one of the great voices of contemporary American literature and as a remarkable Renaissance woman. Poet, educator, historian, best-selling author, actress, playwright, civil-rights activist, producer and director, Angelou is best known for the autobiographical writings *I Know Why the Caged Bird Sings* (1969) and *All God's Children Need Traveling Shoes* (1986). This latter work narrates the period of her life spent in Ghana, and chronicles her friendship with Efua Sutherland. Her volume of poetry, *Just Give Me a Cool Drink of Water 'Fore I Die* (1971) was nominated for the Pulitzer Prize. Since 1981 she has held a lifetime appointment as Reynolds Professor of American Studies at Wake Forest University.

KOFI ANYIDOHO is currently Professor of Literature in the Department of English and Director of the CODESRIA African Humanities Institute Programme at the University of Ghana, Legon, where he also served for over six years as Acting Director of the School of Performing Arts. His published works include seven collections of poetry, two of which are CD recordings of his poetry in Ewe, his mother tongue. As a literary scholar, Anyidoho has published numerous journal articles and book chapters, and has edited a number of major books on African literature. He is a past President of the African Literature Association [1998-99].

SANDY ARKHURST is a retired Senior Lecturer in Drama and Theatre at the University of Ghana. Having been mentored for several years by Efua Sutherland, his studies and teaching have been premised on his belief in theatre as a communal art form. Arkhurst introduced Theatre for Development in Ghana and was part of the 'Drama in Education Movement' in the country. He has taught in Ghana and Nigeria and has directed several major theatre productions in these two countries as well as the USA.

WILLIAM BRANCH (actor, playwright, educator, screenwriter and producer in the United States) first met Efua Sutherland when he was invited to participate in a summer seminar at the University of Ghana in 1963. Thereafter, the two continued their friendship over the years, and when Branch published *Crosswinds: An Anthology of Black Dramatists in the Diaspora* (1993), Sutherland's drama *Edufa* was one of the first he sought for inclusion. Branch's best known works include *A Medal for Willie*, *In Splendid Error*, *Baccalaureate*, and *A Wreath for Udomo*, the latter based upon the Peter Abrahams novel. He has been a Professor at the University of Maryland Baltimore County, a visiting scholar at many colleges and universities. In addition to *Crosswinds*, *African American Drama* (1992), he is the author of numerous articles and reports for *The New York Times*, *The New York Amsterdam Review*, *The New York Post*, and other publications. Among other honours, William Branch has been a Guggenheim Fellow, an Emmy nominee, and an American Book Award recipient.

MARGARET BUSBY of Ghana, as a young university graduate in the 1960s, co-founded the publishing house Allison & Busby Ltd., of which she was editorial director for 20 years. A&B's list included international fiction, non-fiction, poetry and children's books. She was subsequently Editorial Director of Earthscan Publications. She works as a writer, editor, critic, consultant and broadcaster, and has been a judge for many literary awards, including the Orange Award for New

Writers, the Independent Foreign Fiction Prize and the Caine Prize for African Writing. She is the editor of *Daughters of Africa: An International Anthology of Words and Writing by Women of African Descent* (1992), has contributed to many national and international publications and has written drama for radio and for the stage (notably *Yaa Asantewaa—Warrior Queen*, which was presented in the UK and Ghana during 2001 and 2002). Honours she has received include a Society of Young Publishers Award (1970), the Pandora Award from Women in Publishing (1993), the Write Thing's Excelle Lifetime Achievement Award (1997), an honorary doctorate from the Open University for services to the Arts (2004), and an OBE for services to Literature and to Publishing (2006).

JOHN COLLINS has been active in the Ghanaian/West African music scene since 1969 as a guitarist, band leader, music union activist, journalist and writer. He began teaching at the Music Department of the University of Ghana in 1995, obtained a full Professorship there in 2002 and in 2003-5 was Head of Department. He is currently Chairman of the BAPMAF African music archives NGO, a consultant for several Ghana music unions and co-leader of the Local Dimension highlife band.

DAVID DONKOR is Assistant Professor of Performance and Africana Studies at Texas A&M University. As a doctoral student in Performance Studies at Northwestern University he held the Gwendolyn Carter Fellowship in African Studies. Before pursuing graduate studies in the United States, Donkor worked as a correspondent for 'Solid Black' on Ghana national radio, and also as an actor with the resident theatre company of the University of Ghana. In 1992 he received an Entertainment Critics and Reviewers Association of Ghana (ECRAG) acting award for his role in the film 'Shoeshine Boy'.

JAMES GIBBS has, since 1968, taught drama and literature in English at the Universities of Ghana, Malawi, Ibadan, and Liège, and he is currently a Senior Lecturer at the University of the West of England (Bristol). Among his publications are *The African Writers' Handbook* (edited with Jack Mapanje, 1999) and *FonTomFrom: Contemporary Ghanaian Literature, Theatre and Film* (edited with Kofi Anyidoho, 2000). Short publications during the last few years include articles on Ghanaian dramatists (Ben-Abdallah, Asare, Marshall, Mawugbe, Sutherland), on Nigerian writers (Osofisan, Saro-Wiwa, Soyinka) and on British theatre activists/writers (Banham, Dickson, Littlewood). Gibbs is reviews editor for *African Literature Today* and during the last few years his own reviews have appeared in *Africa Today, Position* (Lagos), *Leeds Bulletin of African Studies, Research in African Literatures* and *World Literature Today*. With Martin Banham and Femi Osofisan, he edits James Currey's African Theatre series, and he has edited the seventh title in the series: *African Theatre: Companies* (due 2008).

COMFORT CAULLEY HANSON is a retired Ghanaian senior civil servant and currently manages the Bennet Caulley Memorial School in Accra, Ghana. After teaching in the 1960s she entered the civil service as a Regional Manager in Ghana's Centre for Civic Education. Having served as a Family Planning Education Officer, she was appointed Secretary to the Committee on the International Year and later became the Founding Executive Secretary of Ghana National Commission on Children.

BIODUN JEYIFO is Professor of African and African-American Studies at Harvard University. He taught at his alma mater, the University of Ibadan, and at the University of Ife, and at Oberlin College before going to Cornell in 1988 where, as Professor of English and later Associate Chair of the English Department, he taught for eighteen years. At Cornell, together with a few colleagues, he pioneered the expansion of the curriculum of English studies at both the undergraduate and graduate levels to include the so-called 'Anglophone' literatures of Africa, the Caribbean, South Asia and other parts of the developing world. Professor Jeyifo has worked on the complex connections between literature, critical theory, humanities scholarship and twentieth-century progressive social philosophy. He has travelled and lectured extensively in the United States and Canada, and in Africa, Europe, the Caribbean and South Asia and has published extensively in the fields of drama, African and Caribbean literatures, and comparative postcolonial Anglophone studies. His most recent book-length publication is *Wole Soyinka: Politics, Poetics, and Postcolonialism.*

ROBERT W. JULY, South African, is Professor Emeritus of History at Hunter College and Graduate Centre, The City University of New York. He has previously taught at the University of Ibadan, Nigeria, and Kenyatta University, Kenya. He is author of *The Origins of Modern African Thought: Its Development in West Africa during the Nineteenth and Twentieth Centuries* (1967, 2004); *A History of the African People* (1970); *Precolonial Africa: An Economic and Social History* (1975); and *The African Voice: The Role of the Humanities in African Independence* (1987).

MABEL MLIWOMOR KOMASI is a Lecturer in the Department of English, University of Ghana, Legon where she teaches courses in Children's Literature, Women's Literature and Romanticism. Her research interests include Ghanaian Children's Literature, Women's Literature and Ewe Oral Literature. She has recently published a Bibliography of Ghanaian Children's Story books in English.

FLORENCE LAAST (Nelson) is a retired teacher who served for many years in the Ghanaian school system. As leaders in the community of the Catholic

Church in Ghana, she and her late husband, Willy Laast, helped to establish church congregations and institutions. She founded Saint Martin de Porres School, one of the most highly regarded primary and junior high school complexes in Ghana.

JOHN LEMLY, Professor of English and African Studies at Mount Holyoke College (Massachusetts), has headed the Five College African Scholars' Programme (post-doctoral fellowships to African lecturers), taught at the University of Ghana and the University of Fort Hare (South Africa). His publications include studies of Ama Ata Aidoo, Wole Soyinka, Nadine Gordimer, and Chris Abani.

JÜRGEN MARTINI teaches English Literature and Cultural Studies at the Otto-von-Guericke University in Magdeburg. He has previously taught at the universities of Bremen and Bayreuth. His main interests are the New Literatures in English, Children's Literature and Cultural Studies. Together with Helmi Martini-Honus, he has translated into German a number of novels and children's books from Africa, the Philippines and Aotearoa (New Zealand).

MICHAEL MCMULLAN was a Colonial Service officer in the Gold Coast during the 1950s. He left Ghana in 1960 to pursue a legal career in England. After appointment to the Bench, he became Resident Judge at Wood Green in London.

PENINA MLAMA has just completed a term as Executive Director of the Forum for African Women Educationalists (FAWE), widely recognised across Africa for its leadership, especially in the field of girls' education, with operations in more than thirty countries. A Tanzanian, Dr. Mlama was formerly Chief Academic Officer and Deputy Vice Chancellor of the University of Dar es Salaam.

FEMI OSOFISAN is a Professor of Drama at the University of Ibadan, and one-time General Manager/Chief Executive of the National Theatre, Lagos. In the tradition of activist intellectuals all over the world, Osofisan wears many hats as playwright and theatre director, poet and novelist, critic and theorist of literature, composer and translator, scholar and journalist. He has over two dozen plays in print, plus four novellas, five volumes of poetry, three books of published essays, five edited books; several monographs and essays in learned journals; as well as three books of translation. Among many others, Osofisan has been honoured with the French National Order of Merit Award (1991); the Nigerian National Order of Merit Award—the highest in Nigerian academia (2004), and the Fonlon-Nichols Prize (2006). Osofisan is a former President of the Association of Nigerian Authors (ANA); and the current President of International PEN, Nigeria Chapter.

SANDRA L. RICHARDS is Professor of African-American Studies and Theatre with a courtesy appointment in Performance Studies at Northwestern University. She has taught courses on African-American, African, American drama, and black feminist theories and directed plays at Stanford University, San Francisco State, Northwestern University, and the University of Benin (Nigeria), where she was a Fulbright lecturer from 1983 to 1985. She has published numerous articles on African-American and Nigerian dramatists and is the author of *Ancient Songs Set Ablaze: The Theatre of Femi Osofisan* (Howard University Press 1996). From 2001-2004, she held the Leon Forrest Professorship of African-American Studies that supported ongoing research on issues of cultural tourism to slave sites throughout the Black Atlantic.

AMOWI SUTHERLAND PHILLIPS is an Attorney at Law and an Adjunct Instructor in the Departments of Politics and History, Literature and Modern Languages at Whitworth College in Spokane, USA. She is a board member and international representative of Mmofra Foundation, Ghana, and has collaborated in the design and production of two children's audio books based on the writings of Efua Sutherland.

OLA ROTIMI, Nigerian dramatist, was founder of the Department of Dramatic Arts at Obafemi Awolowo University. His plays, noted for their political satire, include *The Gods Are Not To Blame* and *Hopes of the Living Dead*, which are among the best known and most widely performed of all Nigerian plays. The article in the present volume was included in *Issues in African Theatre*, the last book he edited before his death, in 2000, and which was published, in 2003, by colleagues of his department.

ESI SUTHERLAND-ADDY is Senior Research Fellow, Head of the Language, Literature, and Drama Section, Institute of African Studies, and Associate Director of the African Humanties Institute Programme at the University of Ghana. She has held visiting lecturerships at Manchester University, University of Indiana, University of Birmingham, and L'Institut des Hautes Etudes en Sciences Sociales, Paris. In addition she has held portfolios as Deputy Minister for Higher Education and Culture and Tourism of Ghana; has conducted studies for the governments of Ghana, Namibia, and Ethiopia and UNESCO, UNICEF and The Commonwealth. She has acted as Rapporteur General at several world conferences on education and serves on several boards and commissions and is a member of FAWE and ALA. Sutherland-Addy has published widely on African theatre, film, and music; mythology; and the role of women in African culture and society. She is co-editor of *Women Writing Africa: West Africa and the Sahel* published by the Feminist Press at CUNY. She was awarded an honorary doctorate by the University College of Education at Winneba in September 2004.

MARGARET (PEGGY) WATTS has published poetry in a number of literary journals, particularly *The Caribbean Writer*. She is Editor of *Washerwoman Hangs her Poems in the Sun: Poem by Women of Trinidad and Tobago*. She teaches at the Tampa Florida campus of Springfield College. 'Auntie Efua' was her mentor during the 18 years she and her family lived in Ghana; Efua fed her palmnut soup after the birth of her daughter, and organised the outdooring of Rachel Gyasiwa Nana Adjoa, who read her mother's poem at the memorial for Efua in New York.

HENRY NII-ADZIRI WELLINGTON is a Ghanaian architectural scholar and a practitioner. From 1972 to 2006 he taught Architecture, Urban Design and Settlement Planning at the Kwame Nkrumah University of Science and Technology (KNUST), Ghana. It was during his involvement with community-oriented research and development programmes with his students at the KNUST that he came into contact with Efua T. Sutherland. Wellington has retired from the KNUST to start a new school of Architecture at a private University in Accra. He is currently engaged with research issues in Heritage Studies.

VIVIAN O. WINDLEY is Professor Emerita at The City College of New York, where she specialised in teacher education for children. She gained national recognition as Director of the TTT Project (Training Teachers of Teachers), a programme based in Harlem schools which utilised the expertise of the liberal arts and education faculty in an interdisciplinary approach to teacher education. It was cited by the United States Office of Education as 'one of the most innovative teacher education programmes in the country'. She was senior co-author of the 1971 and 1976 editions of the Houghton Mifflin Middle Grades Reading Programme as well as consultant for Children's Educational Television. She is the author of *Environment and a People's View* and editor of *Building on the Strengths of Children*. Her travels and interest in Ghana have generated several projects of major support for schools and libraries, including the children's park-library complexes founded by Efua Sutherland. She has been a guest lecturer at the University of Ghana, Legon, and for the Ghana Broadcasting Corporation.

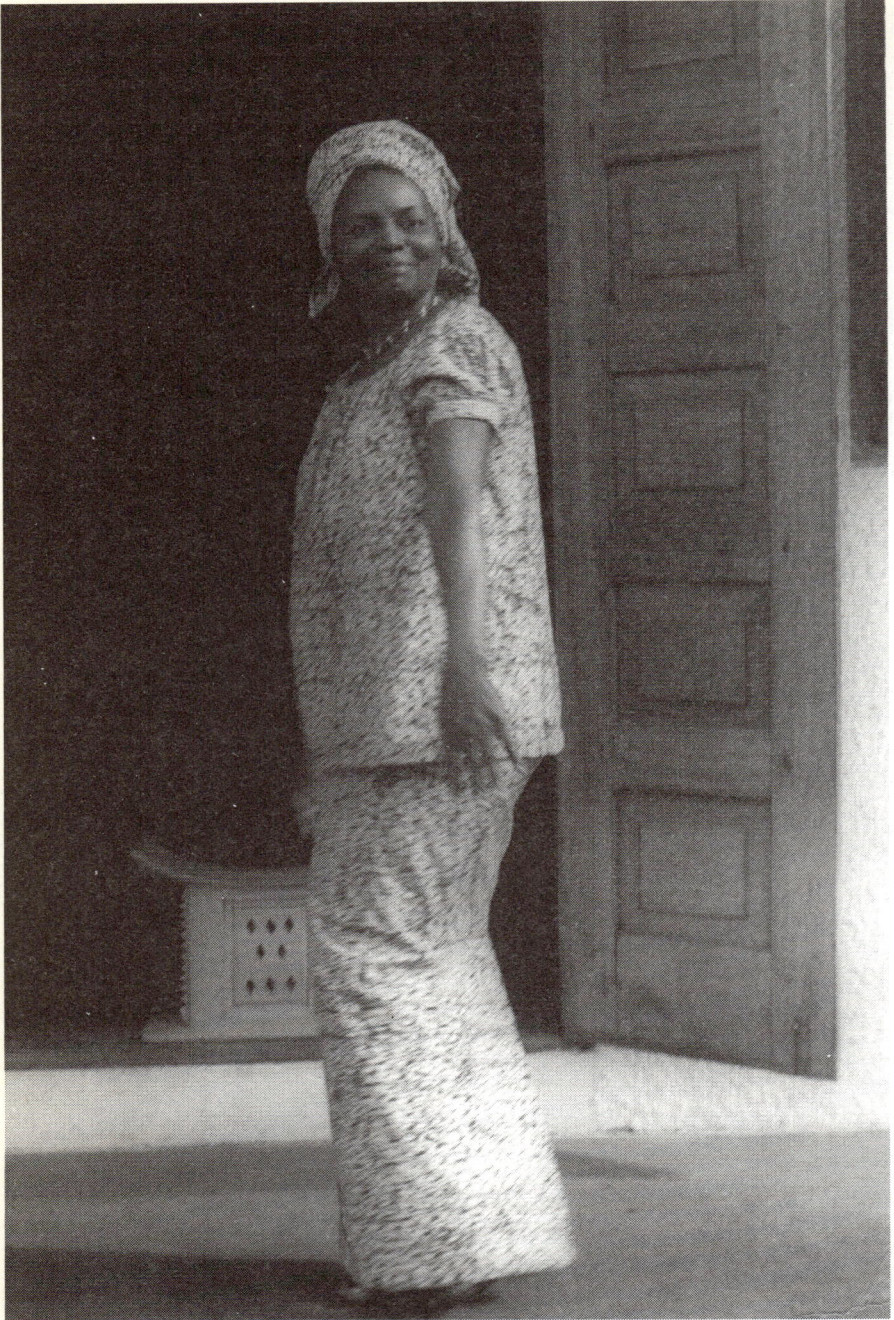

*Efua Sutherland in a playful pose in the doorway of her home "Araba Mansa" in Accra,
Circa 1985. Copyright of photo © Willis E. Bell*

PREFACE

Early in the 1950s, Efua Sutherland arrived at a moment of clarity concerning her creative directions, stating succinctly from her teaching post in Asante-Mampong to a friend: "I think it best to go and find some soil more ready to nurture the sort of development for which I am fashioned." As one of the three children literally mothered in this period along with our figurative artistic and institutional siblings, those words are for me a prescient imagining of the actual physical environments that our mother went on to create and cultivate with purposeful, intentional care, resulting in an impact of no small significance on the intellectual and cultural landscape of her era.

By 1965, visitors to our home would be frequently unprepared but delighted to find themselves in a tree-filled and meticulously kept compound named for her grandmother *Araba Mansa*, incongruously situated on the immediate outskirts of Accra. Here, we experienced an unusual and quite magical childhood inseparable from the exuberant independence-era energies which also produced her own creative writing and launched her life-work in the theatre and literature development movements.

Araba Mansa was but one manifestation of Efua's unified concept of living and performance spaces. Its principal buildings, including the simple lines and red tiled roof of the family house and the nearby writing studio, were conscious models of the traditional courtyards in indigenous architecture, mirrored in her professional work by the Drama Studio for experimental theatre in the centre of Accra, and further evolved in the *Atwia Kodzidan* or Storytelling house in later years. In her own words, the venue of traditional African theatre was not a purpose-built structure, but the courtyard in the Ghanaian home or the area beneath a communal shade tree. In these familiar settings many of life's dramas were customarily played out, and the concept could readily be adapted to spatial considerations in the development of a modern theatre culture.

Certainly, the celebratory rituals established and repeated over time, which attended the seasons of our lives at *Araba*, underscored this and set us apart, occasionally with excruciating self-consciousness for us children, from average urban middle-class Ghanaian families. At Christmas, for example, a large hut constructed just outside the house from fresh palm fronds and decorated with tinsel and flowers in the traditional style would become the hub of social life until the New Year, and an outdoor bonfire would remain alight more or less for the duration as well. The theatrical opportunities offered in this setting were obvious: a tradition evolved in which all the children gathered would proceed with lighted candles and song to light sparklers around the bonfire. Nana

Okoampah—the female chief of Atwia village whose formal association with Efua Sutherland as a cultural resource had developed into a personal friendship—was frequently present to preside with remarkable eloquence over formal family occasions.

The house was a setting no less deserving of attention to detail in our mother's mind than a playwright's stage instructions, and aspects of its design did evoke a stage, particularly within the round space of the courtyard. We first heard full-throated renditions of Negro spirituals here from Maya Angelou. At times the roof literally reverberated with explosive shouts of laughter especially when the likes of the musicologist Nana Kwabena Nketia, and the poet Kwesi Brew or the historian Adu Boahen were present.

In the 1960s, the legendary American folk-singer and social activist Pete Seeger, who was performing at the Drama Studio, was persuaded by her to play a few of his songs privately for two of us in our courtyard because we were laid up with measles and could not leave home. There were other occasions on which international performers would use our courtyard and grounds to limber up their vocal chords or otherwise ready themselves prior to going on stage. Many birthdays and anniversaries, significant arrivals and departures were celebrated, not with material fanfare, but with meticulous attention to aesthetics—freshly mowed grass, pots of arranged fresh flowers and gleaming waxed wooden floors. With her bearing, her natural elegance and the artistry in her dressing, she could not have been unconscious of how well the house framed her personality. The effect, even on those of us who lived with her, was powerful and indelible. For visitors, experiencing the house in its stark simple elegance with her in it could be and often was, completely captivating.

Araba was turned into a natural haven, from its extensive plantings of familiar and exotic trees and bushes from all over Ghana, to the orchard of varied fruit trees from which visitors came to expect hand-squeezed refreshments in preference to the bottled carbonated alternatives served everywhere else. Every plant and tree was deliberately positioned for utility, aesthetics or effect, encouraged with painstaking care to develop a personality of its own. The compound was home to a profusion of birds, which she loved and myriad other creatures including snakes which she could not abide. Above all, it was meticulously managed under her personal supervision or delegated with sensitivity so that we never really felt disadvantaged in relation to her professional work—we could roam freely and discover endless opportunities for play.

We children surmised very early the necessity for our mother to remove herself daily, with her usual support staff of a typist and an assistant, to a separate creative space in her writing studio; an understanding which was often manifested in the breach rather than in the observance, for the Studio's thatched roof and stone-paved entrance way fascinated and beckoned – it was only a minute's excited scamper from the main house. Within its rounded whitewashed walls were contained critical archives and an extensive library of books by Pan-African and world renowned writers. Quite often those same writers—Wole Soyinka, Chinua Achebe, Ama Ata Aidoo, amongst many others—would be present in person. The Studio building also housed the photographic studio of Willis Bell, a close friend who collaborated extensively with Efua in the photographic and architectural components of her work.

There was always a rather joyful carry-over of creative work into the home, so that we were all familiar with the evolutionary pathways of the songs or verses which survived to be included in her plays and those which failed the final cut. If she had been particularly exhilarated on a research trip to a festival or at a theatre workshop, the recordings would be played and replayed at home. Perhaps it was these that reinforced my memories of research journeys taken across Ghana with my mother from the Volta Lake through the Krobo Hills to the marshy lagoons of Keta. In each location, regardless of which part of Ghana we visited, she was afforded an extraordinary level of hospitality and access which, in retrospect, attested both to her own highly professional preparations and to the respect and enthusiasm she showed to those she believed were her expert sources.

In my child's mind, the home studio and the Drama studio stood at either end of a continuum of creative worlds. The low and unique profile of the latter, in downtown Accra, was a statement of courage in itself, dwarfed by the landmark Ambassador Hotel on one side and vulnerable to the encroachment of government office complexes on the other. It seemed to be an upstart institution that would bide its time by day, coming alive at night on performance evenings, many of which I spent in the back row of the open-air theatre to which Efua would retreat unobtrusively to observe the stage action, seeming to be as interested in the audience response as in the play itself.

There were other ways in which we were generally folded into her work—sometimes being given acting and speaking parts in the projects involving children, or accompanying her to the market on costume fabric shopping sprees. As we grew older, there were more serious consultations to solicit our evolving views and those of our circle of young adult friends, many of whom considered themselves sons and daughters of the family. Ralph became a valuable collaborator in book illustration, set design, architecture and landscaping. I advised on matters of legal import, and Esi specialised in professional interests in literature and African studies most closely associated with our mother's work.

During the years of her close association with Atwia village as a research project, we were frequently taken along and encouraged to engage in the life of the village. The day of the annual *Ayerye* festival was always particularly exciting. We would arrive in Atwia early in the morning to find the chief, Nana

Okoampah, presiding over the *abenfie* courtyard full of women preparing food for the expected guests. As the day progressed we would be privy to the full range of consultations on the life of the village, ranging from the provision of potable water and infant vaccinations to school programmes and dispute resolutions. The climax of the day would be Nana's resplendent procession from the *abenfie* to the *Kodzidan* in a positive affirmation of Efua Sutherland's vision for that structure as a multiple-use community space.

In addition to being a gathering place for fellow writers, *Araba Mansa*, for three decades, bestowed its unique inspirational and restorative gifts on a selective and varied group of people from all walks of life and from many different countries. She mentored many young people and welcomed them with unstinting generosity to *Araba*. At times, sheer fun, superior cuisine and boisterous, sparkling conversation were the sole objectives and in this our mother excelled. Her legendary cooking, though ambrosial, was hardly ever served in a timely fashion; yet no dinner guest regretted the wait, charmed as they were by their hostess and rendered mellow by cold beers, fresh juices or the occasional freshly home-tapped pot of palm wine. Often, her guests sat outside on the back verandah or on the outdoor patio in full view of the charcoal brasiers over which meats sizzled and pots of delicious soups simmered. For some of her carefully selected circle of friends in leadership positions in the worlds of business, finance, politics and international affairs, their experiences at *Araba* recalled the more bucolic past of their younger days and were for them a necessary antidote to the pressures occasioned by their urban successes.

Through her constant efforts, *Araba Mansa* did become the nurturing soil she determined to find and it came to acquire an almost spiritual significance. Above all, it was her place of grounding, her refuge and her muse. Whenever possible, she maintained Fridays as days of contemplation and selective exertion. At such times she would walk the grounds, explaining to those of us closest to her, her ambitious vision for a child-centred foundation dedicated to the holistic cultural development of children in Ghana. She intended that a portion of *Araba Mansa* be licensed to her Foundation for this purpose and for years in advance had been putting a landscaping plan in place.

Efua did not live to see this plan fulfilled, though she lobbied extensively for its objectives and was able to establish the legal framework for the Mmofra (Children's) Foundation and preside over its initial Board meetings. In the ten years now of the Foundation's active operation, a hands-on Board whose original membership was personally endorsed by ETS has put many of her ideas into practice in a close community context with funding that is substantially local. Neighbouring schools and children have been the primary early beneficiaries of Mmofra Foundation programmes, which to date include interaction with globally recognised writers, performers, artists and personalities, specialised workshops in image rendition and photograph archiving, the development of a library of world-class literature for children, of health education material for youth and a growing inventory of children's audio-visual products such as the DVD of Sutherland's children's play *Ananse and the Dwarf Brigade*, and book and audio CD versions of the play *Tahinta!* and the folk tale *Voice in the Forest*.

For those most closely associated with this work, the successes and achievements so far are attributable in no small measure to an extraordinary and deep fund of goodwill for Efua Sutherland herself, which survives her physical absence. Numerous people, particularly in the Arts, who would ordinarily command fees and arrangements far beyond the means of the Foundation have given of their time and talents, and indeed continue to do so unstintingly, on the strength of Sutherland's name and reputation alone. There is every reason to hope for a future in which her legacy lives on in the cultural capital of African institutions and enriches the lives of children everywhere.

Amowi Sutherland Phillips
January 2007

INTRODUCTION

I pray you, my dear Mr. Nkrumah, to use all your power to put a Pan-Africa along these lines into working order at the earliest possible date. Seek to save the great cultural past of the Ashanti and Fanti people, not by inner division but by cultural and economic expansion toward the outmost bounds of the great African peoples, so that they may be free to live, grow, and expand.

W. E. B. Du Bois[1]

OUR TASK

Ways and Means of putting talent to work
meaningfully and effectively —
Midwifery processes
Celebration processes
in a situation where the economic battle
leaves other hungers neglected.

Efua Theodora Sutherland[2]

As this book is being finalised, we are in the process of Ghana's celebration of its fiftieth anniversary of Independence. *Ghana@50* is generating various expressions – public and private – of pride, praise, and optimism, as well as of embarrassment, criticism, and cynicism. In other words, Ghana, at fifty, is psychologically healthy. Much is being touted, during this Golden Jubilee, of the material and social progress Ghana has achieved in its half-century of self-government. By the same token this anniversary of political Independence is the occasion for sober reflection on the meaning(s) of Independence itself, particularly when considered through lenses of social, economic and cultural self-determination.

If there is one point in the contemplation of Ghana's Independence that has become axiomatic, it is the assumption/acknowledgement of an abiding Pan-African symbiosis. When the President of the newly independent Ghana stated, 'The independence of Ghana is meaningless unless it is linked up with the total liberation of the African continent', he was indeed speaking of Ghana, the nation-state. But, as his leadership would prove, Kwame Nkrumah's statement was equally an articulation of a theory of an Africa of globalised parameters, which had been operating over generations of Pan-African writing and activism, from E. W. Blyden to W. E. B. Du Bois to Amy Jacques Garvey.

What, in the end, is being celebrated? *What*, in a supra-political sense, *is Ghana*? These questions take on real significance in an era characterised by phenomena such as cultivation of ethnic-heritage cultural policy alongside the imperative of nation-over-ethnicity political consciousness; a Ministry of Chieftaincy and Culture alongside a Ministry for Tourism and Diasporan Relations; the popular music invention 'hip-life', the obvious adaptation of Diasporan hip-hop to Ghana's signature high-life music; socio-cultural debates over national languages in education and over a traditional-wear-Fridays campaign alongside a Presidential grey suit for Jubilee Day; 'Eat Ghana rice' billboards alongside 'Buy American rice' billboards; and such sources of international, continental and regional pride as Ghana's leadership in the United Nations (UN), African Union (AU), Economic Community of West African States (ECOWAS), and the New Partnership for Africa's Development (NEPAD) alongside the popular commentary on HIPC[3] toilets. The symbolism of these characteristics of contemporary Ghanaian life assumes an identification of a Ghana that operates in local, regional, African, and Pan-African spheres while simultaneously struggling to chart a course within the global community.

Now, after fifty years of Independence, the evolution of Ghana can be productively analysed, from a profusion of theoretical perspectives on 'the nation' in its various manifestations. Theories of modernism, post-modernism, post-colonialism, hybridity, and globalisation have been given Africa/ Diaspora-specific focus, particularly with regard to culture, in, for example, Paul Gilroy's 'Black Atlantic', Kwame Anthony Appiah's 'Cosmopolitanism', Nana Wilson-Tagoe's 'Space-Culture-Nation-Home-Narrative', or Stuart Hall's 'Transnationalism'.[4] All of these theoretical approaches help to illuminate the complexities of Ghanaian self-definition, for the nation and for its people, as both negotiate the 21st century.

As one of the hallmarks of his leadership as the first President, Kwame Nkrumah established an Institute for African Studies at the University of Ghana, in 1963. In articulating the mission of the new Institute Nkrumah was, in a manner of speaking, transmitting the charge from his mentor, as quoted in the Du Bois epigraph above. Regarding the task of the humanities and arts Nkrumah issued specific objectives:

In studying the arts, however, you must not be content with the accumulation of knowledge about the arts. Your researches must stimulate creative activity; they must contribute to the development of the arts in Ghana and in other parts of Africa; they must stimulate the birth of a specifically African literature, which, exploring African themes and the depth of the African soul, will become an integral portion of a general world literature. It would be wrong to make this a mere appendage of world literature ...

In this way, the Institute can *serve the needs of the people by helping to develop new forms of dance and drama, of music and creative writing, that are at the same time closely related to our Ghanaian traditions and express the ideas and aspirations of our people at this critical stage in our history. This should lead to new strides in our cultural development* (emphasis added).[5]

Even though 'this critical stage in [Ghana's] history' refers to the moment of Independence fifty years ago, surely that visionary statement by Nkrumah could just as well refer to the point in time where we now stand: nearing the end of the first decade of the 21st century! Could not Nkrumah today experience the following scenario: overhearing a conversation in the Nzema language on a cellphone (whose Akan name *me gyina abonten na me rekasa yi* means 'I'm standing outside, talking') spoken by a man in a sombre Kente cloth getting out of his 4-wheel drive vehicle on his way to his father's funeral at which he will perform a traditional dance – a funeral for which his bereaved family, however, has gone proudly into debt? Such a scenario incorporating globalised trappings into specifically Ghanaian cultural phenomena illustrates the dynamics of contemporary life of the 21st century Ghanaian.

The question is sometimes raised, whether Africans, in their pursuit of the materials of 21st century progress, are risking mortgaging their cultural inheritance? Theories like 'cosmopolitan contamination' and 'Black Atlantic' are challenging us to critically engage notions of 'specifically African literature', 'African themes', even 'our people'. Adapting that cultural inheritance to the job of self-defining development is the work of cultural activism. It was precisely such work that characterised and consumed Efua Theodora Sutherland, inspired by a notion of 're-constructing Africa as a liberating concept and a nourishing reality'.[6]

A Research Fellow at the Institute of African Studies, and subsequently awarded an honorary Ph.D. by the University of Ghana, Efua Sutherland's life's work was a model for the mission of the Institute, as articulated by Nkrumah at its inauguration. Sutherland's 'brand' of intellectual and practical cultural synergy can be summed up with the phrase 'theory and praxis of cultural activism'. Hence, to identify her as a 'Ghanaian playwright' is reductive, as is 'Ghanaian folklorist' or 'Ghanaian children's author'. While theatre, oral traditions, and children's literature are indeed the genres in which she wrote, those creative works were products of theories on the adaptation of oral performance culture, Ghanaian languages, and other indigenous material into stage production; or experiments in the adaptation of children's games, songs, and other play 'texts' into educational materials. These theories, experiments, and studies, became, in turn, the bases from which she founded or helped to found institutions and organs for the dissemination, perpetuation, and application of the cultural capital, to insure their preservation and function in a vital Ghanaian cultural life.

Through her research and her training of researchers, Sutherland fore-grounded the performing arts and artists of Ghana in a truly exemplary fashion. She interacted very closely with the communities in which she did her research, showing a profound respect for them as custodians of a precious heritage and creative artists in their own right. Her hunger for knowledge was palpable as she sought ingenious means to document, give exposure to and produce works inspired by the heritage of artistic expression.

Institutions/organs fostering cultural production in Ghana such as the Ghana National Commission on Children, the Children's Libraries, the National Theatre Movement, The Ghana Association of Writers, *Okyeame* literary journal, Kusum Agoroma Players, *Kodzidan* (Story House) in the town of Atwia, Mmofra (Children's) Foundation, the W. E. B. Du Bois Centre for Pan-African Culture, and PANAFEST (The Pan-African Historical Theatre Festival) – all owe their origin wholly or in part to Efua Theodora Sutherland. As this volume demonstrates, subjects crucial to any reconciling of African traditional culture with the exigencies of globalised, or cosmopolised (post-)colonial, (post-)modern cultural life were the substance of Efua Sutherland's creative and practical enterprise.

The intellectual and artistic community in which Sutherland functioned was inherently Pan-Africanist. She collaborated intensely with a cadre of African movers and shakers in the Arts and in politics, who visited or sojourned in Ghana, such as Felix Morisseau-Leroy of Haiti, Wole Soyinka, Maya Angelou, Coretta and Martin Luther King, Jr., and Ngugi wa Thiong'o. Illustrative of such associations are the conversation in this volume with South African writer Robert July and the last interview given by Efua Sutherland, conducted by Nigerian fellow playwright, Femi Osofisan. Here, particularly, can we appreciate Sutherland's Pan-Africanist position, in the artistic field as well as in the critical connections between the Continent and the Diaspora. In an act of great symbolic sentiment, as she reveals in the interview, it was Efua Sutherland herself who prepared the body of the 'Father of Pan-Africanism', W. E. B. Du Bois, for his funeral, in 1963.

Having grown up under colonialism as part of the generation that was struggling for a new dawn in Africa, the awareness of this wider African world with its firmament of ideas no doubt provided an impetus for dedicated efforts by artists and intellectuals to make a place for the arts in these historic moments. The imaging of Africa's past and future as well as the (re)creation of metaphor and symbolism fit to carry the experiences and aspirations would become a passionate preoccupation. Some among this generation were convinced that rigorous research into Culture and Thought would be essential for providing a firm underpinning for the evolving post-colonial theory and praxis.

The appreciation of Efua Sutherland's pioneering role in the creation of new

African literary and theatrical forms based on the dramatic essence embedded in African life has been intense for those who experienced the process. Those who bear testimony to it include her students, artists and intellectuals from different parts of the world with whom she collaborated. References to documentation on the Ghana Drama Studio and the *Kodzidan* (House of Stories) community project, for example, are to be found in prominent works such as *The Cambridge Guide to World Theatre*, as catalogued in James Gibbs's Selected Bibliography featured in this volume. For many students at secondary and undergraduate level, particularly throughout Sub-Saharan Africa and in certain institutions in the United States, her short story 'New Life at Kyerefaso' and her plays, particularly *Edufa* and *The Marriage of Anansewa* are required texts. This constitutes possibly the largest group of readers who have had exposure to her work.

What is less recognised and consequently accorded virtually no scholarly attention is the fact that Sutherland was a diligent researcher who engaged in a consuming quest for knowledge about the multiple dimensions of the artistic heritage in specific societies and communities in Ghana. She also set out to establish research methods suited to the study of African arts and, in particular, the performing arts. Her quest was for an approach that would liberate African communities from being objects of anthroplogical study and centre them, instead, as sources of a body of knowledge, grounded in abstraction that finds its most powerful expression in the arts, thus giving the arts such a significant role in African society. Sutherland's own essays on these methods and the theories that she developed on notions such as the role of play and the storytelling theatre are largely unpublished although they have been shared in conferences, lectures and training sessons. Her ideas are discernible from their practical application in her experimental work.

In view of the notions distilled by Sutherland from her life-long quest to achieve an understanding of the relationship between the arts and African life and in particular the dramatic arts of Africa, she remains virtually absent from critical discourse on theory developed over the past four decades in the areas of African literature, culture and development. While a few critics, such as Gay Wilentz in her *Binding Cultures*, have placed Sutherland in the context of other women writers, scholarly attention is limited to critical analyses of her plays which do not engage her own ideas about the field.

Given these diverse forms in which Efua Sutherland's artistic and social activity manifested itself, the objective of this volume, then, is to achieve a synthesis of her cultural activist work for Ghana, in particular, and for Africa, in general. The posthumously published article by the late playwright Ola Rotimi, reprinted here, analyses Sutherland's innovative work as foundational for African literary theatre, while the contributions by Biodun Jeyifo and David Donkor examine the Sutherland plays specifically – *Edufa*, *Foriwa*, and *The*

Marriage of Anansewa — for her formal, technical, and substantive achievements. Theatre critic Biodun Jeyifo exposes Sutherland's culturally radical adaptation of a Euripedes play, in her little-noted *Edufa* and the socially progressive import of her *Foriwa*. In Jeyifo's assessment, the relevance of Sutherland's treatment of issues that are of utmost topicality today in all African countries, gives those works permanence in African literary production. Both Jeyifo and Donkor give detailed treatment of Sutherland's 'translation' to the stage of the essential inter-activity between audience and performers from Ghanaian storytelling tradition, a 'translation' for which Sutherland invented neologisms such as *anansegoro*. On the other hand, in our objective to map the breadth of Efua Sutherland's significance in the field of African cultural production, other articles devoted to literary criticism in this volume concern the work of other writers whose work forms a 'community' with Sutherland's, for example, Ama Ata Aidoo and Lorraine Hansberry. Sutherland's engagement as a Pan-Africanist cultural activist is the theme of the memoir by personal friend Vivian Windley, who collaborated with Sutherland to collect books from an African-American partner constituency — no less an African-American institutional pillar than Harlem's Greater Abyssinian Baptist Church — for Sutherland's Children's Library. Or, in yet a different vein, Sutherland's influence as a pathfinder in Ghanaian women's stage performance inspired the contribution here by John Collins, on pioneering women high-life musicians. Thus, this volume, through its own eclectic form and content — literary criticism of Sutherland's writing; literary criticism of others' relevant writing; documented articles on Sutherland's institution-building; and memoirs and testimonies of Sutherland's leadership and activism in its various forms — this volume replicates the holistic form and content of Efua Sutherland's cultural activism.

As a collaborator with fellow writers and artists Efua T. Sutherland is acknowledged as having been the moving force behind the establishment of literary enterprises, particularly the Ghana Society of Writers, established in 1957, and the literary magazine *Okyeame*. Articles in the magazine discussed aspects of Ghanaian culture, announced and reviewed artistic endeavours and featured illustrations using artists' impressions of traditional motifs such as the *adinkra* symbols. This passion took a different form in Sutherland's collaboration with colleagues, such as Kwabena Nketia, to present texts in Ghanaian languages, often taking pride and pains in a creative process of producing translations of these texts into English. A further extension of her impulse to stimulate literary production by Ghanaian writers, Sutherland was a midwife to many a publication, assisting numerous authors of a remarkable range of works. Writers such as Ama Ata Aidoo, Meshack Asare and Kofi Anyidoho attest to Sutherland's tireless mentoring of their work. In this volume Jürgen Martini's interview with Meshack Asare and, indeed, Femi Osofisan's interview entitled 'There Is a Lot of Strength in Our People', reflect the special nature of the relationship that developed between Efua Sutherland and the many talented persons who were beneficiaries of her nurturing influence. As Osofisan candidly states, 'I have edited the interview rather heavily, to hoard to myself those portions which rightly belong only to me. But the following words are a gift she left behind, preciously, and which I am proud to share with you...' Margaret Busby's tribute 'The Pathfinder' gives a poetic iteration of this recurrent theme.

Like many intellectuals and cultural activists of the 'independence generation' Efua Sutherland saw herself as an African with responsibilities that included the representation and validation of indigenous thought, values, and knowledge; the fashioning of new institutions, and systems of thought. Anne Adams draws our attention in this volume to the way in which Sutherland, as well as 'sister' writers Aminata Sow Fall of Senegal and Werewere Liking of Cameroon, tear away at the superficiality of blind adherence to tradition but replace it with a carefully considered reinterpretation of ritual structured to promote the essence of a future ideal.

This role as 'min(d)ers of the culture', especially for the cultural education of children, inspired the creation of an environment for meaningful transmission of cultural heritage. Sutherland held as sacred the duty of bringing up children who were fully conscious to the core of their being about themselves as African. In the testimony of Comfort Caulley Hanson, former Executive Secretary of the National Commission on Children, Efua Sutherland, as chairperson of the Commission 1983-1990, was able to initiate a number of ground-breaking and dynamic children's programmes and projects. These included the promotion of local infant food substitutes; establishment of the Park-Library Complex Project; a Child Literacy Project; and the establishment of a Sociology and Child Research Group. As part of her research work, Sutherland carried out a multi-year Children's Drama Development Project premised on her belief that drama had a huge and unexplored potential in the area of education. Her papers such as 'The Playwright's Opportunity for Drama with Children' (1976) spell out a life-long dedication to the total development of children. In the present volume Mabel Komasi's article provides an overview of Sutherland's writing for children, while Esi Sutherland-Addy offers a detailed commentary on Sutherland's six children's plays, which bear out her utter respect for children as personalities endowed with the ability to perform, which adults have lost.

Besides the theatre's value as a pedagogical medium for children, Sutherland also recognised its potential for socio-historical healing and reconciliation for adults. For Sutherland, theatre has the power to help Africans to confront the deeply ingrained trauma of slavery and colonialism. The Pan-African Historical Theatre Project, now known as PANAFEST, was mooted by Sutherland as a framework for bringing Africans on the continent and in the Diaspora together around long-repressed issues raised by slavery. In her opinion, these are an impediment to the progress of Africans and must be laid to rest. It is of great interest that a number of contributions to the present volume look at the dramatisation of the return of the Diasporan. On this topic Sandra Richards writes about 'Dramatising the Diaspora's Return': Tess Onwueme's 'The Missing Face' and Ama Ata Aidoo's *The Dilemma of a Ghost*. John Lemly also contributes to this topic with a discussion of Hansberry's and Aidoo's first works.

As a form of oral performance, the theatre is naturally adaptable for development projects in Africa. An advocate for women's performance as a tool of empowerment for gender equality in Tanzania, playwright/activist Penina Mlama discusses, in this volume, a 'theatre-for-development' project of the University of Dar-es-Salaam. Today, an acknowledged cultural tool, 'theatre for development' shares Efua Sutherland's conviction from decades ago that theatre has the potential to contribute significantly to social change. Mlama's essay on 'Empowerment for Gender Equality Through Theatre: The Case of *Tuseme*' reverberates with this same conviction and seeks to provide proof of the effectiveness of theatre in providing girls with the inner resources to tackle the intransigent issue of gender inequity in the area of education by training them to speak out (*Tuseme*). It is little wonder that she expresses some frustration – a frustration shared by Efua Sutherland – at the fact that the nation's educational system could not see fit to incorporate locally developed innovations such as *Tuseme* into the core curriculum.

Sutherland's own most famous project of Theatre for Development was the product of her 30-year relationship with the consummate orator, singer and storyteller, Nana Baah Okoampah VI, Chief of the village of Atwia in the Central Region of Ghana. This multi-talented and unique woman leader offered Sutherland the singular honour of opening to her the entrancing world of her stories, and other forms of oral literature for which her community had become famous in its local area. Sutherland's response was to seek to support the community in nurturing this heritage and bringing it to national and international attention. Eventually, having agreed with the community to erect a building dedicated to their unique dramatic form of storytelling, she obtained support from the Rockefeller Foundation to engage the community in building, through communal labour, the *Kodzidan* (Story House) which, today, sits at the centre of the village. The *Kodzidan* project was not merely a building but involved research and training of both the artists in the community and academics and practitioners from all over the world. Indeed the *Kodzidan*, in its heyday has been visited by storytelling enthusiasts, scholars, film makers, writers and statespersons from all over the world. With the demise of the two great women who initiated the idea and the strong effect of the rural-urban drift, the *Kodzidan* today serves more as a communal meeting space and is much less the hub of artistic activity.

Sandy Arkhurst, who reflects on the *Kodzidan* project in this volume, met Efua Sutherland in 1962 as a student working with Sutherland on her search for drama and its functions in African societies. He also worked with her on exploring drama as a vehicle for the development of a modern African reality. We read here Arkhurst's documentary narrative of his experience in the validation and development of the storytelling theatre tradition of the people of Ekumfi Atwia, brought into the limelight by the synergy between the indomitably talented woman Chief of the village, Nana Baah Okoampah VI, and Efua Sutherland. As Arkhurst himself says, this is only the preamble to the story that must be told.[7]

The *Kodzidan* project presents yet another dimension of Efua Sutherland's explorations of African aesthetic expression. Space held a great fascination for her. Ghana's countryside, the heritage of space use for day-to-day and ceremonial activities as well as traditional architecture, are all examples of Sutherland's interest in the values attributed to it. Most importantly, she was taken by the possibilities for adapting the aesthetics and notions of space use for contemporary demands. H. N. A. Wellington's essay on sharing 'the spatial dreams' of Sutherland provides an architect's analysis of Sutherland's engagement with space.

The connections between traditional forms of theatre and contemporary popular performance were a constant subject of Sutherland's artistic theory and practice. Her recognition of the popular arts of Highlife and Concert Party Theatre is today shared with many a scholar. Musicologist John Collins' interest in West African popular entertainment has led him, like her, to participate in and promote these arts and to archive them. He offers in this volume an account of the Ghanaian women's emergence onto the stage of popular entertainment, including a brief comparison to the influence of the church on popular African-American women artists, which, again, emphasises Sutherland's deep fascination with the experience of the people of the African Diaspora. Collins's article also highlights Sutherland's importance as role model and advocate before Government authorities for the promotion of women's cultural performance.

Her stature as a role model and inspiration to women as performers, artists, writers, and scholars was a natural result not only of Sutherland's active example but also of her very persona, as a female African public intellectual. Whether present in UNESCO circles or in the *salon* that was her home, the statuesque presence of Efua Sutherland – attired always in African cloth – commanded the respect that was validated by her intellect and her passion for Africa's potential. And, so, as an early African feminist, Efua Sutherland has left a social legacy of cultural activism. That feminist legacy abides also in literary role models, in Sutherland's play *Foriwa* and the antecedent short story 'New Life at Kyerefaso'. Indeed, this short story, with its self-conscious village-girl protagonist, is the piece through which Efua Sutherland is represented in Margaret Busby's seminal reference work, *Daughters of Africa*, whose 'Introduction' we have adapted for this book. Busby's personal admiration for Efua Sutherland is expressed in her poetic eulogy published in the London *Guardian* and reprinted here.

Attempting to replicate in this volume the holistic nature of Efua Sutherland's work creates a challenge in organising the material for an anthology such as this one. Therefore, although each article has been mentioned in the context of its place in Sutherland's 'sphere', we find it useful to lay out the (confounding/confining) linear arrangement of the pieces for the book. Of equal importance here are critical studies of her own literary publications and those of others engaged with subjects relevant to Sutherland's spheres of cultural production and development. The volume opens with a collection of essays which examine Sutherland's ideas as a thinker in the field of African literature and drama by notable critics who have further been stimulated by the direction of her thought to generate their own ideas on such innovative notions as *anansegoro*. This discussion of Sutherland's pioneering ideas is realised through contributions to the works of other writers and artists, attesting to the growth that has occurred in the now established field of African theatre and literature and, in particular, the blossoming of women in these fields.

The first section includes six critical studies of Sutherland's works: four on the plays (Rotimi, Jeyifo, Donkor, and Adams) and two on the writings for children (Komasi and Sutherland-Addy), as well as three on other writers' works relevant to Sutherland's interests (Richards, Lemly, Martini). The section concludes with Busby's Black women's literary history, of which Sutherland is both a beneficiary and a contributor; and Gibbs's comprehensive bibliography, supporting the studies in the section. The second section is composed of narratives and interviews by colleagues – fellow writers (July and Osofisan), and fellow institution builders (Windley, Arkhurst, Caulley-Hanson and Wellington). The third part consists of personal sentiments of Sutherland's stature and far-reaching influence as a cultural activist and role model. Among the tributes, some are from colleague-friend-admirers: McMullan, William Branch, and Maya Angelou. The others, from those who related to her as 'Auntie Efua', are, nearly all, expressed – not coincidentally – in poetic language: Laast, Margaret Busby, Kofi Anyidoho, mother and daughter Watts, and Ama Ata Aidoo. We hope that this arrangement of the pieces conveys the primacy of the theory-praxis underpinnings of all of Sutherland's work.

As Ghana celebrates itself, recalling the vision of Kwame Nkrumah for Ghana and for Africa, the perspective on Ghanaian cultural heritage offered by Efua Sutherland's work is a valuable base. When we consider any of the 'icons' of Pan-Africanist philosophy – Du Bois, C. L. R. James, Fanon, etc – the role of culture was essential in any strategy for political self-determination. Thus, this volume as a catalogue of Efua Sutherland's Pan-African cultural activism preserves the relevance of her creative, scholarly and institutional legacy. But, as her own work was characterised by a restless, constant searching for the meaning of Independence, in its cultural manifestation, the survival of her legacy means that the searching is to be carried on by cultural activists of today. The survival of Sutherland's legacy should inform Ghana's and Ghanaians' endeavour to process the historical experience, to yield philosophical insight for a self-conscious concept of what it means to be Ghanaian at this point in history. Efua Sutherland's legacy of Pan-African cultural activism abides: it abides in experimentation with the persistent presence of the trickster figure in Ghanaian performing arts; it abides in programmes for children's cultural education; it abides in debates on the form and content of Pan-Africanism in the 21st century, as reflected in the colloquia and performances of the biennial PANAFEST Pan-African Historical Theatre Festival and numerous other objects of Ghanaian cultural heritage influenced by Efua Theodora Sutherland. This volume attempts to record that legacy.

PART I

EFUA SUTHERLAND'S ARTISTIC SPACE

Ola Rotimi

The Attainment of Discovery: Efua Sutherland and the Evolution of Modern African Drama

Born in Cape Coast, Ghana, in 1924, Efua Sutherland (née Morgue), is certainly the first African female playwright/director south of the Sahara. She schooled at St. Monica's Teacher Training College, in Ghana; Homerton College in Cambridge, England, and the University of London's School of Oriental & African Studies, where she specialised in linguistics to supplement her earlier discipline in teaching. Returning to Ghana in 1957 (the historic year of Ghana's independence from British colonial rule), she set up an experimental theatre. This was followed, three years later, by the establishment of the Ghana Drama Studio, which she envisaged as 'a centre for vigorous experimentation in drama …[and] in developing writers'.[1] In 1963, Sutherland was appointed Research Fellow in African literature, with a focus on drama, at the University of Ghana's Institute of African Studies. She subsequently combined this position with that of Artistic Director of Kusum Agoromma – an itinerant theatre group based at the Ghana Drama Studio.

Sutherland's first play *Foriwa*, produced in 1962 and adapted from her short story 'New Life at Kyerefaso' (1957), visualises the ideal of a new nation, highlighting such patriotic motifs as inter-ethnic mutuality, and a positive cleavage with the insularity and petty prejudices of the past. This was followed by *Edufa*. Produced in 1962, *Edufa* is an indictment of materialism spawn [sic] of insatiable self-interests. Her third major play, *The Marriage of Anansewa* (produced 1971), is a social satire and, in all respects, her most successful drama to date. She has been influential to the emergence of modern African dramatic arts in Ghana: first, by her encouragement of newer playwrights to apprentice in her studio; second, and more significantly, perhaps, by her own experiments with the cultural particulars of traditional Ghanaian theatre to serve modern terms of dramaturgy.

Before Sutherland, theatrical expression in modern Ghana took four forms. The first was the 'Folk Drama'. This was a neo-traditional form of display undertaken by itinerant folk-troupes. Their staple fare revealed a penchant for bawdy and bodily jokes spun generally around womenfolk, commingled with traditional dance, acrobatics, music and mimetic gestures – much like the Yoruba *Alarinjo* theatre of Nigeria.

The second form, dating to about 1915, was drama modelled on 18/19th century British examples with characteristic features of witticism and stylistic elegance. Such features predisposed the drama more to being read (rather in the mode of Closet Drama), than to being performed. Plays like Kobina Sekyi's *The Blinkards* (c.1915), J. B. Danquah's *The Third Woman*, and F. K. Fiawoo's *The Fifth Landing Stage* (both written in the 1940s) exemplify this form. By contrast, the third form of modern theatre in Ghana predating Efua Sutherland's efforts lent itself more to performance, as did the traditional-theatre-derived Folk Drama. Like the Folk Drama, it was unscripted and improvisatory. Known as the 'Concert Show of the Two Bobs' (so named after its innovator Ishmael Bob Johnson and his co-star Bob Ansah), it evolved in the early 1920s. Drawing on the examples of America's Minstrel and Vaudeville shows, it developed a specialty in comic gags, song and dance, Charlie Chaplinesque miming and slapstick situations.

The fourth form is the Folk Opera. It grew out of the cantatas/oratorios of local Christian churches, as well as from exposure of indigenous composers to the musical styles of Western European opera and operata [*sic*]. Its focus was on socially engaging issues; however, relegating, as it were, the religious affinities that had borne its emergence. Primary exponents of this form are G. Adali-Morty, who, as librettist, and Saka Acquaye, lyricist, both composed what has been described as Ghana's first opera entitled *Obadzen*. Saka Acquaye followed this up with *The Lost Fisherman*, first written in the Ga language.

Sutherland's first play, *Foriwa*, is more a revival of the dramaturgic preference of the second of the forms identified above. Stylistically, at any rate, *Foriwa* aims at a certain elegance of speech, which, sometimes, appears so stilted as to jar with characterisation, mood and situation. For a quick comparison, let us look at the monologue in which Oni, in Danquah's *Third Woman*, describes the trinity of her personality (the physical, the protective and guiding spirit, and the essential soul), vis-à-vis Edufa's purported speech of remorse in Sutherland's play of the same title. The dissonance between style, on the one hand, and the intimations of mood and characterisation, on the other hand, is striking:

ONI: It is my fortune ... to have such good friends
        companions and partners in adventure.
        The culmination will be our union.
        With such concordance in each companion
        so for life, or life in part, I will assume
        With me is Okra and with me Sunsum.
        (Danquah: *Third Woman*: Act II, sc. ii)

EDUFA: Who thought the charm made any sense? Not I.
        A mystic symbol by which to calm my fears –
        That was all I could concede ... if only I hadn't
        been so cynical. I bent my knee where I have
        no creed and I'm constrained for my mockery.
        (Sutherland: *Edufa*: Act I, sc. iv)

As Sutherland's firstlings in dramaturgy, both *Foriwa* and *Edufa*, like Danquah's prototypal *Third Woman*, reveal flaws reminiscent of the self-conscious bombast so common in Shakespeare's early craftsmanship. Without question, Sutherland's second play, *Edufa*, evinces some improvement: a greater credibility in character delineation, and a marked creative maturation on the part of the author, when compared with the stylistics of the much earlier *Foriwa*. However, it was to take Sutherland some seven years after the premier production of *Edufa* in 1964, to hint of a discovery of her bearings in the search for a form of scripted drama that is at once modern and intrinsically African. This hint came with the production of her third play, *The Marriage of Anansewa*, in 1971 (published in 1975): a hydra-headed satire treating motifs of traditional courtship, betrothal, marriage, burial lore, ethnic paranoia, along with contemporary social foibles as can be seen in the practices of local Christian churches, the chicanery of artisans, and in the desperation of societal opportunists.

In this play, three dramaturgic indices stand out in testimony as much to Sutherland's highly innovative mind, as to the success of her artistic direction. First is language. No longer are the obtrusive, self-conscious linguistic forays. Rather, we are now addressed in a speech that is lacking in characterisation, emotional state, and occasion. Second comes structure. Although the play uses European-style, three-act divisions, Sutherland distinctly weaves into each of these divisions scenic threads pulled sensitively from the warp and weft of traditional Africa's theatrical fabric. Prominent among these is the *mboguw* scenes, intended as interludes for communal dance, singing, comment, and general celebration.

Complementing the *mboguw* to affirm the influence of traditional theatricality in the structuring of *The Marriage of Anansewa*, is Sutherland's hearty use of the play-within-a-play device. Exemplifying this are the scenes depicting:

i.   How shall I find a mate?
ii. Akwasi and Akosua's lesson on pre-marital obligations.
iii. Money extortion in the church.
iv. Bricklayer/painters at work.

The third evidence of Sutherland's maturation as a modern African dramatist in search of cultural identity is her creation, in this play, of a tradition-based, multi-roled figure tirelessly assuming the disparate parts of property-man/storyteller/confidant /commentator and actor.

The contribution of traditional theatre to Sutherland's creative ingenuity does not end with form, of course. Sutherland's style also benefits immensely from traditional oral arts. Her expansive use of praise-poetry in this play is a cogent illustration of this fact. Adulatory poetry, intended to evoke pride in one's being, or in one's exemplary pedigree, is a dominant genre of traditional African orality. To indulge in it is by no means to wallow in megalomania. Rather, praise-poetry (which also accommodated self-praise) is meant to be a metaphor for achievement, an attestation to capability. All this is quite akin, no doubt, to citations of academic or professional distinction in Euro-American custom.

The following example of praise-poetry preserved for Chief-Who-Is-Chief, is noteworthy for the epithets of fierce strength, all of which strive to bolster an intended image of indomitability for the recipient:

Oh, Fire-Extinguisher!
Fire-Extinguisher,
You have caused flame flashes to darken,
You have caused 'I'm Irreversible'
To come to a full stop.

Blazing-columns-of-fire-who-Says I-will-Not-be-Halted
Has come to a full stop.

Masculine-One-Destined-To-Command-To-Victory!
You consume fire, 'abraw'

This you did, this you did,
And therefore do nations say
Well done, and well done, 'abraw'
Have they not heard your fame?

When they hear your fame
Do they not acclaim you in praise-names?

Fire-Extinguisher-Victor who deserves appellations!

Even where 'elevated' parlance appears, as in the next excerpt, a congruence still exists between the motivation of the character and the overall satirical purpose of the parlance itself. Here, Ananse ingratiates himself in a letter to the Chief of Sapa:

I have returned safely home after my visit to you. The little affair about which we spoke seriously, occupies my thoughts. How can I ever forget that you have done me great honour? To show my gratitude, I will guard the object of your interest ... with all the vigilance in my power.... Since forwardness has never been [one of] my faults, I will not even dare to drop a hint that the way is open for you now to begin oiling the wheels of custom. You who do not pay mere lip service to law and custom, but really like them, need no prompting from anyone. Therefore, I will only add that I'm very happy to be, yours in the closest of links in the not too distant future, George Kweku Ananse.

If, in *Foriwa* and *Edufa*, Sutherland takes to sombre contemplation of the virulence of ethnicism and self-interest among the diverse peoples of Ghana, in *The Marriage of Anansewa* she ostensibly resorts to a genial swipe at these vices. A case in point is the response of the culturally older woman, Aya (Ananse's mother), and Ekuwa (Ananse's aunt), to invocations of ethnic fears in the play. Ananse perceives this flaw of ethnic paranoia in the women, and readily exploits it to advance his own stratagem. Ananse has just received news of the impending arrival of all the four chiefs to claim Anansewa in marriage, as promised to each of them personally by father Ananse. Ananse must get the old women out of the scene: the easier for him to breach tradition in tackling the unexpected crisis. He lies to the women that his thriving cocoa farm in the village has just been devastated by unknown arsonists. This news gets the women panicking back to the village to save whatever may be left of the family's estate. But this is not before they have given vent to paranoid invectives at 'tribal' enemies whom they readily conceive as impelled by jealousy:

AYA: People of Nanka!... I knew it would not satisfy you if I didn't remain in rags to the end of my life.
ANANSE: People are bad!
EKUWA: People of Nanka! Laugh with satisfaction, then. Kweku's car will no longer arrive in Nanka and park outside the house of the Nsona clan. Our hope having burnt down to ashes, how is he going to afford spare parts and petrol and tyres? You, who have successfully lamed and ruined him, rejoice then. Pound *fufu* and eat it served with chicken groundnut soup in happy celebration of this victory of yours.... Kweku, if your mother goes, I follow her. Should I sit alone in the courtyard of the Nsona clan house to suffer mockery from the tongues of Nanka citizens? I couldn't.

Sutherland extends this kind of genial treatment of a people's behavioural flaw to the mercenary ploys of modern Christian churches in Ghana, also in the play.

For centuries, petty jealousies, squabbling, and gossiping among women have served comic scenes in drama. In *The Marriage of Anansewa*, Sutherland uses these devices to good effect. We are not accosted, by the result of these devices, with the kind of affected finesse typical of characters in, say, Western Comedy of Manners. Rather, Sutherland applies the devices fitly in tune with characters popularised from traditional Ghanaian theatre by the skits of the ' "Two Bobs" Concert Party'. These devices, needless to say, have also served the comic intentions of other Ghanaian playwrights. The scenes of petty jealousy, squabbling, and gossip among community womenfolk in Ama Ata Aidoo's *The Dilemma of a Ghost* come quickly to mind.

Again, the enlistment of chorus-roles from Ghanaian ritual theatre into the cast of modern African plays is one other evidence of creative exploration into tradition noticeable in Sutherland's theatrical experiments. As noticeable, one might say, as also are her forays into traditional lore for dramatic source-material. It was one of those forays that yielded the hero, Ananse, for this play. In the folklore (*Anansesem*) of the Akan peoples of Ghana, Ananse the Spider is sometimes a hero and sometimes a villain. The association of the spider with trickery and a nimble intelligence arises from the ingenuity of the creature in weaving intricate webs to serve both as home and a trap.

All told, in the evolution of modern African drama, Efua Sutherland will be remembered prominently on two fronts. The first is her contribution to the fashioning of modern African drama through the use of appropriate traditional image, expressive idioms, and structural devices. Second is her abiding commitment to the practice of theatre. In the capacity of director, she has been able to test out the viability of her dramatic experiments, thereby helping to trim the outlines of modern Africa's dramatic form. As is the case with some of her literary contemporaries, the fulfilment of her striving has come with the attainment of discovery. Articulating this vision in her earlier years, she had said:

I am on a journey of discovery. I'm discovering my own people ... there are certain hidden areas of Ghanaian life ... that I just wasn't in touch with; in the past years, I've made a very concentrated effort to make that untrue.

In retrospect, she can now assert more confidently: 'I know my people now.'[2]

Biodun Jeyifo

When *Anansegoro* Begins to Grow: Reading Efua Sutherland Three Decades On

Friends, Anansegoro doesn't take long to grow! There they were, trying, when suddenly Ananse springs up to stand at the door of the room in which his daughter lies, and invoking an oath, forbid anyone to touch his daughter.

STORYTELLER, *The Marriage of Anansewa.*

Nobody expected that she would hold up the festival like a mirror, and make us take a good look at our faces in it. She has asked us to be the men *we say we are, and bring Kyerefaso back to life* (emphasis added).

POSTMASTER, *Foriwa.*

First, a clarification. The re-reading attempted in this essay is not coming three decades after the spectacular arrival of Efua Sutherland on the scene of modern West African drama. That *arrival* took place about five decades ago when I was still in the junior forms of secondary school in Ibadan, Nigeria. Thus, and needless to say, of that arrival, I knew nothing at the time.[1] The 'three decades' indicated in the title of this essay relates to my discovery of the power and sophistication of Sutherland's theatre when I had my first experience of a stage rendition of her best known play, *The Marriage of Anansewa*. The occasion was the staging of the play in 1977 as Ghana's entry for the World Black Arts and Culture Festival, otherwise known as 'Festac 77'. The performance was, at least for me, clearly the best of all the country offerings in theatre in 'Festac 77'. Moreover, though I had of course read the play before I saw that performance, the difference was so markedly dissimilar as an aesthetic and intellectual phenomenon, that I made this point the central issue of a review of the performance that I wrote for one of Nigeria's leading daily newspapers. I would like to make a short recapitulation of what I said in that review as a framework for the readings that I wish to make of two of Sutherland's plays, *Edufa* and *Foriwa*, in this essay.

'Friends, *Anansegoro* doesn't take long to grow!' This statement, which is the opening sentence of the epigraph to this essay and is made by the Storyteller in *The Marriage of Anansewa*, carries considerably different aesthetic and emotional charges in the play as a literary text and the play as a staged or performed event, especially if the latter happens to be the superb production which I saw and reviewed so enthusiastically in 1977. Of course, whether considered as a literary text or as a staged event, the moment in the play indicated by this statement is a nodal one in which the pace of the action quickens considerably and the dramatic action becomes enormously suspenseful. But if the play is encountered *only* as literary text, this moment is nodal only and strictly in a *thematic* sense: George Kweku Ananse, the protagonist, has as usual tied himself in knots, has overreached himself and henceforth in the movement of the dramatic action, his efforts to untangle himself will either ruin him utterly or, conversely, redeem him by a hair's breadth. But as a performance, the moment is nodal in ways that go beyond the (mere) unravelling or consolidation of Ananse's schemes and wiles. For in a staged version of the play, Ananse must not only *think* – or hatch – his plots, he must from this moment to the end of the play raise the performative level of the acting out of his schemes and at the same time effectively and even masterfully mobilise others to perform and act out his schemes and plots with him. In other words, in the medium of the staged drama, this moment in the play is when we come to realise that Ananse has not been acting alone; that all along he has depended considerably on the collaborative performance of nearly all the other characters or performers on the stage with him. One way to clearly perceive the difference being urged here is to see it in terms of the Heideggerian distinction between 'being-in-the-world' and 'being-in-the-world-with-others'. With regard to the former, 'being-in-the-world' for Ananse means that basically, he is on his own and his failure or success depends on his wits, his schemes, and his trickery. But since 'being-in-the-world' is necessarily complemented by 'being-in-the-world-with-others', from the moment when *anansegoro* begins to grow, Ananse's failure or success depends on collaboration given or withheld by the other performers on the stage with him. The difference indicated here is perhaps best comprehended in terms of the distinction between *anansesem* and *anansegoro*, two key terms in the conceptual armoury of Sutherland's theoretical elaboration of her approach to drama and theatre in the modern West African context.[2]

Anansesem is primarily the body of tales about the exploits of Ananse, but the term also embraces the storytelling tradition, the conventions of narration and performance through and in which the Ananse stories are relayed across the generations. *Anansegoro* on the other hand, is the modern art of theatrical performance that Sutherland creatively extrapolated from the more traditional base of *anansesem*. At a basic, methodological level, this extrapolation is a systematisation that entails making more stylised and more precise elements of performance in *anansegoro* like storytelling, poetry, musical renditions including vocal and instrumental extemporisations, and dance sequences. In *anansesem*, these elements are more loosely or informally enacted, while in Sutherland's reconfiguration of *anansesem* into *anansegoro*, the elements are made more precise, more polished and at the same time more expansively suggestive. This is all at the formal or methodological level. But beyond the methodological plane, deep currents of quite conscious ideological and philosophical reflection also inform the differentiation between *anansegoro* and *anansesem*. I know no better way to put this than by saying that in *anansegoro*, the individual-community dialectic is more fully and consciously realised than in *anansesem*. And we are better able to perceive this in an encounter with *The Marriage of Anansewa* as a staged, performed event, especially at that nodal moment in the play when the Storyteller announces portentously: '*Anansegoro* doesn't take long to grow!' For as we have earlier remarked, in the literary text, this moment registers mostly, perhaps even exclusively, as a crossroad of *thematic* developments in the plot of the play when Ananse either faces utter ruination or survives by the skin of his wiles. But in performance, by a subtle twist of both theoretical and practical manoeuvres, *anansegoro* 'grows', because, beyond the wiles of George Kwaku Ananse, every performer on stage contributes mightily to the performative effort to work for a thematic resolution which, in this particular play, makes for a happy denouement, a happy unravelling of the tangled web of Ananse's overreaching schemes. Another way of putting this is to acknowledge that before I actually saw the play in performance, I had only been very mildly aware that *anansegoro* is, as Efua Sutherland herself so insistently urged, a community art. More pertinently, I had only been dimly aware of the individual-society dialectic which, in *anansesem*, tips the balance of forces in this dialectic toward the fate of Ananse, that is to say toward the individual, while in *anansegoro*, the balance is indubitably held in a state of tension, if not indeed slanted toward the community.

In the foregoing account, I have tried to restate the core of ideas and issues that I wanted to communicate to my readers in my review of the staging of *The Marriage of Anansewa* as Ghana's entry for drama for 'Festac 77'. In that review, given the insurmountable constraints of space or scope in the medium in which the review was published, I could not satisfactorily expatiate on my tremendous excitement at discovering the distinction between *anansesem* and *anansegoro*. At the heart of this distinction is the great latitude that *anansegoro* provides for grappling with the contradictions, dilemmas and possibilities of the individual-community dialectic. This is what I intend to deploy as a point of departure for the readings I wish to make of *Edufa* and *Foriwa* in this essay. In other words, and with specific reference to gender identities and contestations, in this essay, I am driven by the following question: when *anansegoro* begins to 'grow', what can we make of the fortunes of the protagonist hero in relation to the fate of the whole society? First then, I now turn to *Edufa*, beginning my observations and reflections on that play by briefly indicating the deliberate, radical changes that Sutherland makes in her adaptation of Euripides' *Alcestis* in her play.

As in all classical plays, the respective plots of *Alcestis* and *Edufa* are simple enough: a husband has invoked the powers of the occult, the supernatural, to substitute the life of his wife for his life, a substitution to which the wife in each case has willingly acceded in the self-sacrificing amplitude of her love for her husband. But there ends the similarities between Euripides' play and *Edufa*. Indeed, the changes wrought by Sutherland in her adaptation are nothing if not startlingly original. Since these are numerous, only the most intriguing need be noted in the present context. Of these, perhaps the most obvious is the fact that in the Euripides play, the wife, Alcestis, is brought back to life at the end of the dramatic action; she is brought back to life by the intervention of Heracles (also known as Hercules), who successfully challenges the powers of the underworld for the life of the wife of his friend, Admetus, king of Pherae. By contrast, in Sutherland's *Edufa*, there is not even the slightest possibility of such providential restitution. The reason for this leads us to one of the most important changes that Sutherland makes in her adaptation of the Euripides play. Simply stated, this has to do with the fact that in Euripides' play, the recourse to the gods, to the occult and the supernatural for the substitution of one life for another is known to the whole community and is indeed elaborately celebrated as an ennobling act which will win great fame, perhaps even deification for Alcestis. It is even claimed that she will become special among all women. In other words, the world of the ritual substitution of one life for another that we encounter in Alcestis is the same as in Wole Soyinka's *Death and the King's Horseman* or, for that matter, the world of the institution and practice of widow burning known as *sati* in colonial British India.[3] In this world where the logic of *noumenon* completely subsumes that of *phenomenon*, to die the death of another who is one of the great ones of the land or the paterfamilias of the lineage; to die such a death is celebrated as a supreme act of nobility and grace. This is resolutely not the world of *Edufa*.

Here the very act or practice of the ritual substitution of one life for another, specifically of the life of a wife for her husband, is shrouded in secrecy and ridden with bad faith, terror and guilt. Where Admetus and the entire citizens of the city state of Pherae openly celebrate Alcestis' self-immolating act, Edufa – the protagonist of the play which bears his name as its title – is endlessly terrified lest the secret is revealed beyond the confines of the family grapevine that it was he who manoeuvred to replace the life of his wife for his own by seeking the intervention of the dark powers of the occult. Indeed, this is the heart of the matter: the occult in Sutherland's *Edufa* is profoundly dissociated from any notion of religious or divine inscrutability, any notion of cultural legitimacy or spiritual grace, all of which subtend the moral and ideological authority claimed by or for the protagonist of Euripides' *Alcestis* or Soyinka's *Death and the King's Horseman*. This may be another way of saying that the occult and the supernatural are thoroughly demystified, even secularised in *Edufa*, but the matter goes much deeper than this. For after all, ritual practices and their subtending metaphysical values are given respectful, even affirmative recognition in *Edufa*. This recognition is most in evidence in the actions of the

Chorus of maidens who open and close the dramatic action of the play; most of these actions revolve around the necessity and possibility of performing cleansing, purificatory rites to avert evil. Thus, if it is not the case that Sutherland in *Edufa* completely withholds religious legitimacy from the occult and the supernatural, why is there nonetheless such a dissociation of the supernatural from cultural legitimacy and spiritual grace in the play? For an appropriate response to this question, it is perhaps best to explore another instance of the radical changes that Sutherland made from Euripides' *Alcestis*. This is the change in the father-son antagonism around the act that enabled the substitution of the life of the wife for her husband's life.

If in *Alcestis*, it is rather difficult to decide whether or not Pheras' confrontation with his son, Admetus, was intended by Euripides as a tragicomic affair with more emphasis on the comedy than the tragedy, there is never the slightest doubt that Sutherland intends the bitter quarrel between Edufa and his father, Kankam, be seen as a matter of the utmost seriousness. In *Edufa*, the father suspects, but is not quite sure that his son has exchanged the life of his wife for his own life. The more Edufa denies the accusation, the greater the moral and spiritual distance between father and son; and it is only after his father has turned his back on him, allegedly forever, that Edufa can then in secret anguish acknowledge the value of the father he has lost by his cowardice and bad faith. How far this scenario is from the moral universe of the antagonism of Admetus and Pheras in *Alcestis* may be gauged by the fact that from the beginning to the end, Pheras admits, even exults in his cowardice: nobody, he vigorously and contemptuously tells his son, was ever intended by the gods or the powers that rule the universe to die in place of another, not excluding parents and their progeny. What is more, Pheras is full of withering disdain for his son's accusation of cowardice from one who is so crassly terrified of the loss of his life that he is willing to let his wife die the death that was meant for him. Indeed, if there is any moment at all in the play when a thick pall of doubt and misgiving is cast over Admetus' nobility and tragic grandeur, it is this instance of his father's erosion of his moral and spiritual equanimity. This, indeed, is the basis of his 'tragic flaw', if one may circumspectly use that term in a play in which, after all, Alcestis is brought back from the dead and restored to her husband, a play that in effect does not end on a tragic note, as does *Edufa*. This 'tragic flow' of Admetus is none other than his failure to acknowledge the all-too common, all-too human fear of death, the universal dread of our inevitable mortality. In other words, though endlessly grieved by the impending death of his wife, Admetus is a man who is nonetheless profoundly at peace with his moral being and, equally important, at peace with his society and culture. The contrast between him and Edufa on his last point is one of the most important changes wrought by Sutherland in her adaptation of the Euripides play and it calls for a careful explication.

It is worthy of note that both Admetus and Edufa are men of great social standing in their respective societies: Admetus is the king of the city-state of Pherae; Edufa is a very 'big man' in the modern, patrimonial African sense of both possessing considerable wealth and consistently and expansively dishing out largesse to all sections of the community. Both are men of substance; each of whom attracts to his person a degree of respect and veneration available to few men and women in the society. But then, there arises the fact that on the crucial issue of seeking the intervention of the occult for the substitution of the life of the wife for that of the husband, Admetus and Edufa meet widely divergent responses from their respective societies. For while no one beside his father, Pheras, indicts Admetus for seeking the intervention of the supernatural to substitute the life of Alcestis for his own, while indeed the act is rooted in deep religious and symbolic sanctions of the culture, Edufa on this same point is totally at variance with his culture to the point that the act is shrouded in great secrecy and is also haunted by unassuageable feelings of guilt and bad faith. This is why for a large part of the dramatic action of the play, Edufa is as much driven by acts and words to prevent his secret from being exposed as by acts to ward off the impending death of his wife, Ampoma. That is why, also, his descent into derangement at the end of the play is as much a consequence of the fact that his secret is at last out as of the fact that Ampoma dies anyway, demonstrating the futility of all his ritual acts to undo the pact through which he has substituted her life for his own. The crazed outpourings of his spiritual collapse at the end of the play are noteworthy in the light they shed on his dissociation of consciousness from psyche:

EDUFA: I told her not to swear. I didn't know that harm could be done.
CHORUS: Not to swear, or harm could be done. Alas!
SENCHI: [Seizing hold of him] Tell me all, Edufa.
         [The owl hoots outside]
EDUFA: [Wildly] Didn't he take that bird away? [He looks at Senchi dangerously] Who are you? Don't restrain me. [Straining with more than natural strength] Where is my leopard skin? I'll teach Death to steal my wives.... Death, I will lie closely at the grave again, and when you come gloating with your spoil, I'll grab you, unlock her from your grip and bring her safely home to my bed. And until then, no woman's hand shall touch me (152-53).

All the pathos and the contradictions of Edufa's sorrowing consciousness – and his destruction – are contained in the first speech of this passage: 'I told her not to swear. I didn't know that harm could be done.' That, and the fact that the women present at the scene – comprising Seguwa and the Chorus of women who had been serenading Edufa – all turn away from him in horror when the secrecy of his pact with occult forces is revealed. With regard to Edufa's violent and anguished protestation that he did not know that harm could come from this pact, there is not the slightest doubt that Edufa passionately loves his wife with a love that is fulsomely requited. Moreover, it is true that Edufa's recourse to the supernatural to substitute another person's life for his own did not initially target his wife, Ampoma; she herself unwittingly falling for the sway of the fetish, the charm. Moreover – and this is the crux of the matter – Edufa merely turned to the occult in a moment of extreme desperation, a moment of deep existential crisis in his life *and he is in equal parts impelled by belief and unbelief in the workings, the efficacy of the occult*. All this notwithstanding, Edufa is ultimately a totally moral and spiritually compromised man in that even in his unbelief, in his fervent hopes that the power of the fetish may be neutralised, he looks to the workings of the occult itself! His 'co-conspirators' in this are his sister, Abena, Sam the idiot *servant*, and Seguwa. In the refracted light of these factors, we can see the dramatic action of the play is doubly haunted, doubly enchanted. There is, first, the haunting pathos of the romantic love of Edufa and Ampoma, symbolised above all by Ampoma's last act as a wife; this being her conversion of her waist-beads to a necklace which she places ritually round Edufa's neck in public. Secondly, there is the 'enchantment' of all the ritual and cabalistic comings and goings of Sam, Abena and Seguwa, as they try to read and manipulate the signs, the auguries of Ampoma's chances for survival in the battle between love and loss, life and death. That the spell, the enchantment, is finally broken – disastrously for Edufa – is revealed in the raging denunciations of one of the 'co-conspirators', Seguwa:

SEGUWA: And yet he buried it. But the deed was done. He buried it, but it was her he buried.

CHORUS: Buried?

SEGUWA: Oh, speak, tongue! Women, you did your ceremony here, but you left the evil one himself behind you. Edufa. He is in there with his victim. This is the day when Edufa should have died. Another has died for him. His wife, Ampoma. She loved him and she has died to spare his life.

CHORUS   One: Died? For him? People don't die that kind of death.

CHORUS: Died? We have eaten here with her, laughed with her.

SENCHI: [Helplessly] Groans in there…like one who stifles agony lest he sheds unmanly tears. I fear it is the worst, my friends.

SEGUWA: Coward! Coward! He is a cursed man. Go. Tell the town about the man who let his wife die for him [She breaks down]. Then go, and tell her mother. Oh, mother! Will someone go and tell her mother, for I cannot look her in the face. I cannot look those motherless children in the face (151-2).

It is indubitably a *woman's* lament, a *woman's* indictment that we hear in these words of Seguwa's bitter jeremiad. This is not due merely to the gender identity of the speaker. Rather, we can discern a specifically gendered inflection in the devastating precision of the indictment. It is about Ampoma's fate as a wife, a *daughter* and *mother* that Seguwa keens. This bespeaks the world of Gayle Rubin's treatise on 'the traffic in women'[4], a world in which all the important axes of female identity are relationally and necessarily determined only with reference to one man or another, whether the given male is a relative or not. The undoubted, though subtle and deliberately understated critique of the patriarchal domination of women that this implies is made all the more potent by the fact that it is linked to an essential patriarchal manipulation of the idioms and values of ritual and the occult. This requires careful elaboration.

We have pointed to the fact that two of the three 'co-conspirators' in Edufa's attempts to invoke ritual acts and values to undo the pact which substitutes Ampoma's life for his own are women. Indeed, Sam, the male idiot servant, is something of an unconscious 'co-conspirator' and is thus far less implicated in the 'conspiracy' than Abena and Seguwa. When this is juxtaposed with the fact that as these female communicants of ritual work secretly to ward off the death of Ampoma, the all-female Chorus also goes about performing rituals of cleansing and purification to rid Edufa's household and the general community of an evil they suspect lurking around. We then begin to glimpse a world view which presupposes a special mystical relationship between women and nature, or rather the elemental forces and energies of nature, conceived collectively as a sort of 'super-nature'. In other words, it is significant that it is only women who are mobilised within the domestic space of the household to neutralise the power of the fetish to take the life of Ampoma, and in the larger community to rid the entire society of evil. Thus, when Seguwa ultimately and irrevocably breaks her vows of secrecy and silence, it is because she has finally come to a proto-feminist consciousness that women's presumed privileged access to 'super-nature' is in fact controlled and manipulated by one man, Edufa, drawing his authority from the institutions and practices of patriarchal hegemony. Similarly, when the Chorus of women learn of this secret and exclaim that 'people don't die that kind of death', this is less an assertion of mere incredulity than the indication of an awakening to the fact that Edufa is not exactly the man they had thought him to be. More generally, it is also an awakening of the female Chorus to the fact that men are well positioned to appropriate and manipulate the ritual functions that women like themselves perform within their culture.

In the light of these themes and issues that we have explicated in the dramatic action of this play, there can hardly be a more topical, more 'contemporary' drama than *Edufa* among the literary works produced by members of what I have in another context called the 'independence generation' of West African writers and intellectuals.[5] Obsession with the supernatural, with the occult, dominates contemporary popular and Pentecostal religion in West Africa. It is a constant and perennial item of news in the sensationalist tabloids of the popular press. More portentously, it is a pervasive feature of the works of the so-called video film industry, throughout the entire continent, but especially in 'Nollywood' of Nigeria. Furthermore, it cuts across all classes and social groups, not only in West Africa but also throughout the entire continent of Africa and indeed many other parts of the developing world. Thus, Edufa is very much a man of these times, and the incredulity of the Chorus statement that 'people don't die that kind of death' is depressingly out of tune with the present age: the newspapers, the video films, and cassette tapes of Christian and Moslem sermons in the marketplace of culture all proclaim that 'people are dying that kind of death'. Indeed, sometimes these inscriptions and accounts hint at the gendered dimensions of the phenomenon which make women as a social group loom large as victims of this 'occult economy' of neoliberal, peripheral capitalism in Africa.[6] In this historic and cultural context, Sutherland's subtle but powerful exploration in Edufa of the invidious ideological location of women in the institutions and practices of the manipulation of the occult assumes a new, unexpected but urgent relevance.

At the surface level, Foriwa is, as a dramatic text, nothing like Edufa. For one thing, while ritual practices and values pervade and dominate the dramatic action of the latter, they play only a minimal, vestigial role in Foriwa. And while one play is a tragedy that ends in utter bleakness, the other play is a social drama whose initial mood of stagnating, crippling anomie lifts at the play's denouement so that the last words, the last intimations of the dramatic action are one of hope and possibility. Finally, the love theme common to both plays is explored by Sutherland in each respective play in completely different ways: one in the haunting, otherworldly idiom common to European traditions of tragic romantic love (Edufa) and the other in the accents of a liaison consolidated on the basis of a 'revolutionary' baptism of fire experienced together by the lovers (Foriwa). Notwithstanding, there are strong undercurrents of theme, characterisation and sentiment linking one play with the other. For in each play, we encounter a community in a deep, even profound crisis of faith, a crisis in which two protagonists, of exceptional endowments of character and will, one male and the other female, stand in the storm centre of the dramatic action.

I would even go so far as to suggest that it is only after one has encountered Foriwa in the play which bears her name as its title, it is only after this that one comes to a due and appropriate appreciation of the strength of will and character in Ampoma in Edufa, since she plays a decidedly secondary role to the protagonist dilemma of her husband, which occupies centre stage in the dramatic action of that play. On this particular point, the impulse – which drives *Foriwa* at the climactic moment of the play to commit herself completely and irrevocably to the daunting challenge of the renewal of her small town community of Kyerefaso rather than go off to the big towns of Ghana – seems to come from the same region of psyche and will as that which drives Ampoma to publicly hang her waist-bead as a necklace around the neck of Edufa as a transcendent sign of her everlasting claim on him. In somewhat similar ways, Labaran, the male protagonist of *Foriwa*, is very like Edufa in the force of the volition that drives him to idealistically set himself apart from other men. True enough, the moral universe in which each of these two protagonists operates and seeks validation for his drives and acts could not be more different, but at the level of comparative generality, it is not too difficult to conjecture that in the same circumstances Edufa would have responded like Labaran to the same set of challenges faced by the latter. After all, even his accusers acknowledge the genuine generosity that defines much of Edufa's relationships within the community. In the final analysis, all of these issues – which strongly suggest subtle points of comparison or even similarity between *Edufa* and *Foriwa* – converged around a claim which was made earlier in this essay for the former. Like *Edufa*, *Foriwa* is a play of the early post-independence period which, many decades later in our present dire circumstances, assumes a surprising topicality, a startling contemporaneousness by the sheer force of Sutherland's visionary projections in her exploration of the central themes of the play. This observation needs to be backed by a careful reading of some underlying, perhaps even 'submerged', aspects of *Foriwa*.

Given how central his character is in *Foriwa*, it is perhaps appropriate that the two prologues in the play, each opening the action of the first two of the three acts of the play, are spoken by Labaran. He is a stranger in the town of Kyerefaso, an outsider. More portentously, he is an *otani*, a northerner in a southern Ghanaian town. The glossary at the end of the play informs us concerning the connotations of that word, *otani*: 'a name by which southerners in Ghana loosely make reference to northern people. It carries derogatory social overtones from the days of the slave trade' (67). But while acknowledging the 'outsider' identity that many in the town ascribe to him, Labaran has wandered across the length and breadth of Ghana; he has seen many sleepy towns sunk in stagnation and decrepitude like Kyerefaso, and he has felt and claimed their despair and anguish as his own. Thus, deep down, he does not feel himself to be a 'stranger' in Kyerefaso. He himself expresses this sentiment eloquently in the first of the two prologues to the play: 'Who is a stranger, anywhere, in these times, in whose veins the blood of this land flows?' (2) This is why Labaran is the only real *man* in the town, where manhood, as indicated in the second epigraph to this essay, is deployed as a trope that stands for either the predicament or the salvation of the whole community, with men, women and children included. Indeed, the most moving speech in the whole play, the speech of the Queen Mother in the climactic third act of the play, echoes explicitly this articulation of *manhood* as a trope of communal and intergenerational identity and possibility:

QUEEN MOTHER   [quietly to the meeting]: Forgive this show of passion. A full heart, like a flood, forces a channel for itself. Sitting here, seeing Kyerefaso die, I am no longer able to bear the mockery of the fine, brave words of this ceremony of our festival. *Our fathers earned the right to utter them by their brave deeds.* They found us the land, protected it, gave us a system of living. Praise to them. Yes. But is this the way to praise them? Watching their walls crumbling around us? Failing to build upon their foundations? Letting weeds choke the paths they made? Unwilling to open new paths ourselves, because it demands of us thought, and good will, and action? No, we have turned Kyerefaso into a death from which our young people run away to seek elsewhere the promise of life we failed to give them here. [Deciding to say no more, she returns to the sheepskin rug and addresses the Linguist] Linguist, those are my thoughts. I knew no way of reaching my people better than with such thoughts than to use this ceremony of our festival as my interpreter. Kyerefaso needs the new life of which we speak, *and men to make it true* (50-51, emphasis added).

The vintage 'founding fathers' theme of this speech is unmistakable. The deeds of the past, of which the speaker asks the gathered assembly to be worthy, are the deeds of brave, far-sighted *men*. Even of the present, living generation, the speech implies that it is men who can be expected to be worthy of the stalwart yeomen of the past. Contextually, this strong accent on heroic manliness as the probable saving grace of the community is perhaps clarified by the fact that though the occasion is a meeting of the representatives of the whole community on the eve of the most important annual festival of the town, the Queen Mother and her daughter, Foriwa, are the only women with speaking rights in the gathering. This is worthy of note, because neither the Queen Mother's speech nor the big issue raised at the gathering – how to break the stranglehold on the community's present and future of a traditionalism which has become an empty, meaningless festivalisation of the past glories of the community – can be deemed to be a naïve, uncritical consecration of reinvigorated manhood providing the bedrock of what needs to be done. For neither in this specific climactic scene nor in other crucial moments in the play is a praise-song to manhood or manliness the expression that occupies the foreground of the dramatic action. That 'honour' belongs to accumulated images and tropes of a society that is sunk in discord and enervation; a society so lacking in energy and perspective that could lead to renewal and innovation that the three protagonists of the play, Labaran, Foriwa and the Queen Mother – the three who, within the whole community alone, bear the seed of possibility within them – are in one way or another convinced that the spark can only come from outside the society. Indeed, this is one of the reasons why this play is so topical now, at this moment in our post-colonial predicament. Kyerefaso stands for countless small towns and villages in Ghana. It stands for Ghana itself, and is comparable to the grim, anomic world depicted by Ayi Kwei Armah in *The Beautyful Ones Are Not Yet Born*; and it is all of Africa, then in the immediate post-independence period and, even more so now, at this moment in history. Given this structure of ideas and effects in the play which run much deeper than the conventional, standard tropes and images of masculinist nationalism, it is all the more remarkable that heroic manliness is such a strong, insistent trope in the play. This can be seen in the following speech of the Queen Mother, a speech she delivers to her daughter just before the passage earlier quoted in this essay from the climactic scene of the play:

Come, daughter, will you not dance? The men are tired of parading in the ashes of their grandfathers' glorious deeds. That should make you smile. They are tired of the empty croak, 'We are men. We are men.' They are tired of sitting like vultures upon the rubbish heap they have piled on the half-built walls of their grandfathers (49-50).

If we persistently encounter in the play this trope of heroic manhood in need of reinvigoration, we are nonetheless enjoined to read it complexly, perhaps even deconstructively. Throughout the play we are so enjoined by the hermeneutic force of strong countervailing intimations of female agency, acting independently of male inspiration or control. However, in the end they combine with the 'heroic' male agency of Labaran and his acolytes, Brobi and Atuo and Postmaster. This suggests that, ultimately, Sutherland's compelling vision in the play points, not to heroic manhood, but to gender equality and solidarity across the sexual divide as the only truly worthy means of meeting the daunting challenges of the age. In moving to the conclusion of this essay, I offer a brief exposition of this observation, this claim.

I began this essay with a brief excursus on that aspect of the title of the essay that powerfully hints at the rich semiotic and interpretive possibilities in the phrase 'when *Anansegoro* begins to grow'. I explained that this marks the moment in the dramatic action of a play – any play – when thematic and performative values in the text combine to clarify the often complex and tangled relationship between protagonists and their societies, specifically and especially in the individual-community dialectic. Applying this heuristic schema now to the dramatic action of *Foriwa*, it is worthy to note that for all the impressive and moving impact of Labaran and his male acolytes and associates in turning things round in Kyerefaso, 'Anansegoro begins to grow' in this play only through the agency of the Queen Mother, supported at the crucial moment by her daughter, Foriwa. For it is finally only on the basis of her inspired decision to use the occasion of the community's most important annual festival to bring matters to a head that things begin to change in the circumstances and prospects of Kyerefaso. At the gathering she is in full control of things, as unpredictable as the outcome of the looming confrontation might seem. And there she plans and enacts decisive strategies and moves even as she knows full well that powerful male members of the assembly are conspiring to de-stool her. The same qualities of farsightedness, restlessness of spirit, and independence of thought and action make the character of her daughter, Foriwa. Indeed, there is a strong hint that Foriwa is 'constructed' out of an inspired reconfiguration by Sutherland of the 'Anowa' myth. In this folkloric myth, the wilful, headstrong and vainglorious heroine insists on always having her way; and she refuses all suitors only to end up marrying a demon or an ogre who comes in the shape of an irresistibly handsome man. Indeed, the brilliant artistic appropriation of this myth by Ama Ata Aidoo in her best-known play, *Anowa*, has become a classic of modern Ghanaian and African drama. I invoke that play because it is instructive that while its protagonist shares similar humanistic and life-enhancing values and qualities with Foriwa, she acts alone and is destroyed as a female rebel against institutions, forces and practices of exploitation and repression underwritten by patriarchy and class privileges. Foriwa initially seems set to reconfirm the negative cautionary lessons of the 'Anowa' myth until she and Labaran mutually discover in each other the saving grace of solidarity, collaboration and equality in friendship and in budding love. If we are to read *Foriwa*, the play, and Foriwa, the protagonist character, as powerful dramatic parables for these times, we must unearth these submerged elements of a subtle, humanistic and non-separatist feminism from the play's surface emphasis on heroic manhood as the salve for a pervasive anomie in our continent which, after all, ultimately spares nobody, no gender, no social class or group.

The programme of experimental theatre which Efua Sutherland began in Accra between 1958 and 1961, and the Ghana Drama Studio which she built to house her experimental work are two of the most important 'happenings' in the creation of modern drama, not only in West Africa, but in the entirety of the African continent. This is a fact that I highlighted in the timeline which I traced for the evolution of drama in Africa in the last one hundred and fifty years in one of the appendices to the book, *Modern African Drama*, that I edited for the Norton Critical Editions (NCE) series on drama in different regions of the world.[7] In the refracted light of this fact, one can justifiably say that one of the crucial instances when 'Anansegoro began to grow' in modern African drama was when Sutherland began her experimental work in the very first few years of the first decade of the post-independence era in Africa. My re-reading of two of her plays, Edufa and Foriwa, in this essay attest to the continuing relevance, the continuing vitality of the legacy she left behind. It only remains for me to draw the reader's attention to the fact that one play, Edufa, connects to a bizarre, sublimely terrifying aspect of our contemporary malaise, while the other play, Foriwa, opens up unromanticised but tangible vistas of the possibility of fresh beginnings. The dialectic remains strong and resilient in Sutherland's legacy; and Anansegoro continues to grow in that legacy for this generation and beyond.

David Donkor

Kodzidan Mboguw: Supplanted Acts, Displaced Narratives, and the Social Logic of a Trickster in the 'House of Stories'

The interior of the Kodzidan in the village of Ekumfi Atwia had grown a little dark with the approach of sundown. The storyteller, located in the stepped-down arena of this community theatre space, paced about as she told the story, surrounded by an audience – quite a throng for this size of space – seated on enclosing platforms. Suddenly the little girl, hardly more than four years old, walked into the arena. The storyteller continued with her performance, paying hardly any attention to the little girl. However, an elderly man in the front row of the audience attempted to shoo her away. The girl ignored him and walked leisurely across the stage, seemingly trying to make her presence felt. Surely this toddler could not be much aware of the little commotion she was causing. Or could she? I watched her closely as she headed back into the audience. Was that a glint of mischief in her eyes I saw, or just a glimmer of innocence? Soon the girl, like the rest of the throng in the building, was focused on the storytelling as if nothing had happened. Well, what, indeed, had happened – anything beyond the simple fact of a little girl walking across the stage while a Kodzidan performance is in progress?

IN SEARCH OF ANANSE

The village of Ekumfi Atwia is a farming community set on a hill seventy-five miles away from Accra, the capital city of Ghana. In the 1960s it was a slimly resourced village with a population of hardly more than five hundred. Nevertheless, what Ekumfi Atwia lacked in material wealth it made up for in a rich and vibrant storytelling tradition and a fervent spirit of self help – here was a community which, despite meagre resources, had successfully raised funds and organised communal labour to construct its own school. While I was an undergraduate theatre student at the University of Ghana, several of my lecturers who had either studied or worked with the late dramatist Efua Sutherland, told anecdotes of how she had encountered Ekumfi Atwia's vibrant storytelling tradition and, impressed, contributed part of her own research funds to the construction of a theatre house in the village.

Sutherland had known the chief of Ekumfi Atwia[1] before her assumption of chieftaincy and got the latter's permission to build a centre to support the village's storytelling tradition. The entire village showed commitment to this project: they selected the location, a site where an important clan house once stood, and contributed their labour – children gathered gravel, women carried cement and young men helped mount blocks. The building went up in 1966. For the people of Ekumfi Atwia, it was a multipurpose centre where they kept funeral wake, met for church services, held official gatherings and greeted visitors. However, they had a keen sense of its importance to storytelling, for it is said that once, when one of the village women spoke about the building, she called it the Kodzidan, or 'the house of storytelling', a name that has caught on in and abroad of the village to this day.[2]

I visited the *Kodzidan* at Ekumfi Atwia in early August 1999, figuratively speaking, in search of Ananse the spider-man trickster of Akan folklore – I was interested in what significance I could derive from Ananse's representation in the stories and performances Ghanaians call *Anansesem*. University of Ghana's Ms. Esi Sutherland-Addy had kindly informed me that the village was putting on a special storytelling event for a visiting group of African-Americans. I was thrilled at the opportunity to attend – for, as she hinted, such elaborate performances had grown rare even in Ekumfi Atwia and that, bar this special event, I had, on my own time-table, a slim chance of seeing the village's much talked-about brand of communal, improvised and participatory *Anansesem* in full expression.

The chance to participate in an *Anansesem* event at Ekumfi Atwia was of tremendous methodological importance to my research. Tricksters, Robert Pelton has observed, appear

'in the myths and folktales of nearly every "traditional" society [...] seemingly trivial and altogether lawless' yet arousing affection wherever their stories are told. They are 'the very embodiment of elusiveness' as they defy social logic and just as skilfully, 'slip out of our contemporary interpretative nets' (1).

However, with regard to the trickster Ananse, I was convinced the problem of elusion derived as much from where scholars cast their 'interpretative nets' as from the trickster's slipperiness itself. Even though the term *Anansesem* refers both to the body of stories *and* to the storytelling *performance* itself (Sutherland 1975: v), and despite that performance is 'a primary arena for the production of knowledge' and a means by which people define themselves and their social world (Drewal 2004: 336), I found Ananse scholars to have demonstrated limited engagement with performance as a meaningful 'site' for exploring Ananse's social logic.

Kwawisi Tekpetey's article, which presents *Anansesem* as a genre of 'narratives' belonging to 'oral literature' (1979: 78), almost completely disregards the performance mode in which these narratives are expressed. Tekpetey makes brief mention of an *Anansesem* audience (ibid: 81) but his implied relationship between this audience and the narratives demonstrates no aspect of the embodied interactivity that is distinctive about performance – the 'audience' may as well be the reader/s of a literary text on the printed page. Furthermore, Tekpetey shows nary an indication that he encountered the narratives, framed as the site of his analysis, in their oral form. Rather, his direct but unacknowledged reference to Rattray's collection of Akan-Asante folktales (1930: 78) suggests that his analysis is based on the transcribed and translated text of an otherwise oral performance.[3]

In his article, 'The Exception Who Proves the Rules: Ananse the Akan Trickster', Christopher Vecsey pays hardly any more attention to performance than Tepketey does. *Anansesem*, Vecsey declares, are 'tales' belonging to Akan 'oral traditions', told at night and on special occasions, recited by all strata of Akan society and disclaimed as truth at a storyteller's commencement of narration. This reference to the storyteller's act of disclamation inches Vescey's discussion towards performance. The reference, however, is exactly that – merely an inch – for every indication is that Vescey has not encountered the tales from which he derives his analysis in their performance from. On the contrary, what he has is abundant evidence in the article that he examined the *Anansesem* in their 'collected' form: as already transcribed and translated texts on the pages of literature by Peggy Appiah., W. H. Barker and C. Sinclair, E. J. P. Brown, Harold Courlander, Frances Sad, Melville J. Herskovits and R. S. Rattray.

In his book, *Trickster in West Africa*, Robert Pelton recognises that *Anansesem* are told 'in a communal setting, in which all the other social and religious apparatus of the society is present in the very bodies of the listeners, who know the stories as the very quintessence of play' (1980: 20). He acknowledges the contingency and immediacy of such play, citing that the audience directly experiences the creativity of the teller as opposed to the reader of a collected story who is thrice removed from the moment of creative enunciation. The references to the setting of event; to contingency, creativity, live experience and embodiment; and to socially situated 'play' – all indicate Pelton's better appreciation of performance as a meaningful site for understanding Ananse's social logic. Unfortunately, his 'close reading' of *Anansesem* derives from texts 'in English, not Akan, printed and collected, not heard individually'. Thus removed from the situation in which the texts were uttered, Pelton, intending to unravel the logic of the trickster in its cultural context, can only 'grapple' with the printed texts 'in solitude, grasping them and the culture out of which they rise only with great intellectual difficulty' (ibid: 21).

Charles van Dyck recognises how linguistic twists and elements of humour are lost in folktale translation and transcription (1980:102). Thus, even more so than Pelton, he details the performance aspects of *Anansesem* expression in his dissertation, 'An Analytic Study of the Folktales of Selected Peoples of West Africa'. Of its five chapters, he commits parts of the first to discussing the storyteller's opening act of disclamation, then dedicates the entire second chapter to describing, among other things, the processes of story acquisition and transmission; the setting of a storytelling event; freedom of expression in the event; the storyteller's manner of delivery; choice of words and other elements of style and artistic virtuosity; and the audience's participatory interspersion of the narration with songs. Despite the detail of his attention, van Dyck does not explore if and how the trickster's social logic is cited in performance. In other words his conclusion about Ananse's significance is derived from the narrative, the textual product of narration, with little regard for how the creative, contingent and collaborative processes of narration itself might account for this significance.

Kwesi Yankah's 'The Question of Ananse in Akan Mythology', challenges folklore scholars' sheer 'content analysis' that disregards how such narratives interact with the lives of those who perform them (1999: 135). For him, the better approach must combine an analysis of Ananse's depiction in the narratives with a study of the 'social context' (ibid: 139-140) and 'stylistic frames' (ibid: 149) of the narratives. 'Stylistic frames', as he uses the term, references elements of *Anansesem* performance, specifically the storyteller's opening disclamation and his/her interactions with the audience's participatory comments. Yankah's placement of the storytelling process, somewhere between the creative manipulation of ontological reality and the candid reflection of socio-cultural truth, hints at parallels between *Anansesem* performance and the ambivalent nature and antics of Ananse.

Despite a hint of parallels between Ananse nature/antics and *Anansesem* performance Yankah does not grasp that as a line of exploration. His contentment with proving the secularity (and thus non-mythic) status of *Anansesem* through its play with reality is understandable given the purpose of his essay. The implication, however, is that the promise that this hinted parallel offers, of understanding Ananse's social logic in performance, remains unfulfilled. My figurative 'search for Ananse' was therefore a desire for a site where I might explore the parallels between Ananse's character and the processes of *Anansesem* — where I might unravel something of his significance in the creativity, contingency and embodied interactivity of performance. When, therefore, Ms. Esi Sutherland-Addy announced that the village of Ekumfi Atwia was holding a storytelling event for a visiting African-American group inside their Kodzidan, I figured that there was hardly anywhere better to experience the forging of Ananse's social logic than in that celebrated hearth of *Anansesem* performance.

THE GENDERED JOUST

The people of Ekumfi Atwia presented two stories. The first, by a woman in her mid-to late-forties, was an aetiological tale purporting to explain the origins of rivalry among women. It went that a hunter once killed an antelope, and brought it home. Afterwards each morning he and his wife, Abena, would consistently discover that someone had done the household chores and fixed breakfast. The hunter vowed to discover the identity of this generous visitor. He hid in the kitchen, kept vigil through the night and saw, to his amazement, that it was the antelope he had brought home that would turn into a beautiful young woman, fetch water, clean the house, light fire and cook the morning dish. Enamoured, he grabbed the strange woman and begged her to stay human and be his junior wife. She initially refused on grounds that the hunter could not be trusted with the secret of her bimorphic identity. Nevertheless, upon an oath of his secrecy she stayed in human form and married the hunter. Abena, however, demanded of the hunter from whence this new wife had come. Against his oath the hunter revealed the young woman's animal origins. In a subsequent domestic dispute between the two women Abena insulted her as merely 'an antelope'. The antelope-woman, realising the hunter's betrayal, transformed back into her animal form and disappeared into the woods.

The other story, narrated by a man probably in his mid-thirties, was also an aetiological tale claiming that the mournful cry of the Owea, the tree bear, is a lament of female treachery. Once upon a time, the story went, all animals agreed to make public their personal *mmrane* or identity-poem, such that it may be recited in memoriam at their death. Owea refused to make his *mmrane* public, not even to his own wife. The wife, unhappy at being kept out of her husband's confidence, asked old hedgehog to hide by and listen while she coaxed the secret from her husband. Unaware of hedgehog's presence Owea finally revealed his identity poem, only to find out at the next council of animals that it had become public. Disappointed, he flew up a tree from where every morning he cries 'Oh, the treachery of woman, the treachery of woman'.

My initial reaction was to cringe at these two tales for they seemed to be little other than misogynistic narratives. However, I became aware that juxtaposed to each other, they offered a reading more complex than pure misogyny. The stories paralleled each other in plots featuring the divulgence of secrets, the betrayal of confidence, a rupture in relationships and the concomitant segregation of self. They are, however, antithetical to each other in at least one way. Whereas the Owea story by the male storyteller portrays a woman's betrayal of man's confidence, the antelope-woman story by the female storyteller depicts a man's betrayal of woman's confidence. The implication is an important aetiological discrepancy between the two tales. The Owea story roots man's suffering in woman's perfidy, the antelope-woman story identifies man's disloyalty as the progenitor of whatever discord may be seen to exist among women.

Just as an inter-textual juxtaposition of the two tales offers an overall reading that exceeds misogyny, a performance-centred and holistic view of the tales offers an understanding that exceeds their aetiological frame. Patriarchy operates to conceal its distortion of gender relations by presenting ideologically laden narratives as 'done deal', 'just so', 'closed' explanations of the world. Therefore, a performance that confronts 'closure' with an 'opening' possesses the political potential to unsettle such ideological operations. Understood holistically the two storytelling acts constitute both opening and closure. The teller of the antelope-woman story, even as she legitimated the spurious co-identification of woman with squabble, displaced it with a counter-narrative of man as the father of woman's discord, a gesture that combines legitimation and subversion in one utterance or act (Drewal 2004: 336). The teller of the Owea story, for his part, gestures to re-close the opening with the narrative of woman as unequivocal mother of man's suffering. Thus, more than sheer aetiology, the two acts together assume the dialogic quality of a rhetorical bout, a gendered joust, if you will, of opening and closure.

THE MBOGUW[4]

The politics of closure and subversive 'opening' also pertains to a feature of *Anansesem* performances known as *Mboguw*. *Anansesem* stories, as Efua Sutherland has explained, are composed with performance demands in mind and are thus not rigidly formed but meant to be given fuller composition and artistic interpretation by the storyteller considered 'author' and 'owner' of the story and therefore possessing the authority of omniscience in the world of the narrative. *Anansesem* audiences, however, have the opportunity to unsettle this authorial identity and authoritative knowledge through *Mboguw*. Literally meaning 'a kicking aside', *Mboguw* does not lend itself to an easy translation concerning *Anansesem* audiences' simultaneous displacement of the storyteller's narration and supplanting of the storyteller's act. In an *Mboguw*, the audience halts the narration and contributes a song, mimed action or comic playlet. 'Contributed *Mboguw*' serialise the story by breaking it up into segments. They are prompted by some sort of inspiration in the performance situation. They may be reflective of mood or aimed at quickening the pace of the performance or inspiring the general assembly. Indeed it is not uncommon for some contributions to be made merely from a high-spirited desire to show off.

In the Ekumfi Atwia performance there were several *Mboguw* contributions. I offer one illustration here. At the point in the Owea story, just when Hedgehog is about to reveal Owea's identity-poem to the council of elders, a young man from the audience enters the storytelling arena with the studied gait of a royal, declaiming 'make way for the chief'. He claims to be a wealthy royal from Asanteland. Despite the fact that Asante people are known for the luxuriant apparel and accoutrements of their royalty, he wears flip-flops and the not-so-elegant cloth of a commoner. Indeed, lacking personal attendants as befits royalty, he serves as his own herald. As the contradiction between his claim to royal wealth and his drab appearance becomes comically obvious, the audience begins to sing: *Adie abia meo! Adie abia meo!* loosely translated as 'I am so poor!' We soon find out that even this man's modest attire is all borrowed. An audience member walks in and claims his flip-flops and the rest resume the chorus: *Adie abia meo!* Another steps into the arena and claims his handkerchief and the audience continues: *Adie abia meo!* Yet another person walks in and claims the very cloth on his back. A struggle occurs as this pretender to royalty pleads for the cloth. He is nevertheless stripped of it, exposing his tattered pair of undershorts. He runs out of the space to the delight of the audience, especially the children in the front seats on one side of the arena.

The audience's seizure of the space and moment of performance constitutes a momentary displacement of the storyteller's narration wherein they supplant the storyteller's act with their own and thus subvert his or her authorship of and authority over the performance. Univocal authorship and authority is often tantamount to narrative closure. Thus, in providing a space for the subversion of the storyteller's authorship and authority *Mboguw* unsettle such very closure. Audiences may subjectively open up the narrative by critically commenting or counteracting the story or, as in the just-described example, flip the story along a completely different tangent. The *Anansesem* storyteller thus emerges as a duplicitous figure, being both and not author of a story in which his role is to give fuller composition and interpretation to a pre-existing text. He or she is a duplicitous figure, being both and not authoritative over a communal art form wherein all present are performers either actively or potentially.

The duplicity of the storyteller extends to the stories themselves. Both storytellers from Ekumfi Atwia began their acts with a frame-setting prelude *Anansesem wonngye ndzi o*, meaning stories are fictions but also meaning, more literally, they are not to be uncritically consumed. At which point the audience responded *Wo gye sie*, stories are meant to be stored, ostensibly to be deployed for critical reflection in one's daily life. In his introduction to a collection of Ananse stories C. A. Akrofi maintains that there is a value of *Anansesem* in the opportunity it offers for a critical and evaluative juxtaposition of the imagined narrative and the practice of everyday life. Consequently the stories acquire a certain ontological duplicity as real and fictional, as actual and imagined. Indeed sometimes the audience jokingly contests the veracity of the teller's story.

Commenting on the storyteller's duplicity, Kwesi Yankah writes that 'the narrator is not a complete liar' given that 'his tale partially reflects the flaws in human society', nor does he completely twist cultural truth. Professed as truthful but challenged as 'lies' and vice versa, the story and its teller are granted an 'open' status – one is neither unequivocally a truth nor a lie and the other is neither unequivocally a truth-teller nor a liar. Both, in each case, are either. This duplicity brings to mind the advice of the Akan proverb: 'When you craft a "lie" craft one with an "opening" such that when you are caught you will have a space for escape.' The verb 'lie' in this case is akin to the usage in African-American linguistics, and signifies a creative, inventive and imaginative impulse in counteraction to the constriction of closure.

THE ANANSE ETHOS AND A TODDLER'S 'INTRUSION'

The duality of the Ananse story, its teller, and the counteractive impulse of *Anansesem* performance towards closed narratives, constitutes the very ethos of Kwaku Ananse, the trickster. Ananse appears in *Anansesem* endowed with speech and a name – the necessary trait of an 'individualised being among'.[20] He also appears as a social being, a farmer married with children, confronting human life-struggles in a village filled with farms and neighbours, and demonstrating a penetrating awareness of human and animal psychology and great familiarity with social codes, both of which he often manipulates to his advantage. The Akan also imagine Ananse as a spider and his wily character is considered an extension of the spider's known craftiness in the Akan world – its mastery of disguise; ability to walk on water or survive under it on accumulated pockets of air, capacity to leap or be borne by wind over great distances; and adroitness at spinning intricate, artistically admirable webs out of its saliva. There is, nevertheless, a vile side that the Akan also observe about the spider creature: an ability to use agility, camouflage and adaptability to deceive and capture prey, and its web, a hangman's noose that entangles the more a trapped creature tries to free itself.

The admixture of craft and deadliness in both the spider and its web corresponds to Ananse's qualities as a master-schemer and mischief-maker in *Anansesem*. For his cunning, Ananse is regarded as *wiadze onyansafo* – the worldly-wise one whose wisdom is greater than all of that of the world together, and which facilitates his trickery. Ananse is, nevertheless, no paragon of virtue: often too clever by half, he falls into foolish mishaps out of greed. He is *pese-menko-menya-nyi*, the selfish one and *dzifodze-penyi*, the greedy one. He is disloyal, cruel, treacherous, unscrupulous, vain, competitive in the vilest manner and insensitive to the suffering of others. He is a parasite exploiting all opportunities to get something for nothing, an insatiable, perpetual malcontent, constantly rebelling against accepted social behaviour. He is a thief, a lecher, an adulterer and an ingrate who knows no inhibitions and recognises no taboos. He is *Apebi-akyere*, the habitual show-off, and *Manbonyi*, wrecker of states or homes. He fosters disharmony and violates his people's trust, acting unscrupulously with relative impunity.

Altogether, then, Ananse is an excessive subversive who arouses affection and admiration while posing the problems and possibilities of his morphological and moral ambivalence – being at once spider and man, artistic and avaricious, dexterous and diabolic, wily and wayward. According to a folktale, Ananse acquired ownership of the stories from *Onyame* the Supreme Being himself. However in dispersing wisdom all over the earth after an unsuccessful attempt at hoarding, it may be said that Ananse's ownership of stories, as in the case of the storyteller, is ambivalent at best, tenuous at worst. When stripped of ambivalence the spider-man gets trapped in his own web of intrigues but is soon able to reclaim duplicity for escape from such confinement.

Ananse's (and by embodiment, the story and its teller's) nature and social logic essentially lie in this impulse to undermine constriction, a feature that intimates individual subjectivity, a potential to navigate power minefields and the ability to activate dialogic possibilities in the face of discursive closure. To see the Ananse ethos manifested in expression, therefore, is to observe those delightful, precarious and duplicitous actions that subvert the closure of meaning. I am convinced that the scenario I described at the beginning of this essay – that seemingly innocuous moment in the middle of the storytelling at Ekumfi Atwia, when the little girl walked on stage – represents an expression of the Ananse ethos.

Efua Sutherland has explained in her writings about *Anansesem* performance that bar the moments when the musical interludes of storytelling are open to general participation, any contribution of *Mboguw*, in the form of comic playlets such as the one I earlier illustrated, is the strict reserve of specialist performers, who do the acting while sharing the performance of the accompanying music. At Ekumfi Atwia, when much of the *Mboguw*, seemingly spontaneous and open to the general audience, were actually quite rehearsed and restricted to selected performers in a bid to present a 'flawless' performance for a visiting group, and when such restriction seemed to have transformed *Mboguw*, ordinarily a gesture of 'opening' into an act of 'closure', the Ananse ethos emerged, embodied in a little girl. The little girl – innocent yet not so innocent in her defiance of a restrictive shoo, accidental and yet somewhat deliberate in her occupation of the storytelling space – unmasked the pretence to open participation, unravelled the seams of stitched-up perfection and claimed for herself Efua Sutherland's desire to place children at the centre-stage, not the periphery, of the Ghanaian theatre experiment. This little girl altogether revealed that Ananse's social logic lies in his ethos and that in performance this ethos is the ultimate *Mboguw*, the definitive displacement of closed texts, the final supplanting of constrictive acts.

John Collins

The Entrance of Ghanaian Women
Into Popular Entertainment

Efua Sutherland helped pave the way for women to gain an avenue into popular music and drama. In this article I will discuss the problems faced by African popular performers (focusing on Ghana) and the various factors that from the 1960s led to increasing numbers of women entering the professional stage and commercial entertainment industry.

With some exceptions, until the 1960s there were few West African women popular stage artists. Up to this time Ghanaian highlife was mainly a male affair (Asante-Darko and Van de Geest 1993: 135), whilst the Nigerian musicologist Omibiye-Obidike says her country's popular music was 'dominated by men' with women popular musicians being generally portrayed by the public as immoral and sexually loose (1987: 4 and 25/6). This disapproval is also commented upon by Aicha Kone, one of the Cote d'Ivoire's top stars, who says 'not all families will accept a woman to be an artist and embrace her as a bride ... they think an artist cannot be a serious person, that she is never at home, travelling all the time' (Harrev 1992: 237).

The low regard for women performers by Ghanaian concert party and highlife band practitioners is manifested in their reluctance to allow women to join their groups; which is why up until the 1990s female parts and voices were practically always performed by men. Mr. Bampoe (Opia), the leader of Jaguar Jokers' concert party told me in 1974 (Collins 1994: 461) that forty women had approached him for a job as an actress-singer, but he had never hired any because women members of the audience would be annoyed to see their husbands admire a real woman on stage. Likewise, the pioneer concert comic, Bob Johnson, said that 'a girl on stage would be branded as a girl without morals' (Sutherland 1970: 15).

Vida Hynes (née Oparabea), who worked as a teenager in the 1960s with concert parties says that there was a similar reluctance to accept women into Okutieku's concert group (Collins 1994:166-170 and 1994: 461/2). The band manager thought it would create bad luck for women to move with men, especially, as Vida Oparabea explains, when females have menstruated and they touch band instruments – as the band may then not succeed. She continues: 'A lot of men in Ghana think that if a female is having menstruation she should not cook dinner for her husband, nor sleep with him – but just keep low.' Oparabea also had problems with some of the people in the towns she played in, who called her *ashao* (prostitute). Her parents even once had her locked up in the police cells to prevent her travelling with Okutieku's group.

Another concert woman who told me (interview May 1991) that she had had family problems is Adelaide Buabeng, who in 1965 ran away from home at sixteen to join the Workers' Brigade Concert Party. Her relatives were particularly annoyed, as she belonged to a royal Awutu family who considered the concert profession as 'hopeless'. Her mother, however, supported Adelaide and gave a bottle of schnapps to the chief each year to allow her daughter to continue her acting career.[1]

There are various reasons as to why African women entertainers were, and still are to a certain extent, belittled. One reason is that the status of all professional popular performers, men and women, is ambiguous as a result of their itinerant life, their youthfulness, their low to intermediate class position and the association between the guitar and drunkenness – compounded by imported artistic attitudes to popular Art and Sacred music and culture. Women popular artists, however, were held in particularly low esteem, and one group of reasons for this stemmed from some traditional African attitudes.

The menstrual taboo that Vida Oparabea mentions was one. Although traditionally women are not forbidden to sing and dance, there was also a widespread prohibition on women using many instruments, which were reserved for men. Amongst the Akans of Ghana, for instance, women are not allowed to play horns and drums (except the *donno* pressure drum) but are allowed to play light percussive instruments such as bamboo stamping tubes, *adenkum* gourds and rattles (see Nketia 1968). There is also a long tradition in African dramatic performance for women's roles to be played by men. This is found in the female impersonators associated with both certain festivals (like the Ga *Homowo* – see Zuesse 1979: 116) and indigenous theatre; such as that of the Mande people and of the Ibo *Okumkpo* theatre with its 'drag' parades (Finnegan: 1970 and Ottenberg: 1971).

These traditional carry-overs that lowered the status of contemporary female popular artists were exacerbated by some aspects of the modernisation/urbanisation process. These include tensions within the extended and polygamous family, an increase in prostitution resulting from the high ratio of urban male migrants, the formal education of women and the introduction of new sexual norms. All these combined together to threaten traditional male authority – which explains why popular texts do often dwell on the subject of sexual tension, marriage treachery, 'good-time' girls, witchcraft accusations and the 'duplicity' of city women (see Yankah 1984: 572 and Waterman 1986: 135).

Before turning to the changes that began from the 1960s that created openings for increasing numbers of women in the popular entertainment field, it should be pointed out that there were always exceptions and that in Ghana, for instance, there were a handful of well-known popular artists in the pre-1960 era.

One of the earliest references to one is in the 1929 Zonophone West African Record Catalogue that mentions the singer Akousia[2] Bonsu, who accompanied George Williams Aingo's Fanti guitar and accordion recordings. Kofi Ghanaba (1975: 730) talks about Squire Addo's discovery in the late 1930s of Aku Tawia who had 'a voice like a nightingale'. The Ga pianist, Addo, subsequently took her to London to record popular Ga songs for Zonophone, including one called 'Tiitaa Nmaa Wolo' (Sweet Canary Write a Letter). About this time the early Axim Trio concert party had been featuring an actress called Lady Wilmot – but she was later replaced by the female impersonator, E. K. Dadson (Braun and Cole: 1995). It should be noted that the konkoma highlife groups of the 1930s and 40s also contained women members, but not as instrumentalists, only as singers and dancers (personal communication Prof. A. M. Opoku: 1992). There were also a few female names in the 1950s, particularly Julie Okine, who sang with the Tempos dance band, and Perpetual Hammond, who acted with the Bob Vans Ghana Trio concert party.

The situation changed during the sixties, however, when women began to join popular groups in some numbers. In the early part of that decade some of the concert female impersonators began to be replaced by professional actresses. These included Asha of Arebela's group, Margaret Quainoo (Araba Stamp), Adelaide Buabeng, Comfort Akua Dampo and Esi Kom of the Workers' Brigade Concert Party and Madame Kenya of the Roches Big Sound. They were followed by the guitarist Vida Rose and the dramatist Efua Sutherland, who both set up their own concert parties in the late 1960s.

It was also in the sixties that the first local female 'pop' started to enter Ghanaian show business. The first were Lola Everett and Charlotte Dada, the latter starring in the 1972 musical film 'Doing Their Thing' about a young girl who, against her father's wishes, becomes a soul singer. During the seventies more and more women moved into the commercial music and recording scene. There was Efua Dorkenoo who, like the late Bella Bello of neighbouring Togo, sang Ewe pop songs; Naa Amanua who performed Ga cultural songs and 'highlife'; and Joana Okang, who sang with the Uhuru dance band. Important Akan recording artistes who also began their careers in the seventies were Mumbea, Janet Osei and Awura Ama. They were followed in the eighties by Abena Nyarteh (daughter of the late Senior Eddie Donkor), and Akosua Amoam, Akosua Agyapong and Yaa Oforiwa who, like Mumbea, worked with Nana Ampadu and his African Brothers guitar band. More recent is Lady Talata Heidi from the Northern Region and a host of female pop artists (Nana Yaa, Lady Burger, Philo Selasse, etc) and local 'gospel' singers who will be mentioned later. The rest of this article will examine the upsurge of female popular artistes since the 1960s by focusing on four major causes: the impact of luck and white foreign stars; the effect of post-independence government policies; aspects of the traditional ethos that have helped rather than hindered women, and the importance of the Christian church as an avenue for musical women.

THE INFLUENCE OF FOREIGN FEMALE STARS

It was the solo singers that emerged in the 1930s in association with jazz and swing music (Ethel Waters, Ella Fitzgerald, Lena Horne, Judy Garland, Peggy Lee, etc) that led to the first layer of African female stars. One of the first was the Zimbabwean singer Dorothy Nazuka, whose career goes back to the thirties and who, according to Makwenda (1990: 5/6) 'specialised in African versions of American jazz favourites'. She was followed by (and also influenced) the most famous popular music star to come out of Africa, Miriam Makeba. She joined the South African Manhattan Brothers close-harmony group in 1952 and later formed the all-female Skylarks, modelled on the American Andrews Sisters (Coplan 1985: 178). The Skylarks in turn paved the way for the Simanje-manje (Now-now) popular music of 1960/70s South Africa, performed by groups such as the Dark City Sisters and Mahotella Queens (see Makeba and Hall: 1987).

In West Africa jazz and swing became part of the local night-life scene from the Second World War period. Ghanaba (1975: 60) refers to the local women, Dinah Attah, who had visited the United States and sang jazz numbers in a 'wild bar' in Accra that catered for wartime American G.I.'s, E. T. Mensah told me (Collins: 1986) that his Tempos highlife dance band, although initially an all-male group when it was formed towards the end of the War, was by 1953 featuring the woman maraccas player Agnes Ayitey and the singer Julie Okine. A year later the Rhythm Aces dance band included a Nigerian singer called Cathy (personal communication Oscarmore Ofori and Betty Mould-Iddirisu: 1992). A stimulus to local dance band women came from the 1956 visit to Ghana by Louis Armstrong and his All Stars that featured the famous blues singer, Velma Middleton (Collins 1986: 23).

Nigerian swing and jazz was pioneered by the late Bobby Benson who, in 1948 and together with his English wife Cassandra (personal communication Kayo Martins 1990), began their Modern Theatrical Troupe in Lagos. The pair danced the jitterbug to jazz and boogie-woogie music played by women saxophone and trumpet players. They were often accompanied by the local Aikins Sisters' singing group and later the Nigerian/Sierra Leonian jazz vocalist, Maude Meyer. Benson's dance band was also the first Nigerian popular music group to introduce on-stage, dancing-girls cabaret' (see Clark: 1979 and Omibiye-Obidike: 1987).

In more recent years it has been soul pop, 'hot' gospel and reggae-singing foreign women who have provided a model for African artists. Kozadi (1973: 276) comments on the importance of Aretha Franklin as well as James Brown for the *kiri-kiri* style of Congo-jazz, whilst Nigeria's top reggae artistes, Peggy Umanah and Evi Edna Ogholi-Ogosi, take their inspiration from Afro-Caribbean women.

Particularly significant is that since the 1960s many world-acclaimed African- American, Latin and Caribbean women stars have actually visited Africa. Millicent Small (Millie) made an African tour in the 1960s; the Brazilian Omo Alakyta performed at Nigeria's FESTAC 77, and Bob Marley's 'I Three' female singers sang at Zimbabwe's independence celebration in 1980. In Ghana a number of African-American women appeared in the 1971 'Soul to Soul' concert, including Tina Turner, the Staple Singers, Roberta Flack and the women members of the Voices of East Harlem. In 1974 there was a visit by the jazz pianist Patti Bown and later ones by Jermaine Jackson, Dionne Warwick and Nina Simone. In the early nineties Rita Marley actually decided to put down roots and settle in Ghana.

THE EFFECT OF AFRICAN GOVERNMENT POLICIES

The cultural and educational policies of the newly independent African states have also contributed to women's entrance into popular entertainment. These policies include the establishment of state and parastatal bands and theatres, the projection of local performing arts through the media, and government-endorsed local and Pan-African festivals. In 1961 the Guinea government set up the Les Amazons dance band within the female gendarmerie which launched the singing career of Sona Diabete. Ten years later the Nigerian government formed Maggie Aghumo's all-female Armed Forces Band, whilst Liberia's Fatu Gayflor rose to fame through their country's National Cultural Troupe. To take one example of women playing at a state-sponsored festival we can take the case of Nigeria's FESTAC 77 where M'Pongo Love, Miriam Makeba, Yatta and Les Amazons and Dina Reindorf's Dwenesie Choir represented Zaire, Black South Africa, Liberia, Guinea and Ghana respectively. Dr. Omibiye-Obidike (1987: 5) claims that the opening-up of Nigerian education to women in her country's post-independence era led them to venture into areas that were otherwise dominated by men, and she refers to the university background of pop-singers Dora Ifudu and Onyeka Onwenu. The Yoruba Lijadu Sisters also had a 'substantial educational background' (Grass: 1988) as did Liberia's Miatta Fahnbulleh (Adih: 1989) and Yatta Zoe (Collins: 1992).

The Ghanaian government created a major avenue for concert party actresses when, in the early sixties, President Nkrumah formed the Workers' Brigade Concert Party. When the Brigade group broke up in the mid-sixties some of its actresses joined the Kusum Agoromba concert party, founded in 1969 by the University lecturer Efua Sutherland and linked with the National Drama Studio.

Since then a large number of concert actresses have risen to fame, many being members of a new brand of mixed-caste television concert party series that began in the early seventies. The first was the Osofo Dadzie series that starred Beatrice Kissi and Florence Mensah, and after it was reconstituted in 1986 the actresses Joyce Agyeman and Mary Adjei. The Obra concert party, formed in 1982, also has a mixed caste that has included Esi Kom, Cecilia Adjei and the group's lead character Grace Omaboe. Her stage name is Maamie Dokono and she is director of the group. Omaboe was at one time the School Drama Organiser for Greater Accra and Cecilia Adjei is a University lecturer.

TRADITIONAL FACTORS THAT HAVE ABETTED POPULAR ARTISTES

In spite of the customary restrictions on musical women mentioned earlier, there are aspects of African culture that have facilitated the appearance of women on the popular stage. The most obvious is that there are African societies that have a tradition of female professional performers which has simply been continued into the present. An example is the *djely mousso* or West African female hereditary *jali* (*jeli*) or griot. They customarily sing, clap, dance and play small percussion instruments that accompany the kora, xylophone (and the guitar today) that are played by men. Many of Mali's current top singing stars, such as Fanta Damba, Fanta Sacko, Tata Bambo, Koutay Kouyate and Ami Keita fall into this category (see Duran: 1989).

Another important feature of pre-colonial Africa was that women were not excluded from the musical sphere altogether; indeed the hunter-gatherer societies of the Kung people of South Africa and the Mbuti of Zaire were completely egalitarian in the music making (see Frisbie 1971:274 and Turnbull 1962: 206). In agricultural communities, too, women played and still play a major role in art production, although women's and men's art often constitute very different spheres of activity (see Hay and Stichter 1984: 114/5 and Drinker 1948: 15). Roberts (1974: 50/1) claims there is a widespread African tendency to regard certain sorts of music and instruments as being for men and others for women. Nketia (1961) refers to the organisation of African music into feminine domestic and maiden songs, and masculine hunting and warrior songs. Let us take a few West African examples.

Omibiye-Obidike (1987: 5) says that Yoruba women have a special realm of music specifically meant for them, and the members of the Sande secret age-set societies of Mende women of Sierra Leone, like the Poro initiation society male counterpart, have their own specific *bundu* drums, instruments and songs (see Van Oven 1981: 21/3 and 46/7). The Tiv of Nigeria have exclusively female wedding songs to welcome a new bride, and Keil (1979: 155) notes there is a marked difference in the way Tiv men and women dance. In northern Ghana there is a twirling dance for Dagomba men called *takai* and another for women called *tora* (see Haydou and Marks 1985: 177). The coastal Fantis of Ghana have the male *kununku* and female *akrod* recreational dance/music (personal communication A. A. Mensah). Similarly, the neighbouring coastal Ga people have the male music of *asafo* warrior companies and what Hampton (1978: 2) calls their 'auxiliary' and mainly female *adowa* preference groups. The Gas borrowed both these *asafo* and *adowa* age-set ensembles from the Akans.

Because Ghanaian women have not traditionally been excluded from music, they have become involved with the emergence of neo-traditional forms (Akan, Konkoma, Nnwonkoro and Osoode; Ewe Borborbor, Ga Kpanlogo, Dagomba Simpa, *et al*) albeit as dancers and singers rather than instrumentalists. Some of these neo-traditional forms in turn (like Koo Nimos 'up and up' music and Ga cultural music) have become commercialised on record and stage – and so have provided women with an access to popular entertainment.

Let us take the case of Ga 'cultural' groups that consciously go back to roots by drawing on Ga folk music. Indeed, *Wulomei*, the name of the pioneering group of the early seventies, formed by Nii Ashitey and Saka Acquaye, is the Ga word for both indigenous priests and priestesses. This popular genre has subsequently introduced large numbers of Ga women to the stage and recording studios. The women sing, dance and play small percussion instruments, whilst the men sing and play at local drums and guitar. Both sexes play the *atenteben* flute. In fact one of the most well known of these Ga 'cultural' groups, Suku Troupe, is actually run by a woman. This is Naa Amanua who is an ex-vocalist of Wulomei.

THE CHURCH AS A ROUTE FOR WOMEN POPULAR PERFORMERS

Just as the church (especially the Protestant one) has provided American and European women with a road to music making, so too has it facilitated the entrance of African women into the popular entertainment field, particularly the African separatist churches that have been so much influenced by the Protestant Methodist, Baptist, Pentecostal and charismatic churches. The African separatist churches continue the indigenous custom of dancing and clapping during worship and the membership of these churches and their choirs contain a high proportion of women.

In Ghana these churches became particularly important for popular music during the country's economic decline of the 1970s when the music industry partially collapsed and a considerable number of musicians had to go abroad to continue their careers. At this point in time many guitar band musicians began to join the choirs that were run and financed by the local separatist churches. This in turn led to the growth of local gospel and 'gospel-highlife' groups that are guitar bands fronted by sexually mixed four-part harmony choirs singing danceable Christian songs. Prior to this, guitarists and guitar-bands had been associated with drunkenness and the footloose life of itinerant bands, so few women were involved with them. However, when the guitar-bands went under the patronage of the church, Christian families found it difficult to forbid their daughters joining them. As a result, after the 1980s a whole new generation of women singers rose to fame. These, to name a few, include Mary Ghansah-Ansong, the Tagoe Sisters, Stella Dugan, Josephine Dzodzegbe, Mavis Sackey, Evelyn Boate, Esther Nyamekye and the Daughters of Glorious Jesus. Bender (1991: 109) mentions a similar situation in Nigeria where there are a great number of mixed and even all-female choirs, maintained by the various independent and Aladura churches. He cites the example of the Good Women's Choir of the Christian Apostolic Church of Ibadan that has released many record albums.

This move from secular to sacred that happened during Ghana's economic problems of the seventies has parallels with the United States; for with the Great Depression of the 1930s and consequent collapse of the record industry, Thomas Dorsey, Ethel Waters and many other American blues and jazz artists, moved away from the secular 'devils music' and began to play gospel music, i.e. 'hot' gospel. This infusion of popular music into the black church explains the blues and jazz influence on pre-war hot-gospel artists like Mahalia Jackson and Sister Rosetta Tharpe; and ultimately, in the post-war era, on Diana Ross, Nina Simone, Dinah Washington, Roberta Flack, Aretha Franklin, the Staple Singers and the other gospel-trained soul and pop stars who have contributed to the feminisation of African popular music.

Moreover, it was from the postwar boom period in the United States that many African-American gospel singers moved from sacred music to secular and commercial 'doowop', soul, motown and disco dance music. Although the process of the sanctification of popular entertainment has happened much more recently in Ghana than it did in the States, there is now the beginning of a corresponding sacred-to-secular trend. Today some Ghanaian men and women gospel artists are moving into the area of commercial dance-music recording. Indeed, church-trained women gospel singers are now a major resource for the female session-musicians in Ghanaian recording studios for local 'pop' releases.

Penina Mlama

Empowerment for Gender Equality Through Theatre: The Case of *Tuseme*

INTRODUCTION

The world has seen protracted efforts towards eliminating the deeply rooted gender inequalities in all societies. The inequalities, which span the economic, political and social fabric of life, are very complex and have proved formidable and tremendously difficult to erase.

Significant success has, however, been scored in a number of areas. Massive political campaigns internationally and nationally have resulted in major policy changes and political commitment to create the right climate for gender equality economically, politically and socially. The United Nations world women conferences (Mexico 1975, Nairobi 1985, Copenhagen 1989, Beijing 1995, New York 2000) had a big impact on making governments all over the world put gender on their development agenda.

Assessment of the status of gender equality shows significant progress in terms of narrowing the gender gap in relation to the provision of equal opportunities for participation in development. Increased participation has been recorded in politics, economic production, education and management. Legislation has given women many rights previously denied to them.

Despite all this tremendous progress, attainment of gender equality in all spheres of life is still a far cry. Major challenges remain to be conquered to ensure opportunities are provided and utilised effectively to make both men and women participate on an equal footing in all aspects of development.

One of the major challenges in this respect is the lack of gender equality empowerment for both men and women. Socialisation processes in most societies in Africa clearly delineate gender roles, responsibility and status on a patriarchal basis whereby the man is superior in all sorts of ways to the woman. Attitudes are inculcated, fostered and cemented from the time the child is very young that man is superior to woman. The nature and degree of that superiority differs from one culture to another but the underlying factor is that there is no equality when it comes to gender.

In this context, the man is socialised to believe that he is superior to the woman, that he must make the decisions, he must fend for the family, he must show physical prowess, and for all this the women must revere, respect, worship and obey him without question.

The woman, on the other hand, is brought up to believe in her inferiority to man: she must be subservient, let the man make the decisions, not speak out, not challenge the man especially in public, serve the man without question and believe in the intellectual superiority of the man to lead, to own property, and be in the forefront in everything.

This socialisation process, which unfortunately goes on unabated, poses the greatest challenge to any efforts to bring about gender equality economically, socially or culturally. In a way, it negates the very foundation of gender equality because in this case, both the man and the woman are disempowered for gender equality. Until a time is reached that the mind of the man is transformed to believe that the woman is equal to him and that of the woman to believe that she is equal to the man, there will be no gender equality. But transforming that mind-set is the greatest test of all.

THE BACKGROUND TO TUSEME

The *Tuseme* 'let us speak out' programme is an example of a practical intervention dealing with this challenge of empowerment for gender equality. Founded in 1996, *Tuseme* is an outreach programme of the Department of Performing Arts, of the University of Dar es Salaam, Tanzania, for secondary schools. A survey of the status of participation of secondary-school-age girls in public life and education indicated severe inhibitions resulting from the socialisation discussed above. Generally girls felt constrained to speak in public; their self-confidence and self-esteem were low, participation in classroom interaction was characterised by shyness, their social relations with boys subservient. This contributed to low academic performance and inadequate participation in asserting themselves as equal members of their society in many aspects.

The objectives of *Tuseme*, therefore, are to empower girls to understand the gender constraints to their academic and social development, give the girls a voice to speak out and express their views about the identified problems, find solutions and take initiative to solve the problems. This includes empowering the girls to give their views concerning factors leading to such problems like school drop-outs, teenage pregnancy, sexual harassment, gender discriminatory practices inside and outside the classroom and any other gender-related problems identified by the girls themselves. The girls are also empowered to find ways through which they themselves can actively participate in the process of solving the identified problems. With the activities taking place at the school and community level, *Tuseme* has several unique features.

One is its unique process of empowerment through the theatre-for-development approach. As mentioned above, women often display the inability to speak out in public, shyness in front of men and high levels of self-confidence. Studies on the participation of women in theatre have, however, shown that the inability of women to speak in public or their shyness has nothing to do with their ability to do so. In traditional theatre performances all over Africa – such as dance, drama, storytelling, which are indeed very public performances, often done to large audiences – women are very vocal, confident and effective communicators. One only has to attend a wedding dance to witness how sharply and ably women analyse, assess and articulate the social dynamics in the community.

Their assumed shyness or lack of confidence, therefore, has more to do with the forum for public speaking in question than their inability to speak out in public. Of course expecting woman to make a speech in a public meeting challenges their confidence, because public meetings are the domain of men in the community, and women are not given the opportunity to participate in such meetings; thus they do not develop any skills for public speech. On the other hand, they are exposed to theatre performance from a very early age and develop the necessary skills for public performance.

The *Tuseme* programme, therefore, decided to pick on theatre as the medium of communication for the empowerment of the girls. The reasoning behind the choice is that, if one wants to give the girls the opportunity to speak out, the most effective way of doing that is to give them a medium of communication they are well versed in. So, theatre was the medium of choice for *Tuseme*. Theatrical forms familiar to the girls and of their own choice, including dance, drama, storytelling, rap, recitations and song are used by the girls to speak out and express their views.

The second main feature of *Tuseme* is the focus on the girls themselves. Advocacy for girls has often taken the form of people speaking on behalf of girls, speaking about the girls or speaking to the girls. The girls themselves become passive bystanders with little attention paid to their own viewpoint, expectations and desires. This approach has often led to the wrong strategies being adopted to improve the status of girls or failure to produce meaningful results.

Tuseme has adopted the approach of making the girls themselves the main players in the process of empowering themselves to speak out. They identify the problems, they analyse them, and they suggest solutions and take action to solve them.

The third feature is the involvement of other stakeholders. It is understood that the gender-based problems affecting girls emerge out of a complex social construct with many players. Even if the girls take an active role in solving those problems, the other players must also play their role, otherwise the efforts of the girls will only hit a wall. For example, where boys carry the attitudes of superiority over girls, any level of empowerment of girls to defy this superiority can be met with resistance from the boys. It is necessary, therefore, to empower the boys to accept that it is fine for the girls to be equal to them.

Similarly, teachers, both male and female, are socialised into the male-superiority construct. If the girls are empowered otherwise, the teachers who wield authority in the school can easily frustrate the efforts of the girls to solve their gender-based problems. Studies have shown for example that sexual harassment is rampant in many schools due to the attitude of teachers who see women merely as sexual objects for their pleasure. This is a major cause of schoolgirl pregnancy and school drop-out. In order for the *Tuseme* girls to solve these problems, the teachers, both male and female, must be actively involved in the process.

Furthermore, many of the gender-based problems faced by the school girls are rooted at home, in both the family and the community at large. For example, it is parents who decide to marry off their school-going daughters. It is the parents who demand that the girls perform many household chores before and after school thus leaving the girls with little study time and too fatigued to concentrate in class. The community as a whole often puts little value on the education of the girl-child as compared to the boy and, therefore, takes no action to support the girl to be taken to school, to stay in school, or to perform well.

Tuseme, therefore, involves all stakeholders in the process of empowerment of the girls. The girls take a central and leading role but all the other stakeholders actively participate in the *Tuseme* process.

THE *TUSEME* PROCESS

The *Tuseme* process has stages as shown in the following table:

No.	Process	Activities	Expectation
1.	Preliminaries	Facilitators discuss with the school authorities the intention to carry out a *Tuseme* process.	The school authorities and community are ready for the process.
2.	Familiarisation	Facilitators introduce *Tuseme* to the relevant authorities in order to familiarise themselves with: – The social set-up of the school community – major groups that constitute the school community, relationship with the neighbourhood etc. – The physical set-up of the school, boundaries, library facilities, sports grounds, etc and to determine whether they are adequate or not.	To better understand the working environment. To get preliminary information on the subject matter.

No.	Process	Activities	Expectation
		– The academic performance of the school in general and cohort group in particular. Employ the use of creative dramatics to create rapport and a condusive working atmosphere.	
3.	Data collection	Divide participants into small research teams and assign them to interview a certain number of community members about issues related to the goals and objectives of *Tuseme* (strengths and constraints). Ask the teams to submit their findings in writing.	To get information on the issues of concern that impede social and academic development of girls.
4.	Data analysis	Data analysis process is undertaken as follows: • List all the findings. • Cluster/group the findings/ issues that are not related to the topic. • Verify the authenticity of the findings.	
		• Prioritise the findings in order of urgency. • Classify the findings according to their similarities and differences (clustering and collapsing). • Find out root causes of the findings. • Find possible solutions to problems. • Identify responsible people or parties to help solve different problems.	

No.	Process	Activities	Expectation
5.	Theatre creation	Discuss in groups which issues from the data analysis you want to include in your performance. Select forms of art, which you are competent and comfortable to use. Create a theatre performance on the selected issue by involving everybody in the group in the creativity and performance. The performance should be created in a way that it can provoke discussion on solutions to the identified problem. Select one person to play the role of a joker (one who will lead the post-performance discussion after the stage presentation). Ensure that costumes, props and scenery are designed and available.	Participation of all cohort members
6.	Performance	Discuss with the participants and the school administration about the possible day and time to do the performance. Make sure that the entire community is invited to the performance. Do a formal performance to an audience of the school and surrounding community.	
7.	Post-performance discussion	Immediately after the performance, hold a discussion with the audience. Make sure the joker involves all stakeholders in the discussion. The joker should avoid answering questions but challenge the audience to answer the questions instead. The joker should make sure that all issues are discussed thoroughly.	

No.	Process	Activities	Expectation
8.	Action Plan	Involve all the stakeholders in formulating an action plan for the implementation of the action agreed upon to solve the identified problems. Carry out this exercise either immediately after the performance or the following day. Action plan usually involves the *Tuseme* cohort group although it is also possible to do it with the entire school community. Whatever the case, the action plan should be endorsed by the school administration for it to be effected. The exercise is done on a chart which indicates the following: • Problem • Root causes • Solution • Activities • Time frame • Responsible person/part • Resource/budget • Indicators	
9.	Creation of Clubs	*Tuseme* clubs are formed in the school Elections are held for office bearers	

(Makoye: 2004)

The *Tuseme* club – formed, led and run by the students themselves – became a permanent structure at the school to serve as the beacon for the implementation of the action plans agreed upon and monitoring of results and their impact. The objectives of the clubs centre around empowering the students, both boys and girls, but with particular attention to the girls, to be self-confident, assertive, disciplined, and proactive in academics. The clubs also encourage the students to have positive attitudes and values, respect for each other, set high goals and share ideas and experiences. *Tuseme* clubs organise many activities in the school, including performances, debates, guidance and counselling, peer education on life skills, study groups and open days for the community. *Tuseme* clubs also contribute to a national *Tuseme* newsletter through having a club editorial board.

Once every year, all the *Tuseme* schools come together in a *Tuseme* festival, to share experiences on the action they have taken to solve the problems identified. Activities at the festival include theatre performances, empowerment workshops, discussions, visits to academic institutions and industry, discussions with national-level role models and academic activities, including exposure to science, technology and ICT.

HISTORICAL DEVELOPMENT OF TUSEME

As mentioned earlier, *Tuseme* was founded in Tanzania in 1996. Over the years, *Tuseme* has been established in thirty secondary schools all over the country and has recently been introduced in ten primary schools in Kilosa district. The Ministry of Education stated in the Secondary Education Sector plan that *Tuseme* would be scaled up and introduced in all secondary schools in the country between 2004 and 2009.

In addition to establishing *Tuseme* in the schools, a programme of training has also been undertaken. A pool of about fifty resource persons was drawn from theatre artists, educators, and community development workers. The department of Fine and Performing Arts is also training its students in the *Tuseme* process. This pool of resource persons provides the facilitators that work in the schools.

Two teachers from each of the *Tuseme* schools have also been trained in the *Tuseme* process. The training is geared towards imparting skills in democratic school management, artistic performance and gender awareness. This training is important in order for the teachers and the school management to create space for the empowered students, especially bearing in mind the fact that schools in Africa normally operate on authoritarian management systems. It is also important to note that the *Tuseme* process calls for the transformation of the students and the school environment. The teachers, therefore, need to be equipped to manage this transformation positively. The heads of the schools also undergo *Tuseme* workshops for the same purpose.

The MIALI Training Centre founded in Dar es Salaam in 2002 has also conducted training of resource persons into the *Tuseme* process. The success of *Tuseme* in Tanzania led to its introduction in other parts of Africa. In a collaborative effort between the Department of Fine and Performing Arts of the University of Dar es salaam, the Forum for African Women Educationalists, FAWE, and MIALI, *Tuseme* has been introduced in schools in Rwanda, Senegal, Kenya, Ethiopia, The Gambia, Namibia, Guinea, Mali, Chad and Burkina Faso.

In June 2004, during a Policy consultation that brought together ministers and senior officials from ministries of education from twenty-seven African countries, *Tuseme* was presented as a best practice in girls' education in Africa. The aim was to convince the represented ministries to adopt, scale up and mainstream *Tuseme* in their national education systems.

MAJOR ACHIEVEMENTS OF TUSEME

Tuseme has shown significant success towards empowering girls in various ways. An external evaluation commissioned by SIDA of *Tuseme* in Tanzania, conducted in 2002, concluded that there were clear indications of empowerment for the girls who have gone through the *Tuseme* process. The empowerment is reflected in the increased self-confidence and assertiveness through speaking out and expressing their views.

The Headteacher of Bagamoyo Secondary School in Tanzania is quoted as saying: 'I have noted that the students who have gone through the *Tuseme* process in my school are not intimidated to say whatever they feel is not working well around them within or without the school' (Makoye: 2004). In 1998, *Tuseme* students in Msalato Secondary School in Tanzania successfully took up the matter of a teacher who was not academically competent by asking school management to replace him (Materego: 1999).

Tuseme girls have confronted or reported teachers who harass them, who do not turn up to teach or come to class late. They have challenged school administration where things are not working well. An important point to bear in mind here, though, is that the *Tuseme* process enables the students to handle all these issues in an intelligent and amicable manner through engagement in critical analysis, dialogue and discussion.

Tuseme school managements have admitted that their initial fears over empowerment of the students have been unfounded, because in actual fact *Tuseme* has become a very useful ally to school management in the smooth running of the schools. Members of *Tuseme* pride themselves in being people of high integrity, discipline and highly motivated to succeed in what they do. The Headmistress of Mgugu Secondary School admitted, for example, that she was pleasantly surprised when she reported to the school as a new headmistress to find that she had a very light work load because the students actually ran the school in all areas relating to student management themselves (FAWE: 2003).

Tuseme schools have also shown big improvement in girls' academic performance. Passes (at division one to three) in the national O-level examinations for Msalato Secondary School, rose from 22% in 1995, before the introduction of *Tuseme* in 1996 to 45% in 2003. Students selected to continue to A-level improved from 20% in 1996 to 90% in 2003. At Bagamoyo Secondary School the pass rate increased from 22% in 1995 to 44% in 2003 and transition to A-level from 9% in 1995 to 25% in 2003 (Makoye: 2004). The *Tuseme* process has also significantly contributed to improvement in academic performance at the FAWE Centres of Excellence in Kenya, Senegal, Rwanda and Tanzania.

At Kajiado primary school in Kenya, the average score in national examinations improved from 66% in 2000 to 75% in 2002. Transition to secondary school improved from 67% in 1997 to 85% in 2001 and to 100% in 2003. The Rwanda FAWE girls' school produced the 2 top girls in the 2002 national O-level examinations and 6 out of the top 10 in 2003 were from the school. At the CEM Grand Diourbel Secondary School in Senegal, the pass rate went up from 27.62% in 2002 to 54.9% in 2003 (FAWE: 2004).

Tuseme schools have also shown a significant reduction in dropouts due to pregnancy. For example, at Songea Secondary School in Tanzania school pregnancy dropped by 62.5% between 1999 and 2001. Between 1997 and 2004 there was one case of pregnancy at Bagamoyo, four in Msalato (Makoye: 2004).

At the FAWE Centres of Excellence the pregnancy statistics for 2001-2003 are:

AIC Kajiado Primary School, Kenya – 3 out of 499 students (0.6%)
FAWE Rwanda Girls' school – 2 out of 740 students (0.3%)
Mgugu Secondary School, Tanzania – 1 out of 275 students (0.5%)
CEM Grand Diuorbel, Senegal – 0 out of 275 students (0%)

The girls from the *Tuseme* schools have also reported the elimination of cases of sexual harassment by the teachers (FAWE: 2003). This is due to the fact that the teachers know that because the girls are empowered they are bound to take up any issue of sexual harassment. On the other hand, since the teachers are also empowered through the *Tuseme* process, they become part of the effort to eliminate sexual harassment in the school.

Increased gender awareness among teachers, school management and the community surrounding the schools is another important achievement of the *Tuseme* process. Support for girls' education, willingness by teachers and the community to support the girls and assist them to eliminate the gender constraint to their education has become apparent in the *Tuseme* schools. Teachers have become proud of the improved performance of the girls and have gone out of their way out to help where originally they would not have done so. For example, in many of the *Tuseme* schools the teachers are willing to give extra tuition to the girls who need it without charging, which is the practice otherwise.

The *Tuseme* spirit also generally gives the whole school community a sense of belonging and pride in themselves. These examples go to show that there is much value in the empowerment of girls.

THE TUSEME THEATRE PROCESS AND THE EMPOWERMENT OF GIRLS

The above-mentioned achievements have much to do with the *Tuseme* process itself. It was mentioned earlier that *Tuseme* uses the theatre in the empowerment process. The theatre process in the form of dance, drama, song, story telling, rap, recitation and such other forms has been the core of the success in making the girls come out of their shells to speak out and express their views. *Tuseme* has discovered that, once the girls are given the opportunity to express themselves through theatre forms, they do it without any inhibitions. In actual fact their participation in theatrical performances seems to flow very naturally.

The same is true for the teachers and members of the community. As described earlier, all the stakeholders participate in the process and none of the categories of the stakeholders showed any inhibition in participating actively in the theatre performances both as performers and audiences.

It became clear through the *Tuseme* experience that people – men and women, boys and girls – actively express themselves and speak out when the theatrical medium is applied. This may be due to the entertainment characteristic of theatre, which makes it fun to participate in. Another factor could be the familiarity of the medium to the community.

Theatre performances, such as dance, storytelling, recitations and dramatic skits are forms, which members of the community participate in throughout life. They have, therefore, mastered the skills for using such forms for expressing themselves. It should be remembered also that theatre plays an important educational role in African traditions. As such using theatre to speak out on problems, as is the case in *Tuseme*, is a very familiar practice in many African societies.

The girls in *Tuseme*, as well as the boys, have always come up with fantastic songs, dances, dramatic skits, stories, and other theatre performances portraying their views of the gender-based problems they face and their analyses of the causes and possible solutions. The numerous reports on *Tuseme* workshops at the University of Dar es Salaam, Department of Fine Art and at FAWE have many examples of such artistic creativity. Themes have included negative attitudes towards girls' education by parents, pregnancies, sexual harassment, forced marriages, sugar daddies, peer pressure, bad school leadership, gender-insensitive school environment, the impact of poverty, divorce, HIV/AIDS on girls' education, to mention but a few.

An important point to be noted here is that these artistic creations were by the girls themselves; and even by so doing the girls built their confidence to speak out.

CHALLENGES EMERGING OUT OF THE *TUSEME* EXPERIENCE

A number of challenges have emerged out of the *Tuseme* experience.

First, the realisation that even though so much has been said about the need to liberate women from the cultural attitudes that foster their oppression, very little change is happening on the ground. Working at the level of the school and community has shown how deeply entrenched these cultural values and attitudes are at the schools and the communities around them and how they continue to negatively affect gender relations.

Secondly, it became clear that the education systems where *Tuseme* was introduced have no programme towards the empowerment of both girls and boys for gender-equality issues. This was true for both the main curriculum and extra-curricular activities. There is, therefore, a big demand for the *Tuseme* kind of process if the young generation is to be equipped with skills with which to assert themselves as equal partners with the opposite sex for personal and national development.

Due to the negligence of this need by the education system, the teachers and the school management system are not equipped to handle empowerment for gender equality. Indeed, even the simple gender awareness is in short supply in most schools. The author recalls a personal experience where, during a *Tuseme* training workshop for secondary school teachers, one male teacher confessed that he had been teaching in girls' schools for nineteen years and he had had no idea how gender constraints could so negatively affect the girls. He added by saying that he shuddered to think just how much damage which he as a teacher had caused to so many girls in those years and insisted that this training must be given to all teachers as a matter of urgency.

The third challenge relates to boys. It is often assumed that because the men are given a superior status in the society, then the boys are fine and when it comes to gender issues, they are part of the enemy. The *Tuseme* experience has shown that the boys are suffering from the fact that people do not realise that they also need empowerment to handle gender equality issues. Having been socialised to believe that they are superior to women, they are often at a loss as to what to do when situations challenge their superiority. Often they are also struggling between logic that tells them that girls are equal to them intellectually or otherwise and society pressure that expects them to behave in a superior manner to women. Peer pressure on gender issues seems to be harder on the boys, pushing them to treat girls in ways that they know is not right. Consequently, attention needs to be directed to the empowerment of boys to handle gender equality.

The *Tuseme* process managed to empower the boys so well that they comfortably espoused and accepted the idea of gender equality and actively participated in enabling the girls and themselves to be empowered. A case comes to mind of a boy from Ruvu Secondary School who was a leading athlete at the school and was selected to be in the school team for the national school competition. But he chose to participate in the national *Tuseme* festival, which was taking place at the same time. He admitted to the author that he presented to his teachers and his fellow male students that he saw more value in building up his gender skills through *Tuseme*.

The fourth challenge is structural. How can the *Tuseme* process be mainstreamed in the normal school system? So far *Tuseme* has operated as a project outside the normal school curricula. The *Tuseme* activities are conducted outside the normal curriculum even though the ministry of education and the school management accepts them officially. In Tanzania, for example, *Tuseme* has now been taken up as a programme of the Ministry of Education. Still the *Tuseme* activities remain extra-curricular. The question is how can the empowerment of both girls and boys, as done through the *Tuseme* process, be mainstreamed into the education system?

The fifth challenge relates to the place of the theatre in the education system. Most school systems treat theatre as an extra-curricular activity. Theatre has also been used to serve educational campaigns on such issues as HIV/AIDS, environment or health and sanitation. In most cases, the students are audiences to messages delivered through theatrical forms. The difference with *Tuseme* is that the students themselves are the creators and communicators of the messages and as a result of which they get empowered by owning both the message and the process of delivery.

It is important, therefore, for the education systems to pay more attention to the potential to empower the young people contained in the theatrical process and use it more as a liberating process for both girls and boys. There is enough evidence from the *Tuseme* experience that theatre has great potential for that.

CONCLUSION

In conclusion, it can be said that *Tuseme* has proved to be a powerful process of empowering girls as well as boys to overcome the deeply entrenched unequal gender relations and inhibitions. It is hoped that this *Tuseme* experience will open more opportunities for young people, especially girls, in Africa to be given the opportunity to acquire the skills with which to handle and overcome the rampant and complex constraints to meaningful and equal gender relations.

Mabel Komasi

Efua Theodora Sutherland: Visionary Pioneer of Ghanaian Children's Literature

Formal European education was introduced into the Gold Coast during the middle of the eighteenth century, when the Reverend Thomas Thompson, an Anglican missionary, established the first school in Cape Coast in 1752. The development of a reading culture among the people in the country was a major part of the aims of the various missionaries and colonial merchants who began working in the then Gold Coast. Producing scribes and clerks for their commercial establishments; and for the missionary enterprise, teachers and catechists to read and interpret the Bible and allied literatures for would-be converts was foremost on the missionary agenda. So was equipping the local people with the requisite skills to be able to read the English Bible, thereby helping to propagate Christianity.

Written literature for adults thus could be said to have begun with the introduction of formal education, and, consequently, literacy by the colonialists. Although there is some evidence to suggest that to the north of the Gold Coast, some people had already learnt to write Arabic, this was not widespread. It was employed, according to de Graft Hanson (1993: 17), mainly for 'the more mundane and purely utilitarian activities of keeping official records, maintaining correspondence between kingdoms and for preparing amulets and charms for those who had need of spiritual protection' rather than for literary and creative purposes.

The long period between the establishment of the first school in 1752 and the emergence of books written specifically for children in the late 1960s makes it appear as if the emergent writers such as J. Benibengor Blay, Asare Konadu, Ayi Kwei Armah, Bediako Asare and others (Angmor 1996: 39-43), who were beginning to make a name for themselves in the field of adult literature, did not regard books for children as worthy of their attention. In the Ghanaian context an additional *raison d'être* for the minimal interest shown in local creativity was the availability of inexpensive foreign books. By Independence, however, the creative stimulus was awakened in Ghanaian writers as a result of the ferment of ideas that accompanied the Independence drive.

Before the middle of the eighteenth century, however, parents and grandparents drew upon the stock of traditional Ghanaian folklore to entertain and educate both young and old. When we turn to other African as well as

Ghanaian children's literature, it is clear that traditional literature, particularly folk tales, is crucial in its beginnings.

The pioneering efforts of people such as Efua Sutherland, who were committed to the cause of children's literature, must be acknowledged. Equally important is the growth of Ghanaian publishing houses, such as Educational Publishers and Manufacturers Limited, Royal Gold Publishers, Quick Service, Afram Publications and recently, Sub-Saharan Publishers, who publish children's books. This development has also eliminated the thorny problem of the foreign exchange which, hitherto, used to stifle publishing abroad. Here again, we must acknowledge the role that Efua Sutherland and others played in helping to establish the indigenous Afram Publications, so that the creative works of emergent young writers could be published.

The pioneer writers of children's books therefore made use of folk tales, myths and legends from the oral tradition, which constitutes a body of literature in its own right with a special significance for children as a primary resource. Some of these writers merely translated the tales into English; in some cases, they collected and transcribed them in the Ghanaian languages; others went beyond transcription and translation to adaptation. Another group of writers simply used these traditional tales for creating other imaginative stories, drawing on the techniques and other features that they found potent in the oral tradition. Some Ghanaian writers who retold folk tales for children include: J. O. de Graft Hanson in *The Little Sasabonsam* (1972), *Papa and the Magic Marble* (1973), *Papa and the Animals* (1973), K. B. Keelson in *Storytime with the Animals* (1974), Hannah Dankwa-Smith in *Some Popular Ananse Stories* (1975).

Although Efua Sutherland's main contribution to Ghanaian literature was in the field of drama and the incorporation of Ghanaian folklore into the dramatic traditions of this country, her other major interest was in the field of developing a suitable literature for Ghanaian children. She was the first Ghanaian writer to take a serious interest in writing for children. Teacher, poet, dramatist and academic, she put into practice what can be regarded as the cornerstone for the production of reading material for children. As a teacher, she recognised the role of 'play' in enhancing the learning process of children. In view of this, her first book for children was appropriately titled *Playtime in Africa* (1960). This was soon followed by another pictorial essay, *The Roadmakers* (1960). Later, she wrote a short story, *Obaatan Kesewa* for children, which was published by the Bureau of Ghana Languages in 1967. As far as can be determined, Sutherland was the first Ghanaian writer who attempted to produce a book with an indigenous background for children in Ghana. Prior to this period, before and immediately after Independence, there were scores of cheap books of foreign origin for Ghanaian school children to read. Hence, many of the emergent writers thought it was more profitable to produce books for adults.

Efua Sutherland initiated various programmes in drama at the Ghana Drama

Studio affiliated to the Institute of African Studies of the University of Ghana. Like other African scholars, she recognised the very strong connection between oral literature and literature for children. As a consequence of her work in the establishment of experimental theatre projects such as Kusum Agoromba, Sutherland organised school children in and around Accra through the Children's Drama Development Programme of the Drama Studio. *Vulture! Vulture!* and *Tahinta* were published together in 1968 and constitute her best known publication of plays for children. *Children of the Man-Made Lake* was also published posthumously in 2000. Her unpublished plays for children include: 'The Pineapple Child', 'Nyamekye', 'Tweedledum and Tweedledee', and 'Ananse and the Dwarf Brigade'.

In the past, the scanty critical interest shown in literature for children in Ghana was probably due to the fact that the number of indigenous children's books was not large enough to deserve critical attention. However, during the past 40 years or so, increase in the writing and publication of books for children in Africa demands that a closer look be taken at this literature for the purpose of critical evaluation. In the mid-1970s, various seminars and workshops on writing and publishing for children were organised. These workshops and seminars helped to establish the awareness that Ghanaian children need to read books related to their cultural background. The credit for this awareness goes to the emergence of a well-established and informed community of writers with the perception of childhood as a distinct period which merits its own literature.

Although Sutherland wrote for both children and adults, critical material on her work centres mostly on her adult work, which was published later than the work for children. Almost all the secondary sources one can find on Sutherland's work are about her adult plays. Although there are scattered references to her life-long passion for writing for children and general attention to establishing a literature for children, one realises that not many critics have attempted to draw attention to Efua Sutherland's work for children. What accounts for this omission?

We could assign several reasons for this lack of critical attention to her children's work. It may be that her children's work does not embody profound insights that deserve critical evaluation. This would constitute an anomaly, if it were the case, because one would have to read the work to evaluate their philosophical quality. On the other hand, it could also be a consequence of the low status of children's literature as an academic discipline. A few decades back, in the 1970s, children's literature did not have status as a discipline that could reward serious research. This essay is, therefore, offered as a means of acknowledging Sutherland's contribution to the genre of Ghanaian children's literature.

Much as we acknowledge her role in developing theatrical and dramatic conventions in Ghana, we must also not lose sight of the enormous contribution she made towards encouraging young writers to follow her lead and write for children. Her concern for children translates into the many schemes she initiated on their behalf. She was the convener of two seminars for playwrights' organised under the Children's Drama Development Programme of the Ghana Drama Studio, University of Ghana. Added to these efforts which brought the production of children's literature to the notice of potential writers, Efua Sutherland also established the Mmofra Foundation: a not-for-profit cultural organisation for children, which established after her death, a Language Club based at her home, *Araba Mansa*, where children go to read, tell and perform stories while learning about the different aspects of Ghanaian culture. Examples of the outcome of this venture are the re-issuing of the rhythm play *Tahinta* with an accompanying audio cassette as *Tahinta! A Rhythm Play for Children* (2000) by Afram Publications, and a DVD version of *Ananse and the Dwarf Brigade* produced by Film Africa in 2006 featuring some of the children who were members of Mmofra Foundation Language Club.

Through her extensive contribution to the development of Ghanaian literature in general and children's literature in particular Efua Sutherland has carved for herself an enviable name in the history of literature in Ghana. The group of writers who wrote and published for children in her wake could be said to have been influenced by her single-minded dedication to the cause of literature for children.

Efua Sutherland was an indefatigable worker who poured her energies into enlightening people about the necessity of preserving what is valuable in Ghanaian culture for the benefit of future generations. That is why her most important concern was to get the children, who are the strongest link to the future, to appreciate the beauty of African culture and carry it forward to the next generation. Sutherland's efforts on behalf of Ghanaian children encouraged the government of Ghana to set up the Ghana National Commission on Children, which she eventually served as chairperson.

Her clear vision about the importance of preserving Ghanaian culture made her realise that, in whatever mode the African writer chooses to work, it is significant to note that he or she has a specific role to play in society. The writer is always placed in a sensitive position because s/he is aware that his/her output must have relevance to the cultural norms of his/her society. This is similar to the views of other committed African writers such as Chinua Achebe, who observes that: 'The writer cannot expect to be excused from the task of re-education and regeneration that must be done. In fact, [s]he must march right in front' (1975:45). Sutherland realised that the writer must be in the forefront of the 're-education' and 'regeneration' that needs to be done through the moulding of the sensibilities of their readers, especially children. She believed that children must be nurtured on the cultural images that should give them a positive feeling about themselves. She therefore remarked in an interview with

Lee Nichols in 1981 that she started writing seriously for children in 1951 when she noticed that the books children were reading in those days 'had nothing to do with them, (they) had nothing to do with (the children's) environment, their social circumstance or anything. And so I started writing' (Nichols 1981: 279). Though the traditional oral literature existed for both young and old, there was very little of what could be described as written national literature for Ghanaian children. It is in this light that we should see Efua Sutherland's contribution to the establishment of a national literature for Ghanaian children as fully realised.

PLAYTIME IN AFRICA

Playtime In Africa, Sutherland's first publication for children in 1960, has earned a more definite place in the history of Ghanaian children's written literature than any other children's book, not only because it marks the beginning of the genre of written children's literature in Ghana but also because it makes use of poetry, a genre that is not extensively represented in Ghanaian children's literature. *Playtime in Africa* was published by Brown, Knight & Truscott in London. Sutherland achieves two goals with this publication: she gives children a book filled with pictures of their favourite activities, games and plays; she also provides them with the descriptions of these activities in easy-to-read verse. Even for children who cannot read, the pictures are explicit enough for them to guess the kind of words that follow each picture. Since children are already accustomed to the games represented in the pictures, it can be assumed that they would find as much pleasure in looking at the pictures as they would if they could actually read the poems. Therefore, through the medium of play, Sutherland encourages children to learn to read and enjoy themselves in the process.

In modern times, ideas in writers' minds are put on paper first, and then an illustrator is found to render the idea in pictorial terms. Sutherland – the first writer in Ghana to give expression to the term 'picture story' – inverts this order, turning the creative process inside out. Rather than rely on an illustrator to translate the idea in her mind onto paper, she looks for a photographer who captures the activities of live children on film. She then proceeds to write down the description of these activities, using the pictures as a guide.

Particularly noteworthy about *Playtime in Africa* is the medium in which Sutherland describes the games: poetry or rhythmic speech. The antipathy that most students develop towards poetry later in school can be ascribed to the culturally irrelevant poems they are made to learn by rote when they are children. A nursery rhyme such as 'Baa, baa, black sheep, have you any wool?' except for the rhythm, has nothing that the Ghanaian child can relate to. Sheep in Ghana hardly have any wool, nor is a woollen garment an item of clothing a Ghanaian child is familiar with.[2]

The pictures in *Playtime in Africa* depict happy children at play. Some of the games, such as *Ampe*, were and still are mostly played by girls. The self-explanatory poems that accompany the pictures capture deftly the rhythm of the game:

Clap as you jump, fling out your foot,
Sometimes the left foot, sometimes the right,
You will score when your foot meets mine.
I will score when our two feet cross.
No boys can join our jumping game
It's *Ampe*, and it's just for girls (p.4).

The narrator identifies herself as a girl and the rhythm and cadence of the words are also reminiscent of the soft and feminine nature of girls. The author, however, makes sure that no child is excluded from the pictures and the fun. She represents both boys and girls in play situations that are entirely natural. On the next page, she includes boys with this counter identification:

We boys think soccer is the best game of all.
We like to run after the ball, kicking, dribbling,
and passing it from player to player right into the goal (p. 5).

Whilst both *ampe* and football are scoring games in which boys and girls strive to show that they can 'best' each other, they are played in the spirit of healthy competition.

Role-playing is one of the ways in which children learn and prepare themselves for their adult roles later in life. Between the ages of four and six, girls will commonly imitate mother and boys develop a fascination for bicycles and cars. There are pictures of girls making believe they are adults preparing food, whilst boys fidget with an oversized bicycle or play at fishing. The lines that follow the pictures express these sentiments:

Our peanut stew tastes just like Mother's.
Girls can work just as their mothers do.

And boys?
Well, boys are always with bicycles –
riding, mending, getting hungry as wolves (pp. 32-34).

Sutherland's simple poems demonstrate to children that poetry can be made relevant to one's own environment and that it can also be fun. At a conference on the study of Ghanaian Languages at the University of Ghana, in May 1968,

Sutherland advocated that: 'Poetry teaching in the Ghanaian Languages should begin in Class 1 and be developed steadily… Capitalising on the vitality of poetry in Ghanaian life is going to open up children and more adult students to a better reception of poetry in English' (1969: 30).[3]

Sutherland's poems represent and extend the various traditional games that parents and grandparents used to play when they were children and which she is anxious to pass on to children. In addition, some of the poems in *Playtime In Africa* give children cultural education in the kinds of games that used to be played by both adults and children before television and other 'modern' forms of entertainment such as films and video games appeared on the entertainment scene. At the top of the picture of a game of *Oware*, the traditional Ghanaian marble game, comes this light, descriptive poem:

We don't talk too much when we play *Oware*,
We have to watch and think.
It's our special kind of checkers.

We move our marbles from cup to cup,
and soon, if we're clever,
we can win them back
in twos, and threes, and fours (p.14).

The descriptions are simple enough for even children who have never seen or played the game before to have a mental image of how to play the game when they come across it. The uncomplicated language in which the descriptions are couched makes it easy for children to handle; there are no difficult words to struggle with and the rhythm simulates normal speech as much as possible. Given the familiar conversational structure of the poems, it is likely that children may not even notice they are reading poetry. The effect of Sutherland's approach lies in her attempt to get children to enjoy these simple down-to-earth poems. Her intention was that their poetic sensibilities would be nurtured on the culturally relevant experiences represented in the poems.

Another notable characteristic of Sutherland's style is the self-inclusive viewpoint from which the descriptions of the games are transmitted. She alternates between the singular 'I' and the plural 'we'. This has the effect of making the voice of the personae in the poems the same as the voices of the participants in the game, effectively drawing the readers also into the game. A clear demonstration of this technique can be found in the poem about the xylophone:

Ah, now I can wake up the xylophone's gongs –
all the way up and down.
The gongs sleep in each long plank 'til I knock.

Then they wake and make me tunes —
any tunes my hands ask.
Today the tune is for the dance of the deer
It is a very special dance.
Be careful, hands!
If you ask wrong,
the music will come out all wrong (pp. 28-29).

Children's highly developed imaginative faculties are called into play, using the interesting image of sleeping and waking gongs. The hands are also given an identity of their own, such that they become independent of the 'I' of the poem. Also, the writer introduces another cultural phenomenon to children. Those children who are not familiar with the xylophone, a musical instrument from the northern part of Ghana, get the chance to experience it vicariously through Sutherland's picture as well as the insightful description in playful language.

THE ROADMAKERS

The Roadmakers is another picture book published by Sutherland in 1961. In the preface to the book, which seems to have been written with children as well as adults in mind, she reveals her intentions:

Ghanaians live in a time of construction and fundamental change... [we are] children of an ancient people with our roots deep in Africa's soil; converts and victims of the many human, ideological and material influences which have found their way into our country by land, sea and air. Our fathers knew nothing of the new roads of technological advance and industrialization ... but they left us excellent paths of human relations and wisdom that we intend to save.

Although the writer clearly has in mind physical construction of the infrastructure needed in the building of a nation, it is very apparent that she also sees cultural identity as something that needs to be constructed. For her, the task of nation building does not only involve concrete and steel, but also fashioning a national identity that would correspond with the high hopes for the future of the newly independent country. The title of the book, *The Roadmakers*, reveals and emphasises the roles the author perceives herself and others playing in the construction of the cultural identity of the country and its people; that is, creating new roads to link the past with the present. Implicit in this is a dialectic between Sutherland's desire for reasonable progressive change and her anxiety that the change will bring along with it the seeds of destruction of Ghanaian cultural identity.

Efua Sutherland's belief in the existence of an interconnection between the past, the present and the future is revealed in her deep anxieties about the inimical influences of Western civilisation on the African traditional way of life. Consequently, Sutherland's ideas about the focus of knowledge to be imparted to children diverged significantly from what the average adult in society saw as important. People with less commitment to the preservation of the traditional values only see the superficial benefits of 'progress'. Her work for children seeks to address the perceived dichotomy between culture and progress. She suggests, therefore, that it is the responsibility of committed adults to take steps to preserve what is valuable in Ghanaian culture and, more so, transfer it to the children. We must, therefore, see her constant harping on the need for documentation as her preferred medium of capturing history in pictures, poems, plays and stories for the children 'so that children or the next generation would know history in order to create a new reality for themselves...'

Meena Khorana (1998: 2), in concert with other practitioners of children's literature, observes that there is 'the need to examine children's and young adult[s]' books to determine what adults believe is important for the younger generation to know, what cherished values to pass on and how they equip children to lead the nation in the future. A survey of this children's literature indicates a new cultural nationalism is being forged to counter the effects of imperialism.'

Countering the effects of imperialism, colonialism, neocolonialism, and post-colonialism seems to be the responsibility Sutherland assigned herself and other writers for children. As a first step towards fulfilling this responsibility, she sought to implant Ghanaian values in her child readers before Western ideas catch up with them and dilute their appreciation of African culture. She, more than anybody else in Ghana, realised that the allure and glitter of the material culture that the West endorses is difficult to resist as children grow into adults. Sutherland therefore saw the wisdom in giving children a thorough grounding in the vital knowledge necessary for the survival of traditional wisdom. She sounds a warning to readers:

And if we are not to continue losing our children to the towns, they must get from their education the initiative for enterprise, the practical ability and the adjustment to the environment of their villages which are vital to their survival there (*The Roadmakers* 1961: i).

In *The Roadmakers*, Efua Sutherland assumes the voice of a prophet or a seer, accurately predicting the consequences of the indiscriminate adoption of Western ideas and values which are not compatible with African ones. She must be credited with the vision and far-sightedness that recognise the effects of rapid modernisation and industrialisation on the psyche of the Ghanaian even before they happen. Although she was aware of the benefits that modernisation and industrialisation could bring to Ghanaians, her apprehension about the erosion of cultural values that would follow in their wake is very real indeed. Her advice then is to adopt a gradual approach, basing our eventual choices on '...a reassess [ment] of our views and our values... [in order to] choose a clear direction'.

There is evidence of a constant tension within the writer's vision between the adult Ghanaian's duty of preserving the traditional culture for the benefit of the younger generation, on the one hand, and acknowledging the benefits of advances in the form of education and technology, on the other. She further cautions her readers:

> What we cannot buy is the spirit of originality and endeavour which makes a people dynamic and creative. Wisdom has recognised this and raised a voice which might well save Ghana and all Africa from *continuing the error of looking outside herself in determining the road of progress* (Preface: ii, italics added).

Khorana also admits:

> While recognising the importance of progress, writers also want to inculcate in young readers a respect for tradition, sense of community, time-honoured beliefs and customs, kinship with nature and the land... (1998: 9)

Efua Sutherland's insistent warning voice is almost drowned out now by the clamorous noise of progress and technological advance. She lamented, four years after Independence, in the Preface to *The Roadmakers*, about the already discernible effects of Western civilisation on Ghanaians, both young and old:

> [we] are converts and victims of the many human, ideological and material influences which have found their way into our country by land, sea and air. The least desirable tastes and values of the outside world reach us through films and junk we import. A problem of delinquency is arising. We are distressed to have Borstal institutions in a society which believes that the responsibility for children is a sacred privilege of the family.

That future has caught up with us. Efua Sutherland strove to give meaning to the *Sankofa* principle, which, in Anyidoho's estimation, is 'a view of life in which the present is in constant creative interface with the past, but always with expectations of future harvests as their essential driving force' (2000: 79). The Sankofa bird, a mythological figure, which constantly reaches into the past as it flies into the future, is an appropriate metaphor within which to locate Sutherland's vision for Ghanaian society. To avoid the national death that

Casely Hayford alluded to in *Ethiopia Unbound* (1911), we must not '...despise our language, our customs and our institutions...' (1969:17). 'Neither must we forget how much [we] have lost in passing from [our] ways to those of the white man' (Kobina Sekyi: 1974). Like Sekyi, Sutherland 'believed in modernisation, but modernisation tempered and controlled by the creative and integrative elements of tradition' (Sekyi 1974: xxii).

The photographs that make up *The Roadmakers* as well as *Playtime in Africa* were taken by Willis Bell, Sutherland's associate in 1959, during an extensive tour of Ghana. The photographs do not chronicle anything out of the ordinary, except perhaps to document life as it was lived in Ghana in the late 1950s. However, if we place them side-by-side with Sutherland's overriding concern to document moments in the history of the nation and keep it in trust for future generations, then the simple children's book assumes the stature of a historical treatise on the history of a nation's growth. The first few photographs portray the old generation and the new one, signified by an old truck – what is usually referred to in Ghana as a 'mammy-truck' – about to cross an old bridge side-by-side with a more modern bus crossing a steel bridge. The implication is clear: the old must co-exist with the new; the co-existence of the past and the future in the present. This message follows through in the next few pages where images of people hard at work both as a community and as a specialised group are presented to strengthen the idea of working together, hand in hand in the present, for the benefit of the future.

The deep philosophical caption that announces the next section: 'Only a fool points at his origins with his left hand', reinforces the idea that it not only behoves us as Africans to respect our traditions, but also to inculcate that respect for tradition in our children. For how can one engender respect for something in another if one's own commitment is less than firm? To point at one's birthplace with the left hand is synonymous with admitting that one has become so alienated from one's origins that one is bereft of the wisdom found in traditional communities. The very idea of pointing at one's birthplace with the left hand is considered sacrilegious in Ghanaian culture.

It is not for nothing that Sutherland invokes this adage. Her commitment to the preservation and transmission of Ghanaian traditional heritage to children comes across very urgently in this particular pictorial essay for children. She is particularly conscious of her responsibility of reminding Ghanaians not to get rid of their past in their haste to embrace the future. The future is important, but it must be carefully planned for in order to ensure a stable society later.

Efua Sutherland expresses this belief in the necessity of the positive aspects of the past being linked with those of the present through the comment on page 15 of *The Roadmakers*: 'The wisdom and the achievement of the past is our guide.' She has thus assumed the role of cultural historian, charging herself with the duty of restoring cultural pride in the Ghanaian through the child. The identity split that the tension between the two ways of life that she perceives – the traditional as against the modern, the Ghanaian/African as against the Western – may become more difficult for children to negotiate in the face of the frontal assault of the images of Western ideas of 'progress.' Concerned adults in our society therefore need to take the initiative in giving the young a sound cultural education in the hope that whatever harm Westernisation may perpetrate on their psyche can be mitigated. Efua Sutherland's voice reminds us: '… [We] have also acquired too many confusions from history' and we have become 'converts and victims of the many human, ideological and material influences' (Preface) assailing us from all directions. Her voice speaks a warning heralding the approach of danger. The pictures, therefore, represent the continuum of life from birth to death. The inscription 'No man rules forever on the throne of time' sums up the idea that is represented in the picture of a grave and mourners at a funeral: 'We are not going to live forever; what we can do to preserve our heritage, let us do it now.'

Sutherland's third book for children, *Vulture! Vulture!* and *Tahinta* (1968) marks the intensification of her interest in children's drama. As mentioned earlier in this paper, Sutherland's main interest is incorporating our folk tales into the dramatic form. She must have recognised the dramatic potential in this children's play-song, *Vulture! Vulture!* She therefore capitalises on the lovely and lively melody, already familiar to children, to introduce organised drama to them.

On the whole, Efua Sutherland can be credited with setting in motion the genre of written children's literature. Now the genre has expanded even beyond what her dreams were for Ghanaian children's literature. Now her vision for the incorporation of cultural education into the reading material for our children is realised in the many publications of folk tales that are available in Ghanaian bookshops for children to read. Hopefully, many children will be nurtured on the cultural values that were so important to Sutherland and which she promoted with vigour. We can therefore credit Efua Sutherland with laying the necessary foundations for establishing a national literature for Ghanaian children.

Esi Sutherland-Addy

Creating for and with Children:
Efua Sutherland's Children's Plays

INTRODUCTION

That the world of the child held a fascination for Efua Sutherland is evidenced consistently in her research and writing, dating from the early 1960s. For the picture book *Playtime in Africa*[1] with photographs by Willis Bell, Sutherland created a flowing poetic text composed in childlike cadences to accompany the photographs of children at play in a wide variety of circumstances in Ghana during the late 1950s and early 1960s. The intensity of her preoccupation with the insights to be gleaned by playwrights from children at play, peaked within the period 1967-1980, when she created and produced experimental drama for children. *Vulture, Vulture!; Tahinta; Children of the Man-Made Lake; Tweedledum and Tweedledee* and *Ananse and the Dwarf Brigade* were all produced during this period with the first three being published. More significantly, these plays formed part of an integrated body of work aimed at creating with and for children, comprising poetry and stories, action research projects, academic papers, course syllabuses and short courses.

Sutherland was convinced that one could not write drama for children if one did not understand the play life of children. Her germinal paper, 'The Playwright's Opportunity in Drama for our Children', delivered at an Institute of African Studies seminar on writing and production of literature for children (5-10 April 1976), definitively encapsulates Sutherland's thoughts. This essay, more than any other, sets out succinctly the paradigm which she had been developing since the 1950s. She first of all sets the broad social and ideological context for her commitment. Sutherland posits in this paper that drama is a process of composition and that writing may be one of several possible emanations of a piece of drama. She was confident that she had embarked on a process of discovery of African society's established ideas about the art of drama, in concepts, form and practice:

> ...I belong to the breed of Africans who have to engage in this finding-out exercise, and thus I hope that the *prescription* will be interpreted in the same vein as the proverb – [If the alligator surfaces from underwater to inform you that the crocodile has a lumpy mouth he is not to be refuted] (Sutherland 1976: 2 emphasis added).

To Sutherland, then, by the time she was writing this essay she had consolidated the findings from her research, her thoughts and her convictions sufficiently to posit a paradigm for composing drama for Ghanaian children. From her observation, play is the child's natural means of exploring the human and natural environment of his or her existence, of learning how to exist with and within them and for resolving the problems he or she encounters in the process (ibid: 3).

She cites children's ability to simulate and imitate life with great spontaneity and absorption. She considers these to be 'ideal dramatic processes at which they (children) are supremely masterful'. She encourages playwrights to regard children as composers of their own drama, asserting that playwrights should compose as if they were a 'participating partner or play mate' (ibid: 4). Her reasons for recommending detailed observation of child play become apparent later on in the paper, where she makes the following point:

If he is privileged to observe the play in its entirety, that is, from how it begins , to how it develops and ends, noting every aspect of its expression, he ends up, in essence, with a play script which he himself could never have created (ibid: 9).

She also goes on to portray the observation of children at play as an efficacious method for developing the skills in what she calls 'the delicate art of creating plays for children'.

In a bid to develop these ideas, Sutherland established the Children's Drama Development Programme: a 5-year project funded by the VALCO Trust Fund.[2] The project was used to collect information about children at play both in formal and informal terms. The roles assigned to children in the traditional festivals and rituals were also studied.[3] In addition to this, a children's theatre laboratory was established at the Ghana Drama Studio[4] which offered groups of children from selected schools the opportunity to explore theatre in a variety of dimensions while at the same time learning about African culture and picking up basic techniques for the stage. Playwrights were also identified and brought within the ambit of the project to counter the trend of writing plays in wooden and ponderous language for children, by developing skills in the composition of imaginative and lively plays. By the end of the period some ten plays had been developed and tested.[5] These plays were produced for public consumption but were never commercially published although copies exist as part of the report on the project.

The purpose of this paper is to examine the extent to which Efua Sutherland's own plays were influenced by her convictions about the synergy between creating drama for children and children's play. Specifically two key contentions held by her will guide our study of her dramatic work for children:

- Firstly, that children's play provides an inexhaustible and profoundly rich resource for creating drama for children; and
- Secondly, that children should be given recognition for their masterful competence in creating drama.

To undertake this investigation, we shall examine four of Sutherland's children's plays paying close attention to structure, dialogue and language and characterisation as possible indicators for assessing whether Sutherland was able to live up to the ideals she sought to prescribe to persons aspiring to write plays for African children. These plays are *Tahinta, Vulture! Vulture!, Children of the Man-Made Lake* and *Ananse and the Dwarf Brigade*. A synopsis of each is provided below for ease of reference:

TAHINTA (1968/2000)

A young boy goes fishing in the Birim, a river reputed to be full of fish and alluvial gold, and running through the fertile forests of the Eastern Region of Ghana. He leaves home very happy but almost despairs as his attempts at catching a fish nearly fail. Suddenly, he hears a splash in his fish trap: he has finally caught a lovely mud fish but just as he gets ready to leave the riverside, a ghost comes walking across the river, and snatches his fish. Even his strong father who comes to help him cannot retrieve his precious catch. The boy threatens to tell his mother, but as his father explains 'A ghost is a ghost' (Sutherland 2000: 17).

VULTURE! VULTURE! (1968)

A vulture perches sadly in the sun. He is feeling lazy and hungry. His wife sends twice for him to come and eat appetising dishes. He refuses both times, offering the meals to the children. However, when he is finally told that there is a dead rat 20 days old waiting for him, he perks up and happily sets off to eat his favourite meal, making it clear that he is not about to share this with his children.

CHILDREN OF THE MAN-MADE LAKE (2000)

The people of the ancient Apaaso Village situated on the bank of the river Afram in the Eastern Region of Ghana are told that the government is about to build a great dam across the great river Firaw (Volta) that will in turn cause their own river to flood. Apaaso is destined to disappear under the flood together with seven-hundred other villages. The children in school are told that a lake will be formed which will be the biggest man-made lake in the world. A town meeting is held to receive the government officials. Every one in the village is confused and sad.

It is 1963. The flood does come, spreading closer and closer. The villagers must prepare to leave their old village for ever. The children of the village must help their parents to pack their valuables, dismantle their homes and take a terrifying trip across the lake to New Senchi, their new resettlement village.

After seven years the children from Apaaso have grown into young adults and have adjusted to their new life with numbered homes, tractors and factories. The beautiful essence of their traditional culture, however, lives on. There is excitement in the air, for one of them, Yaa Amponsah, has come of age and is to be out-doored. So is the new queen mother of the town. As they get ready for the festivities, these adolescents reflect on their journey from Apaaso and their awe-inspiring experiences since then. They do not understand everything that has happened but they know one thing: they will never be the same again.

ANANSE AND THE DWARF BRIGADE (CIRCA 1970)

Ananse, the wily 'man-spider', abandons his family and goes far away to establish a farm just for himself. He gets to a strange clearing where the slightest noise activates a rumbling voice. Greatly frightened, he answers the voice's questions, explaining why he is there. The voice commands the Dwarf Brigade to appear and help him. The Dwarf Brigade is a terrifying and highly organised but mischievous group of dwarfs. They help Ananse make his farm and he does nothing but dance and read newspapers. They seem to know something he does not know and even as they work hard they also laugh a lot.

When the crops are nearly ready for harvest, Ananse's wife Okonore and his son Ibrahim Ananse appear at the farm. They try to pluck some of the corn and activate the voice who, on hearing their story, orders the Dwarf Brigade to come and help them to harvest. Shortly the farm is totally destroyed. Ananse arrives and is wild with disappointment and anger. As he hits his wife, the Dwarfs are commanded to help him do so. However, when he makes the mistake of thumping his chest triumphantly and immediately, the ubiquitous voice commands them to turn on him. As he is pummelled, his only escape from further punishment is to turn into a spider and to slip through their hands into his web.

STRUCTURE

Formula games, play songs and choric stories are seen by Sutherland as proto-type community drama. In her research notes, the writer also identifies insult games, games of self-assertion, games which imitate events – child-made dramas, all of which are resources upon which she calls for composing the plays under study.

In many storytelling traditions in Africa, the choric tale is often classified as a juvenile form. Indeed Hausa- and Dagaare-speaking societies, for example, consider it below the dignity of men to indulge in such forms. These tales are mostly or totally based on, or propelled by, a melodic chant or song. While songs feature as part of all the plays cited above, they are structurally based on different genres. 'Pete! Pete!', (Akan for Vulture! Vulture! pronounced 'Pet eh! Pet eh!' from which *Vulture! Vulture!* is derived) may be classified as a play song/formula game.[6] These songs accompany games played by groups of children with a leader. On the other hand, *Tahinta* is a choric story in which the entire story is recited with the narrator chanting the verses and the audience taking up the refrain. Indeed, there are at least two different versions of this story, one from the Akan Twi-speaking tradition and another from the Akan Fanti-speaking area. The version retold and expanded by Sutherland is the latter.

She sees these formal play songs and choric stories as providing the opportunity for creative rhythmic composition involving mime and physical exercise. This she denotes as motional activity which can be elaborated with verbalisation and song.[7] In the case of *Vulture! Vulture!* the author sticks very closely to the original text, exploring techniques of statement followed by expansion and parallelism associated with some types of oral poetry.[8] These are useful techniques that make it possible to substitute slightly modified statements within the same breath group. For example, in response to a question raised by the Vulture about the meal prepared by his wife, he is told that it is fufu and palmnut soup. In Sutherland's version, there is semantic parallelism in which a second verse is created substituting roast chicken for fufu and palmnut soup in Part Two of the play.

By the time we reach Part Three, which is the climax of the play, we are lulled by the regularity of the rhythm and may be unprepared for the ironic twist of the finale when the Vulture finally gets what he wants. This is again achieved by a surprising semantic switch while the rhythm remains deceptively consistent.

Tahinta is structurally more of a departure from the traditional story because the author takes liberties with the structure by intensifying the role of the participating audience or chorus. She does so by creating space for them to engage in substantial dialogue which sometimes involves commentary on the action, beyond the lines of the refrain and also by extending the refrain itself:

Tahinta
Kind River Birim!
Tahinta

Whatever happens,
Tahinta,
Let him catch his fish
Tahin Tahin Tahin Tahin
Tahinta.
(Sutherland 1968: 19)

Sutherland's plays may also be based on the dramatic interpretation of the plot of an oral tale. In this case, the plot is more closely followed. Thus in *Ananse and the Dwarf Brigade*, Ananse is the traditional greedy, selfish spider-man character who courts severe punishment in the end for his greed.

Structurally, the playwright builds into her theatrical pieces for children informal aspects of children's play such as 'imitation of life through mime'. Action in *Ananse and The Dwarf Brigade* is quite physical and sometimes even tactile. It involves the imitation of detailed physical movements involved in farming such as slashing, stumping, raking, stacking and turning up the earth. The Dwarf Brigade executes marching drills both as a realistic imitation of the military and also as a depiction of movements of these forest beings as depicted in mythology. Their toes, for example, are said to point backwards. This provides child actors with ample opportunity to let their imagination run free. Again, in the final scene when the dwarfs are instructed to help Ananse beat his chest, it is a field day for children who love tactile action. In productions of this play which we have observed, (e.g., January 2001) the actor who played Ananse was pummelled by little fists and as he rushed to make his exit, the children literally tumbled upon him.

Humour here is slap-stick and provides an opportunity for spontaneity and momentary indiscipline. This is also true when the dwarfs are required to laugh in the stage direction, 'Loud laughter from the dwarfs', which appears frequently thoughout the script.

CHILDREN WITH AGENCY

In all of Sutherland's plays, children not only constitute the majority of characters but are imbued with strong personalities. They drive the plot and often determine the denouement of the play. In *Ananse and the Dwarf Brigade*, it is true that there is the voice, referred to as Nana (Grandfather or Royal one), who commands the dwarfs and brings them into the flow of the drama, but there is no question that they know what they are doing. They raise Ananse's hopes by creating a beautiful farm, but they have no difficulties in demolishing it just before the fruits are ready for harvest with the destructive glee that children are so capable of. They themselves are liminal creatures, appearing to be of ancient origin and yet remaining forever children. The dwarfs are depicted as impish beings with power. They can be very rigid in their behaviour but are unpredictable. They disappear, and reappear, and are allowed to do things that would plausibly be frowned upon in disciplined family life such as whistling.

Again, the dwarfs are only happy to oblige Ananse by hitting his wife Okonore on her mouth and absolutely delighted to rain blows on Ananse who, unable to withstand the punishment, turns into a spider. These scenes depict role reversals where children, who are often subject to corporal punishment in Ghanaian society, are able to thrash a badly behaved adult. The free-for-all implied by this episode again provides children the opportunity for complete abandon to respond to their basic instincts, uncomplicated by binding social norms of behaviour and etiquette.

In *Children of the Man-Made Lake*, child characters are of another ilk. The children are endowed with wonderful insight. Beyond echoing the discourse of the adult world about the events surrounding the construction of the Akosombo Dam, they have their very own thoughts. The writer is able to evoke the sense of wonder and bewilderment which the experience necessarily implies. Characters like Kwasi Akroma, who hides in a tree to think, and Ansah Kofi , who makes the most startlingly sensitive statements in the midst of the apparent frivolity of conversation among friends, imbue the text with a disturbing, yet moving reflectiveness. For example:

ANSAH KOFI: Isn't it surprising? When we travelled here on the lake it was so frightening! And now people are travelling safely on it to the north and safely back again. And yet something puzzles me always. It is not like old Apaaso here at New Senchi. Why? Why? Kwesi Akroma?

KWASI AKROMA: What do you mean Ansah Kofi?

ANSAH KOFI: I don't know. I often think about it but I don't know why. And when I think about it, it makes me unhappy. Strangely, I think about water when I think about it sometimes. Is Kwesi Amproma right? Is water a spirit? Are our mothers right? Is water a god? Why don't you anwer me? Why are all of you so silent?

(Sutherland 2000: 114)

In this extract, despite the cheeriness in the air, apparently depicting a people reconciled with a new beginning and cognisant of its advantages for future development, the unresolved issues which carry on in the psyche of this displaced community resurface in this metaphor. The child finds it difficult to define what 'water' should mean to him and, by implication, to his community.

Again, The Boy in *Tahinta* experiences a range of emotions making him a rounded character with integrity. He starts the day gaily and experiences the disappointment of failure as he tries again and again to catch a fish. He slides towards despondency only to be filled with anticipation as he hears a sudden splash. His exhilaration is palpable as he discovers that he has trapped a fish. This makes his terror all the more believable as the Ghost comes across the water to snatch his fish. Having called on his role model, his father, to retrieve his fish he is full of hope and confidence that he is fully defended. It is for this reason that he is crestfallen and somewhat indignant about his father's failure to overcome the Ghost. He thus threatens to apply the ultimate sanction: humiliation before his father's wife. Indeed the momentum of the entire play rides on the emotional experiences of the boy.

The group is an essential character cluster related to children which is featured in all four plays, capturing a variety of group dynamics for theatrical effect. For example, Sutherland explores the structural potential of this dynamic in the rhythm plays by keeping up the refrain throughout the play, so that the protagonist is in constant and somewhat formalised communion with his 'playmates', as he would have been if he had been engaged in a formula game. In *Vulture!Vulture!* the chorus takes on the familiar mode of goading the protagonist and holding him in suspense. Vulture is plied with food that he does not find palatable, and one cannot help wondering if the little vultures' invitation is not made with tongue in cheek.

The Chorus in *Tahinta* is more empathetic to the Boy and echoes his moods, acting as his alter-ego. For example, Boy begins to comment excitedly on the fight between his father and Ghost. Excitement mounts to a crescendo as the chorus takes on a typically rousing cheering around a good fight:

Chorus: Tahinta
They are fighting
Tahinta
Bim! Bam! Bim!
Tahinta
They are struggling
Tahinta
This way! That way! This way!
Down! Kudum!
(Sutherland 1969: 32)

Having produced this play several times, I have noted the glee with which the chorus often takes on this part, closing in on the main actors as they would on the play ground and getting louder and louder.

Children of the Man-Made Lake, on the other hand, is constructed around groups of children in different contexts. This play seems to have provided Sutherland with the latitude to elaborate on the potential of the group dynamic without the structural constraints imposed by formulaic games or the choric story. From scene to scene, child characters of different ages (and in some cases gender groupings), elaborate the plot and determine the mood and direction of the play.

In Part One, for example, girls, on their way to fetch water, introduce us to the rites which symbolise the stability of the community of Apaaso, confident in the immutability of its traditions. Indeed towards the end of Part One, this confidence is expressed by the Women's Leader who says:

The festival has begun. Sing mothers of Apaaso, now, about the land that is ours. Our land, through which flows our generous river, Afram.

(Sutherland 2000: 99)

The girls are discussing the terror which they felt about the rain storm of the previous night. Their parents are certain, though, that the storm, as always, was a sign of a bumper harvest, and the girls laugh as some of them describe how they expressed their fright the previous night. However, there is some dramatic irony built into the scene, for perhaps this is not a laughing matter, nor does the storm represent the predictable bounty which their parents and ancestors have learnt to expect. The storm and the terror that this evokes in the girls could be seen as a premonition of an event, worse than the most horrid nightmare of the people of Apaaso. The device of foregrounding the child's experience of social reality is sustained throughout the play.

In Part Two, the school setting is used to convey authoritative information from teachers to children. The seemingly naïve questions of the children betray the scepticism and denial of their elders. As happens throughout this play, though, the notion of 'children without a care in the world' comes through very forcefully. For example, in this scene, when they are subsequently told that there is an important meeting for which school must close after the first lesson, their reaction is: 'Yee! Holiday!' The atmosphere in the school is full of disruptive behaviour. For example, the naughty little Dentaa distresses one of her classmates who reacts as follows:

Dentaa says I didn't bath this morning. *Laughter from class.* I bathed! My mother won't let me come to school if I don't bath.

In tropical southern Ghana, the banter around bathing occurs very often as some children try to get around this daily ritual. The group dynamics here evoke the insult games found in many classrooms and playgrounds around the world, in which an individual child may be at the mercy of a group. Here, these insult games are spontaneously created with cruelty typical of power-play among children.

In Part Three, the child characters are broken into their gender groupings to enable the play to cover the multi-focal nature of the hasty preparations finally being made in the face of the reality of the flood. The girls, staying close to home, reflect on the cultured space and the once-built environment which is disintegrating in the face of the floods or being dismantled by the very hands that built it. They speak of the symbolic treasures which the women are trying to save. They also look forward with some trepidation to the impending journey.

The boys, on the other hand, cover the uncultured space – the bush and the river bank – bringing back home news of the reaction of the flora and fauna to the flood. The two groups merge as they turn to playing games even as the sacred ancestral stool is being moved, marking the abandonment of the cultured space which their people have known for so long. The poignancy of the moment is highlighted by the fact that the children are playing as if nothing of great import is happening.

In Part Four, the children of Apaaso have arrived in a new and somewhat unsettling environment. In this scene, sticking together is a matter of survival. Ansah Kofi, at the end of this scene, says: 'Kwafo, we will go in a group as you said.'

The writer brings the child characters together again in the final scene set seven years later. The group is built up as the scene progresses. There is talk of out-doorings and possible marriages. It is a scene of children and a society in transition. This is a group in adolescence, straddling childhood and adulthood, the old and the new. Typical of persons in that age bracket, they share (if in a rather competitive and raucous manner) their discovery of new worlds and skills. They anticipate adult life – careers and marriage. They are truly friends, covering each other's backs and caring for each other. For example, they all worry because *Asarebea* who has gone to the port city of Tema has not returned and they decide to go to the roadside to meet her. Their discussion even turns philosophical and reflective.

And yet for all this adult behaviour they are still children at heart. Kwesi Akroma still spends time in his favourite tree haunt. Again, when the children hear the sound of the bus belonging to the new wax cloth factory situated at the brand new industrial town of Akosombo built near the dam site, they chase after it with cries of 'Akosombo Textiles'.

Sutherland's child characters are, therefore, complex personalities. Whether depicted as a collective or as individuals, their experiences are not predictable. While they are children they are not depicted as adjuncts to adults but as self-sufficient beings, interacting with the society and with their environment on their own terms and in their own right. The protagonists of both: *Children of the Man-Made Lake* and *Tahinta* are children. They are placed in the texts neither merely for reasons of verisimilitude nor representing adults. In terms of composition, she depicts them as existing in their own space and perceiving the world from their own point of view, negotiating their way based on their own resourcefulness.

Structurally then, Sutherland can be said to have demonstrated aspects of the creative partnership between adults and children that she recommends should exist between children and playwrights. In her case she seems to enter into the world of children and to present it such that they can display their creativity naturally and indeed engage in play as the core dynamic for action.

LANGUAGE, STYLE AND PLAY

Language is both a means and an end in Sutherland's work, and when she writes for children it seems to take on an even more important diversity of roles. As she clearly states in 'The Playwright's Opportunity in Drama for our Children', she finds that too many plays written for children lack '...the freshness, flexibility and imaginativeness of dialogue which characterise children's authentic verbal expressions and exchanges in that venue [of free spontaneous play]' (p.10).

Furthermore, she advises playwrights to use audience-conscious language (p.15).

In her hand-written notes on 'The Training Aspects of a Children's Drama Workshop Programme' Sutherland has the following bullet points:

• The principle of Mother-Tongue Priority.
• The Bilingualism Objective (from mother tongue – English).

Sutherland was concerned about the school environment as both a space in which the speaking of indigenous languages was disparaged (the 'No Fante Spoken Here' syndrome); and one in which English was taught unimaginatively. For her, this led to a jeopardy of imposing incompetence on children and suppressing their creativity. Sutherland elaborates these two principles in her work and appears to be seeking to make Ghanaian children confident about formally developing the multilingual skills which they use in their communal and play lives.

In the first place, Sutherland's approach recognises that many Ghanaian children have at least two languages but only use these multi-lingual skills in the informal settings such as the market or the playground. The playground offers the opportunity for code-switching and for creating and composing in different languages including English.

In all four of the plays under discussion, Sutherland appears to have engaged in much experimentation with the stylistics of multi-lingualism. In *Vulture! Vulture!* the simplest rhythm line from the original song is maintained throughout the play. Although an effort is made to create variety by various means such as twists in the plot and a dynamic application of parallelism, there is no doubt that the text and prosody closely follow the original Akan language.

Furthermore, the diction which she applies to her texts is palpably childlike. The author especially validates the play-language of children. For example, dialogue in Sutherland's plays is often a convincing imitation of conversation among children. In Part One of *Children of the Man-Made Lake*, the girl characters discuss their reaction to the storm.

KWABEA: The storm last night made me so afraid. Asarebea, weren't you afraid?
That thunder. It was so loud. I was scared.

ASAREBEA: Yee! Do you know what I did? I covered up my head with my cloth.
And I shut my eyes tight; tight like this. And I put this finger and this finger in my ears.
Laughter from all the girls.

KWABEA: Oh, Asarebea, you are so funny.

ASAREBEA: I didn't like it. What did you do, Daakowa?

DAAKOWA: Me? *Loud voice with laughter.* I moved close to my mother and held her tight.

THREE VOICES: Hee! Daakowa! *Loud laughter from all.*

ASON: I listened to the wind. Didn't you hear that whistling. Hy – Hy – Hy. Hwee!
Hwee! Everywhere. This morning there are leaves all over our courtyard. I'm glad it's Brother's turn to sweep.

Again the story that the children in Class One tell in Part Two of the same play is extremely simple and has an infantile ring to the diction.

OFOSUAA: There was a little bird. And he went and stood on elephant grass. And the elephant grass cut his food. And he flew away. Then he went and stood on a pepper plant. And the pepper plant hurt his wound, bad, bad, bad. And he cried and cried: 'Amako aka me kurom.'

CHORUS: Oya hyew! hyew! hyew!

The phenomenon of children boasting and exaggerating in their narrative culture is employed in *Children of the Man-Made Lake* to good effect. The hyperbolic description of the pylons carrying electricity from the hydro-electric plant at Akosombo towards the Port City of Tema is one such case. Ansah Kofi claims to have seen thousands of them.

In this play Sutherland uses juxtapositions to underline the almost unbearable trauma of the community, precisely by breaking into the pathos with apparent childish banality. This is achieved in part through the manner in which children express themselves. For example, Ansah Kofi, a child in the same play, is impishly curious and dares to defy the taboo of observing the removal of the Royal Stool, the very soul of the people of Apaaso, from its sacred abode to be transported across the water, signifying the final abandonment of the ancestral land. This solemn moment is broken by Ansah Kofi saying almost off-handedly: 'But I want to see! Ah! Kwafo, let's continue our game.' That one casual line juxtaposed against the description of these solemn events by the other children and their awe of it, far from being dismissive, highlights them.

At all times there is a childlike playfulness which averts the sense of the tragic but often amplifies the poignancy of the situation being presented. The communal sense of bewilderment is transferred into the children's world of play, making the inexorable advance of disaster more bearable. The children wonder and muse over their impending fate. There is solidarity among the children of Apaaso who are the most vulnerable victims of the evacuation of their people in the face of the powerful political force of the national government and the immense natural power of the dammed waters of the Volta River and its tributaries. By the end of the play even though there are moments of nostalgia and some bewilderment, they take collective ownership of the future which is theirs to own. In her notes, Sutherland calls this 'play power', defining it as follows:

'This is the child's use of the means drama affords to overcome his bewilderment about a world that dishes out to him – conditions and challenges not of his making' (undated notes).

A WORD ON THE DENOUEMENT

As we conclude our examination of the notion that a playwright might consider creating plays with and for children, we are struck by the denouement of all four of Sutherland's plays discussed above. In none of the plays does she as author take a moralistic position. Texts written for children in Ghana such as retelling of tales, are often highly didactic and moralistic. While the plays certainly have a number of embedded messages, these are quite complex. For example, the Dwarfs in *Ananse and the Dwarf Brigade* who are agents of retribution are mischievous imps, not holy angelic beings. The Ghost gets away with the Boy's fish in *Tahinta*, while Vulture in *Vulture! Vulture!* is off to eat a dead rat. At the end of *Children of the Man-Made Lake* the children are trying to sort out as best they can a deeply traumatic experience of displacement. In other words, these denouements contribute to the removal of the adult as an intrusive agent of dominant power, constraining the element of play and creativity. There is something for the children to think about and come back to.

A description of her work as a dramatist would have demonstrated the elaborate processes of self-education in which she engaged in order to prepare herself to write plays that would make it possible to recreate the world of the child on stage. Suffice it to say that her four plays discussed above demonstrate the choices she makes in terms of compositional structure, characterisation, language and style to meet her own highly rigorous standard of writing plays with and for children.

Jürgen Martini

Meshack Asare: Transforming Folklore into Children's Literature

In his contribution 'The Oral Tradition and Children's Literature in Ghana', given at the symposium on African Youth Literature, organised in 1986 by the German Commission of UNESCO at the International Youth Library in Munich, Meshack Asare mentioned other Ghanaian writers of children's literature, among them Efua Sutherland.

'Efua Sutherland…experimented a lot in children's theatre, using material from folklore. She was interested in the subtle ways in which such materials were used for education and instruction. She produced a number of plays for children such as *Ananse and the Dwarf Brigade* and the ever-popular *Vulture! Vulture!* They are both superb examples of traditional counselling in which one is merely shown two opposite characters and left to identify himself with one' (Deutsche UNESCO Commission, ed., African Youth Literature – Today and Tomorrow, Bonn 1986, 45-46).

Asare places himself in this tradition:

Like the other writers [in Ghana], I have got my orientation from folklore. However, I must also say that I started with quite specific concerns, which required that my ideas should come from more sources within the folklore than folk tales. I aimed to attain a deeper understanding of the culture and that way attract more appreciation for it. For this reason, my search has been for those qualities that are exclusively and identifiably ours but by virtue of their universality have some relevance and value for others. *Tawia Goes to Sea*, *The Brassman's Secret* and *The Canoe's Story* try to attain this broadly human, cross-cultural identity (ibid: 46).

Meshack Asare was born in 1945, in Nyankomase, Ghana. He studied Fine Arts at the University of Science and Technology in Kumasi. After graduating from that university, he taught for twelve years in American International schools in Ghana, from 1967 to 1979. During that period, he also took an extension course in Educational Psychology from the University of Wisconsin, Madison. He also holds a degree in Social Anthropology from the School of Oriental and African Studies in London.

Early in his career he contributed an essay and illustrations to the book *Ghana Welcomes You*, published in 1968 for the American employees of the Volta Aluminium Company, and illustrating *Akosua in Brazil* by Alero Olympio and Cecile McHardy. In 1970 he began his career as a children's book author and illustrator. Apart from his work devoted to writing and illustrating for children and younger readers, as Nancy Schmidt said of him at the time, he is also 'a practising artist who makes glasswork, murals, and fountain sculpture' (Schmidt: 33).

His first two books, *I am Kofi* and *Mansa Helps at Home*, both published in 1971, deal respectively with the daily chores of a young boy and girl. The text is a very simple first-person narration, suitable for smaller children, but the illustrations in black and white already show the accomplished artist, with great love of detail in the depiction of everyday scenes from the point of view of a young child.

Already in *Tawia Goes to Sea* (Accra 1970) Asare's ideas can be detected about children's literature in Ghana and particular regions of Ghana, combining a very precise geographical knowledge with regional traditions and history. The fishing community is as minutely depicted as the protagonist, Tawia, and his role in the community. Asare combines a dialectic view of history with an artist's and writer's imagination. Text and illustrations are fully integrated; neither is ancillary to nor dependent on the other. In his awareness of the particular role children play in the tradition of many African societies, as 'messengers whose presence is a gift from the other world' (Cott, *Pipers at the Gates of Dawn*, New York 1983: 189) – thus linking the past with the present, reversing the process of Western socialization, where children are universally depicted as in a state of ignorance – Asare places particular importance on the role history has to play as a continuing past-present relation.

In his award-winning *The Brassman's Secret* (Accra 1981 – Noma Award for Publishing in Africa 1982), the child-viewer and reader can identify with the achievements and failure of the book's hero and protagonist, Kwajo, as the book takes its beginning in the present and ends there. Asare gives a complete impression of the local economy, the intricate network of generations and its function, and the relation between work and leisure.

In choosing the gold weights as the central metaphor, Asare manages to convey a sense of change, in that the gold weights, formerly utilitarian and aesthetic objects, have now become a commodity in the tourist trade, still having both functions, but now with a different meaning. Through a dream sequence, a very traditional device in children's literature, Asare brings both levels, the past in the present and the present in the past, together. The wisdom of the gold-weights coming alive and carrying proverbial meaning, is the vital link between past and present, between animate and inanimate perceptions of the world. Asare manages to show that proverbs, gold weights or *adinkra* patterns have a meaning for present-day society. It is in the dream sequence that Kwajo re-discovers the forgotten meaning of the *sankofa*-bird, with its head turned backward toward its tail. When Kwajo cannot remember its particular meaning – 'Remember the past!' – and tries to rush past the bird in order to at last collect the treasure, the sankofa-bird turns round and attacks Kwajo. The past is not dead; it comes to life and asserts its power. Whereas the heap of gold-dust to Kwajo signifies wealth and power, the brassman and the other gold-weights show him the way to appropriate behaviour, real strength and power which lie in the perception of the past as an integral and vital part of the present. In his illustrations, Asare manages to intensify the effect of the text, in that he employs complex size-variation. In the dream sequence, for instance, the tiny gold-weight takes on human dimensions, being of equal size with Kwajo. The inanimate tool and plaything has suddenly come alive, and it uses its drum-stick in different gestures to warn or advise and, finally, to bring the dream to an end. Similarly, in the dream sequence, the holy shrine, where the treasure is hidden, has an almost oppressive size. *The Brassman's Secret* is, as J. O. de G. Hanson, another famous Ghanaian author of children's books, argued in his book *Children's Literature: The Ghanaian Experience* (Accra 1993: 39), 'in a sense an adventure story even though all the action takes place all in a dream…'

> Such stories exercise a particular attraction to children because children have a strong love for action, they find it exciting if it involves overcoming perils and other obstacles in pursuit of a specific goal to be realised by a character that they can readily identify with. And such a character is invariably or more generally one that is young, strong and courageous. Their innate sense of curiosity makes them wonder what is going to happen next right up till the end (ibid: 39).

It is fascinating to compare the black-and-white drawings in the 1981 edition with the full colour edition of 2002. The black-and-white drawings seem to give settings and figures a far more austere expression than the softer full colour versions. The first edition works through its contrast and rigid lines, showing details for instance in the *adinkra* patterns lacking from the illustrations of the new edition.

Other examples of the intricate fusion of picture and text can be taken from Asare's later books, *Chipo and the Bird on the Hill* (Harare 1984) written and illustrated for his daughter and published in Zimbabwe, or his beautiful way of describing historical processes through the perspective of a century-old tree that is cut down and turned into a boat used by Ghanaian fishermen, in his book *The Canoe's Story* (Accra 1982).

It is Asare's declared intention to eventually cover all regions, traditions and historical periods of Ghana from different perspectives and points of view, in order to supply the Ghanaian child with a deep sense of the importance of history. The books published so far can only convey a limited account of the effect the whole series may eventually have, as not all of the books, although completed, have been published, due to the difficulties of the publishing industry in Ghana. *Meliga's Day* (Accra 2002) takes us to the north of Ghana. In contrast to *The Brassman's Secret*, the setting is more rural, with wide spaces filled with animals, trees and shrubs. Although weaving, pottery and tannery are mentioned and shown in the book, it is the cattle and the goats and animal husbandry that are at the centre of the story. The culture of the northern community is described in its relation to the ancestral spirits and to the earth, to nature and to music.

Sosu's Call (Accra 1997) combines the description of a particular region of Ghana with a narration about a handicapped boy who is able to warn his village of the approach of a storm threatening to destroy the village, by slowly and laboriously making his way to a drum, which he finally manages to use for transmitting a rhythmic warning signal to the men working in the fields. For this very moving book, Asare won the 1999 UNESCO Prize for Children's and Young People's Literature in the Service of Tolerance as well as the 2001 IBBY Award for an Outstanding Book for Young People with Disabilities.

In his 1989 Munich address quoted above, Asare, however, declared his intention to contribute to an attainment of 'cross-cultural identity' in and through children's literature. This can be exemplified on the one hand by drawing attention to his children's books about other African countries (*Chipo and the Bird on the Hill*, 1984, on Zimbabwe; *Children of the Omumborombonga Tree*, 1990, on Namibia; *The Magic Goat* 1997, on Lesotho, and most recently, *Ighewi's Return*, 2004, on Botswana); and on the other hand through books like *Seeing the World* (1989) or *The Cat in Search of a Friend* (published first in a German edition in Austria in 1984, in English in 1986). The latter books tell universal stories, for instance about the possibility of finding out about one's own power without having to rely on the help of outsiders, as is shown in the folk tale about the cat seeking protection from other animals. *Chipo and the Bird on the Hill*, 'with its characteristic sepia drawings on light tan paper' (Schmidt: 35), describes a very similar search to Kwajo's in *The Brassman's Secret*, this time for the meaning of a 'Zimbabwe bird'. While Kwajo has to be taken to the past through a dream sequence induced by the brass figure, Chipo uses a more realistic device, by making Chipo and her partner Dambudzi (troublemaker) take themselves and the reader on a tour of the stone buildings and their various crafts and rituals to finally gain a view of the sacred birds hidden in the stone buildings. Their breach of the rules forbidding them to gain this view is forgiven by the chief, and all children will in future be allowed to view the birds. The riddle of the Zimbabwe bird, however, is left unexplained at the end of the book. The journey into the past, as in *The Brassman's Secret*, is the frame to get the child readers interested in exploring the past of their own country or any other country themselves, since Asare's aim is not to write yet another history book.

The Children of the Omumborombonga Tree was commissioned by the Namibia Project in 1990, in order to celebrate Namibia's independence in the same year. Different from his book on Zimbabwe or later on Botswana, the Namibia Project provided Asare with a basic outline of the story, the story of a creation myth 'about a man and woman who emerge from the large old tree with special powers into a beautiful world of plains, rocks, a large river, and animals, where people of the fire and of the rock already live' (Schmidt: 36). Asare's illustrations to this creation myth – in which the coming together of the different peoples living in Namibia is described as a concept of successful hybridity – are in full colour, with great detail spent on the characteristics of Namibia's landscape. In contrast to European illustrators of African children's books, Asare manages, in all of his books, whether situated in Ghana or elsewhere in Africa, to distinguish landscapes and people, by drawing attention to distinct signs and features. Illustrations and text are based on painstaking research in the countries or regions concerned, of which his latest book to date, *Ighewi's Return* (2004), is a superb example. Asare's research in Botswana made him conclude that there was no proof that the artists of the cave drawings of the San in Botswana were male. His artist in the tale, which once again uses the frame structure of a dream, is female. Unfortunately, the illustrations, with the exception of the book's cover illustration, are in black and white only, due to the format of the series in which the book was published. If the cover illustration is compared with published examples of San cave drawings, the particular sensitivity of Asare to material from outside his own Ghanaian experience can be noticed. The eland, an animal not to be found in Ghana, is drawn beautifully and shown in the process of being drawn and painted.

Asare's books, though set in particular regions, countries and traditions, have a universal appeal. His capacity to relate a textured and sometimes critical image of the past stresses the fact that the past has not been lived and lived through only to disappear in textbooks or conventional historical novels about 'great moments' of history or biographies of 'great men' and only rarely, 'great women'.

History in Africa, is an integral part of folklore and in many traditions, interwoven with mythology in various narrative forms. Secondly, history does not describe slots within linear time. It is rather an account of time manifesting and expressing itself in human action. It is not a dimension of time but rather, of reality and therefore belongs with the transcendental order. The calls to define the 'African self' and 'clarify and prophesy' both require material of unique efficacy; material which connects to the primal, ancestral source and with any possibility, pure and true to the 'native' character. The African writer reaches this source, and when he has found his material, tries to use it to describe a reality which includes all of its possible dimensions.[1]

Interview with Meshack Asare
29 January 2005

JM – Well, Meshack, what I wanted to find out is your association with Efua Sutherland, and what you told me is you first met her in the sixties or in 1960 and were in contact with her until you left in 1984. Perhaps you would want to say something about your first association and how that developed?

MA – Actually I first met or we first met at the Arts Centre or what you call the Arts Council in Accra. That was just around the time I was doing an apprenticeship, just a short work project at the Africa Centre before I started university. And she was working with the Director of Arts: he actually was presidential advisor on Culture, someone called J. H. Nketia. There was a circle of people, a small circle of people; and at that time there were many things happening in Ghana; people like Dr. Du Bois, you know, and a number of these people were actually living in Ghana. I had contact with such adventurous people, but Efua Sutherland was actually one of the people who arranged that there can be a scholarship to study art at the University of Kumasi, and that was in 1963, I think. And from then on actually we were in touch, because she was also doing something I was very, very much interested in. I always liked books and I liked reading as a child; but at the time I was growing up there weren't any children's books, books for children, and I remember struggling through my father's books and magazines. So it was something I always wanted: books for myself, books to read. And when I went to study art, it was in my mind that I should be able one day to make books for children because I was already thinking of illustrated books, books with pictures.

When I was at university, some of the people in this small, small circle, called Cecile McHardy and Alero Olympio both were in Brazil to research on the Ghanaian influence or African influence in Brazil. Cecile came back with a story about a little Brazilian girl who was about the age of her own daughter back in Ghana. The story was short; she said: Well, can we make this story into a book? And I read it and said: Yes, but is that all?' 'In that case, can you illustrate this? Can you illustrate it, do the drawings for the book?' And I did and that was my first illustration of books. But that wasn't the end of it. Now I came back and realised that there was only one person apart from Cecile. There was only one person that I knew who was doing anything for children, who knew anything at all about how to work for children, how to write for them or how to tell them stories, and that was Efua Sutherland anyway. This is because she was developing theatre in Ghana, but I discovered that she was also interested in doing theatre for children, in writing plays for children and not just plays, but taking from tradition, from folklore, from the games that children played and the songs that they sang, and turning this into theatre that would be performed. I was very much interested in that. So when much, much later I decided actually to write myself, I looked around, and she was the person to discuss with. By this time the other person, Cecile, was not in Ghana anymore.

I didn't know any other writer who was writing for children; they were all writing novels and textbooks and mainly for adults; but here was this very, very well educated person; highly, a research fellow at the university who was interested in writing for children. I would have found it much easier to write for adults at the time; I actually started that way. But on a number of visits to the Central Library, where I picked up children's books, they were all foreign, from elsewhere, from Europe mainly or from America or from the Eastern European countries mainly; and when finally I wrote my first story, *Tawia Goes to Sea*, I thought: Well, now I have written this story, but I have written it as if I was writing for an adult, as if I were telling the story to an adult; so now let's see, let's get some opinion, and of course I went to, I took it to Auntie Efua. So we sat and she read through it and made some suggestions and some corrections, and they were all about language. Now, that was very, very, very important. It was important, because of the way we learned the English language, how we actually acquired the English language, mainly through textbooks.

And then we grew up to usually administrative English that we hear. It's like other African countries all about the world. But you see in South Africa or in Namibia there were Europeans living, some British English people, also mixed with the [Africans], though the English language was not their mother-tongue. And [they] also learned, [they] also had the chance to hear more from native English speakers who lived amongst them. It wasn't like that in Ghana. And the English language in Ghana tended to be installed, quite formal, rigid. And now I had written for the first time a book and wanted this book to be read by children. The first thing I had written that had been published were the contributions for the book *Ghana Welcomes You* for adults. But now I had written, spent some time to observe some activities and written about it with a ten-year-old in the middle of it. Therefore, the language had to be that of a child. So, initially, she was a very important mentor for me.

In addition to that there was something else that I discovered: she was also interested in the cross-over from tradition into modernism, into the hybrid creation that would become the modern culture of Ghana, that Ghana becomes part of the modern world, or Ghana brings something from its traditions as it matures into nationhood. She was interested in this. It's an area that she spoke very well, very powerfully and beautifully and convincingly, but she also wrote about, and a particular example was her idea of how tea, tea drinking, also became a Ghanaian custom from observing the English people. We acquired that custom of tea drinking, but we made it into something of our own anyway, and the way we made it something of our own was to call anything of the sort 'tea'. That could be coffee, it could be cocoa, chocolate or whatever, but it was either tea-tea, or coffee-tea or chocolate-tea, or whatever; and I took this as important reference for what I, too, for how I would have to observe the changes around me and how I would find a role in it all for myself and for what I thought to contribute. So the whole idea of creating an image of ourselves, of what we are as Africans with our own traditions and customs, but bringing this image, to refine ourselves, to create or construct an image of ourselves which would become part of the world, which would be seen by the world – was something that I discovered from her. She made it quite clear; and a lot of our exchanges were about this theme, about the processes of achieving this, of defining or re-constructing, actually constructing this image, of the African in the world, being part of the culture of the world, but getting it from or using our traditions, bringing these, reconstructing them, reshaping them. She spent a lot of time training people in the theatre, but she again was quite interested or concerned that our idea, the traditional idea of drama was not exactly the same as the Western idea of drama.

Drama for us was still very, very religious. Child-naming, for example: When the Gas are naming a child or the Ashantis are naming a child, it is a religious occasion, but also there is drama, plenty of it. Everything is arranged and there are roles and everybody plays these roles, and that was our idea of drama; and it occurred in our festivals, in celebrations, big and small. But here was a time to try to create a Ghana drama studio or theatre, and students were brought to be trained to teach drama. So what do we do with the traditions? With what drama is to us? And she again made it the heart of the development of theatre in Ghana. Again, that the idea of the concert party in Ghana would be recognised and respected and built into modern theatre. Perhaps also the idea of drama as it is; as it actually is part of our religious customs and traditions; would also be part of the [development] and these are also some of the things that we spoke about.

My part, really as I realised the importance of reading, of children's literature, and the fact that I had learned to write, and I had learned to draw, and I had also learned to observe the world around me – so what am I going to do with these skills? What is my contribution? What is my role going to be and how am I going to direct this role, so that it becomes useful, in the long term? I realised in this role, in this image-building, in constructing the image of the African, still going back and referring to her own work, the work that she was doing, with the attention that she was paying to our traditions; for example, trying to dramatise a game that children play as children mocking the vulture: 'Vulture,

vulture, pity, pity! Your mother is calling you, your mother wants you.' And then Vulture asks: 'Why is my mother calling me? What does she want of me? My mother ...Why is she calling me?' And then being told: 'Oh, your mother wants you to come home to eat.' This, for example, is a game. But she spent some time to develop this into theatre for the children. She actually wrote a book and published it and a number of things. The butterfly, for example, again: songs about the butterfly that children play with; she took this again and developed it into theatre for children; tried to make a book about it. So she made children's literature, children's play, and a child as a person so important. And our exchanges again centred, of course, on the importance of bringing some of our traditions into modern usage, current usage and modern systems. The last time we worked seriously together, I think, was in the 'Orientation to Ghana' programme. It was my job to look for academics and specialists to contribute stories. And again we sat and spoke a lot and found people to contribute [to the programme] for us...still, the theme of identity of traditions, of the transformation in the merging – what you want to do. She was very knowledgeable.

JM – Did she play any role in politics?
MA – Her role...not as far as I can see. That side wasn't too obvious or too open. I think there was some kind of activism, but rather focusing on culture and I think she believed in some kind of culture purity or purism, whatever you like to call it, and if she took part or participated in culture, it was to ensure that cultural interests were not overlooked.
JM – As language goes most of her work is in English as well...
MA – Is in English and in Fanti. When we met, we used both languages; we spoke English and Fanti.
JM – The plays are for children...
MA – The plays for children, mainly in English, but she used Fanti-words like *fafanto*, 'butterfly', she used and created sounds like *fa fita fita fa*, onomatopoeic, derived from the Fanti language, but then was part of the English text.
JM – I've read them and I was fascinated by them. Were they read all over Ghana?
MA – Around Ghana in the schools. They were absorbed and probably disappeared into the educational system somehow. I don't know about how her work is utilised, how they keep it alive or how they use it now. But it looks like a very, very enriching experience for the educational system, for schools, primary schools, secondary schools. She wrote short stories, but mainly dramas.
JM – There is a very vicious portrait of her in one of Ayi Kwei Armah's novels. Is she also a figure who is controversial?
MA – I have no reason to talk of her as a controversial person. She was forceful, but she also knew what she wanted; she knew what she wanted and she got

what she wanted, but usually she fought just like anybody else fought. She was approachable; very, very approachable, I mean; I spent a number of afternoons, when she was still working at home with her papers. She still had time to talk and read through my own work.

In the sixties, when I was going to school, there were people from everywhere and I attended school with people from almost every part of Africa, with teachers from almost every country in the world and there was this consciousness that that was the end [of colonial rule]. And we knew, because at that time, let's say in the Gold Coast, in Ghana, it looked as if the world had just opened for everybody in Ghana, for us in Ghana, and we also wanted to be – either we wanted to be, but also we were obliged to be – part of the world, of a broader world and I was already there. I was defining *me*, finding myself and reconstructing, constructing an image of myself into the world. And she was thinking – she thought that way already. Later she was developing the drama studio in the late 60s. She developed themes along the lines of our concert parties, which involved more songs and dance in drama. But she also knew about Shakespeare, and about all of those people and what they had done, and the systems that were the norms of the world and tried to bring them together. This is also, I think, what I have been doing, within myself, with my own need: why, for example, there weren't any books for children, about African children with African characters, Kofi and Ama, living in their own home in Ghana and their own adventures and activities. There were stories…I mean, I read about Jack and Jill and about Red Riding Hood and wolves. My idea was to recognise Ghanaians as legitimate characters fit for a book, fit for stories to be told about; that our lives would be fit for stories to be told about; that our life experiences could be described in the form of a book. That was my initial interest, and she was doing that already and therefore she was a fine support to my ideas.

JM – Is there any frustration involved in her later career as well, because obviously the situation in Ghana…
MA – Yes, there was. At the time when I left Ghana, people in her group were under suspicion and not only that, but also her projects, and the finance, the departments. You were under suspicion if it was known that you went abroad and came back and you had contacts abroad.
JM – Did she always stay?
MA – She did. That's right. It shows her toughness.

Anne V. Adams

Revis(it)ing Ritual: The Challenge to the Virility of Tradition in Works by Efua Sutherland and 'Fellow' African Women Writers

Rituals, by their very nature, are archaic; but human society that invents rituals to punctuate its life on earth and beyond is dynamic. Practised since time immemorial, rituals are carried out in accordance with the precedent of earlier generations, even though circumstances may have changed. Their meaning is symbolic, and celebrants are less conscious of a ritual's substance than of the function it serves in the fabric of the society. Because of the dynamism of human society, rituals, as quintessential bearers of cultural tradition, are eventually affected by pressures of movement and change. Hence, some rituals might be lost; others may remain but lose their substance or become perverted. For African societies, the pressures on culture exerted by the exigencies of contemporary life are cutting into the fabric of traditions with each generation. If rituals are to retain their symbolic validity in punctuating the individual's and society's life, in the face of such cultural pressure, then the substance of the rituals must be made to accommodate the dynamism of society itself. They must be consciously revisited with an eye towards making indicated revision.

The issue of the relevance, retention, and reform of communal ritual is central to Efua Sutherland's pair of co-generic works, the short story *New Life at Kyerefaso* (1960) and the play *Foriwa* (1967) (hereafter frequently referred to together as *New Life/Foriwa*). In subsequent decades we see this same issue being treated by other writers, notably the Cameroonian Werewere Liking, particularly in her 'chant-novel' *Elle Sera de Jaspe et de Corail* (1983) and the Senegalese Aminata Sow Fall in her novel *Le Jujubier du Patriarche* (1993).[1] For all these writers, the revisit/revision treatment of traditional ritual is realised through a structural accommodation of the text, no matter what the genre.

Consistently, the metaphor for the revisiting and revision of the ceremonies is some form of 'rebirth' or 'regeneration'. For Sutherland the centrality of the theme is indicated from the very title of the short story 'New Life at Kyerefaso' and from the opening lines of the prologue of the play *Foriwa*, spoken by the young 'foreigner' Labaran: 'Kyerefaso has long been asleep...The town has slept itself to raggedness.' Whereas the short story treats this theme implicitly rather than explicitly – hence the utility of the title's pronouncement – the play articulates the 'regeneration' theme repeatedly: in fact, in the mouth of every major character. It is this very repetition of the theme in *Foriwa* that signifies the 'contagion' of the concept among the townspeople, underscoring its centrality in the writer's vision. With Werewere Liking, the theme of regeneration through ritual is converted into the very form and substance of the 'chant-novel' *Elles Sera de Jaspe et de Corail: Journal d'une Misovire*, becoming the fabric of the work. The title proclaims, through geophysical metaphor [of jasper and coral], the qualities, the 'stuff' from which the future 'new race' is to be moulded explicitly within the text. The objective of the narrative is the execution of an 'initiation' of the townspeople, by calling for a new, refashioned language, a new discursive form, to communicate the society's desperately needed cultural regeneration. With a somewhat different focus, Aminata Sow Fall's *Le Jujubier du Patriarche* 're-constitutes' an extinct ritual, because the traditions formerly supported by it had eroded to a state of barrenness. Dwelling on the perversion of family caste heritage and its retrogressive power with regard to the common weal, Sow Fall invokes the socially therapeutic power of community ritual for regeneration. While Efua Sutherland's play opens with the pronouncement of the urgency for regeneration which will ultimately stimulate the revisiting and revising of the ritual, Aminata Sow Fall's novel begins at the end, or objective, with the reconstituted ritual.

Besides the general thematic interest in regeneration through ritual that the four works share, the phenomenon that is most striking in comparing them is the fact that, in all four, the ceremony in question is presented twice, in absolute or in referenced action, i.e. revisited or re-enacted twice within each text: once to review the state of decay that its celebrant community has reached in terms of the meaning of the ceremony, and again in its restored, revived form. Thus, with each of these texts, the theme of re-investing the ceremonial rituals with a contemporary validity drives the structure of revisiting and revising. The modalities are diverse: Sutherland's idealistic didacticism of the short-story-in-folk-tale-form *New Life at Kyerefaso*[2] or the straightforward sociocultural realism of her play *Foriwa*; Liking's allegorical 'chant-novel'; Sow Fall's writing of the *griot/griotte* into the narrative of historico-social realism. The structural determinant common to these texts is the 'before-and-after' perspective – revisiting and revision – of traditional ceremonies, in the representation of the theme of regeneration through ritual.

To appropriate Efua Sutherland's own language from *New Life/Foriwa* and to recall her pioneer position in contemporary African literature, she was a 'path-finding Mother'. For, from a chronological as well as an aesthetic point of view, her work forms part of the foundation on which the contemporary production of written literature by Africans rests. The artistic commitment to preserving traditional Ghanaian forms in verbal arts while borrowing also from Western conventions, an aesthetic principle now subscribed to by most African writers, is a hallmark of Sutherland's *oeuvre*. But the terrain of this pathfinding Mother extended, from the beginning, beyond her writing to the founding of institutions or organs of historic significance in Ghanaian artistic life, such as the Ghana Society of Writers, the Ghana Drama Studio, and the literary journal *Okyeame*. Devoting her energies fully to such projects of cultural development in Ghana in her last years, Efua Sutherland fulfilled the role which she calls, in *New Life/Foriwa*, 'road-maker', advancing the work initiated by the pathfinders. For Sutherland, creative writing was thus one of the many forms of 'minding [Ghana's] cultural heritage'.

As a demonstration of her artistic interest in reconciling African traditional beliefs and practices to the realities of contemporary life, the 'sister' pieces 'New Life at Kyerefaso' and *Foriwa* – the short story followed by the expanded and somewhat re-focused play – critique three aspects of the social fabric of a town: a) the expectations imposed by the community upon a marriageable young woman; b) the community's suspicious perceptions of a compatriot who comes from outside their region; c) the degenerated homage to historical glories by a people who no longer live up to the ethics and achievements in which they take hereditary pride. In the short story, the centre of gravity is the consistent, principled rejection of all the local suitors by the Queen Mother's beautiful daughter, Foriwa, who is finally won over by a man from a different region, whose energy and ideals of work and progress for the town not only captivate the maiden but ultimately revitalise the stagnating community. For the play, however, the emphasis shifts to the resourceful 'outsider's' initiatives, embraced by *Foriwa*, to reverse the stagnation and decay of community development, and the true significance of the annual festival in re-dedicating the townsfolk to advance the achievements inherited from the forefathers and foremothers. Thus, Sutherland employs different strategies to treat the same thematic elements, achieving a complementary effect.

Of the three social issues listed above that are critiqued in *New Life/Foriwa* the first two are intimately linked. The stranger from another region achieves what the local men cannot: he wins over the mind and, consequently, the heart of the independent Foriwa; and, with his initiatives for renewed enterprises, he brings new vision and energy, 'new life', to the town of Kyerefaso. Indeed, what Foriwa had been holding out for was simply a partner to share the rebuilding, the revitalisation of Kyerefaso; whereas in the short story, set in a traditional village, those revitalisation proposals centred on farming, the restoration of homes, and the production of traditional crafts. The play, set in a recognisably contemporary town, extends the revitalisation ideas to a bigger agricultural project as well as to a bookshop, with the prospect of re-opening the defunct local school. Thus, the 'stranger' comes, offering his hand and mind, for the development of body and mind in Kyerefaso.

The 'stranger' Labaran, a university graduate, is characterised by his modesty and his deceptively unassuming aggressiveness in initiating action that he sees as beneficial to Kyerefaso. He has inspired two otherwise aimless youths to acquire training and establish a cassava plantation, and has encouraged the disillusioned postmaster to expand his shop to accommodate a book-supply business for school-children in the area. These two projects that will build body and mind also involve physical development for the town, exploiting land that has yet lain not just unproductive but festering as a spontaneous garbage dump. To the educated, progressive-mindedly rebellious Foriwa, who could see 'nothing alive' in the men of Kyerefaso, those qualities in Labaran have the effect of a spiritual aphrodisiac.

This figure of the compatriot from another region who is viewed and treated as a stranger is crucial to Sutherland's imperative for integration and partnership among the diverse ethnicities of Ghana and, by extension, of Africa – a theme resonant of the Nkrumahist ideology of the time. It is Foriwa who questions the town's references to this recent arrival as 'stranger':

FORIWA: Where does he come from?
POSTMASTER: [*with a broad grin*] His face should tell you that. He is a stranger.
FORIWA: I mean, is he Ghanaian?
POSTMASTER: Oh, yes. From the north.
FORIWA: And they call him stranger here?[36]

The third issue critiqued by this pair of works, that of the reinvestment of traditional celebrations with contemporary validity, holds a central place in Sutherland's writing as well as in all her other enterprises as a 'cultural worker'. For, in working to 'mind Ghana's cultural heritage', Sutherland also *mines* that heritage for its potential in establishing policies and structures to undergird Ghana's material and spiritual progress. The annual festival celebrated at Kyerefaso in *New Life/Foriwa* involves, of course, the harvest thanksgiving but also, fittingly, the Asafo companies' pathfinding, path-clearing ceremony and their stylised re-enactment of the feats of the conquering ancestors who had won their territorial birthright through blood and thundershot. Designed to inspire pride in the hearts of the people for their strong and virtuous heritage, this observance provides the keystone of the townsfolk's self-image. However, when the Queen Mother, a benevolent and progressive sovereign, challenges the Asafo men to show their own accomplishments to substantiate that self-image, they lose their tongues, for they have no substance to support such a self-image.

As a significant early project of self-consciously African written literature, Sutherland's *New Life/Foriwa*, which was first published in 1960, suggests a productive paradigm for assessing literary treatment of ritual-revision for efficacy in contemporary life. The coincidence of repetition of the critical ritual, for purposes of revisiting and revising them, has motivated this comparison of the Sutherland pair with the Werewere Liking and Aminata Sow

Fall novels. To this end I have constructed a paradigm for assessing the ritual's relevance to contemporary life of which the concepts of *revisiting* and *revising* are central, supported by the others:

reflect > REVISIT > *review* > REVISE > *revive*
(For purposes of distinguishing, brief working definitions from the American Heritage Dictionary are provided here: **reflect** – think or consider seriously; REVISIT – visit again; *review* – examine with an eye to criticism or correction; REVISE – change or modify; *revive* – impart new health or spirit to)

Specifically, the imperative to REVISIT the ritual is motivated by reflection on the situation. The REVISITING itself, which is the response generated by the *reflection*, permits a collective *review*, whose result is the second response, the REVISION of the practice. The outcome of the REVISION is a *revival* of the original significance, but with new substance. Applying the paradigm to Sutherland's *New Life/Foriwa* texts, we find that the REVISITING is stimulated by the Queen Mother but affirmed by the actions of Foriwa and, indirectly, by Labaran also. It is the Queen Mother who has *reflected* on the 'fluff' to which the rituals of the annual festival have been reduced:

QUEEN MOTHER: I have decided to speak. For a long time, I've been trying to find a way to make the people of Kyerefaso see; to see at least that for our ancestors, custom was the fruit they picked from the living branches of life. The lesson is long overdue (25).

Disgusted with the state of affairs and implying a threat to cancel the festival, the Queen Mother calls for a mock-festival on the day before its scheduled opening, to air the case with the council of representatives. This mock-festival serves specifically to REVISIT the time-honoured ceremony, to interrogate its substance. And, so, when the Asafo standard-bearer has recited the closing line of their litany 'We come to offer our manliness to new life', and his men lay down their guns at the Queen Mother's feet, she makes her formulaic response: 'All is well, then. The gun is laid aside. The gun's rage is silenced in the stream.' To this she quite eloquently appends the simple question which brings about the *review* of the whole exercise: 'Now hear me. What's going to be your weapon from now on?' No response is offered by the celebrants who had just finished chanting; 'We are those who roar and cannot/be answered back/Beware! We are they who cannot be answered back.' Filling the vacuum of the men's speechlessness, the Queen Mother continues her impromptu *review* and examination, with an eye to criticism and correction: 'Are your weapons from now on to be your minds' toil and your hands' toil? Is that the meaning of this dedication to new life? Where are you, women all? Come, join the men in dance, for they are offering themselves to new life' (49). All are dumbstruck; they simply are not prepared for this 'attack' (after having 'laid down their guns'). Continuing, the Queen Mother pursues her *review* of the deterioration of their ritual, concluding with the call for 'new life':

> The men are tired of parading in the ashes of their grandfathers' glorious deeds...They are tired of the empty croak, 'We are men. We are men'...Their brows shall now indeed be dusty, their feet indeed thorn-pricked, and 'I love my land' shall cease to be the empty croaking of a vulture upon the rubbish heap... Sitting here, seeing Kyerefaso die, I am no longer able to bear the mockery of the fine, brave words of this ceremony of our festival. Our fathers earned the right to utter them by their deeds...But is this the way to praise them? Watching their walls crumbling around us? Failing to build upon their foundations? Letting weeds choke the paths they made? Unwilling to open new paths ourselves, because it demands of us thought, and goodwill, and action? ...Kyerefaso needs the new life of which we speak, and men to make it true (50-51).

This *review*, with its impassioned chastisement and challenge, contains also the material for REVISION; or, the REVISION resides implicitly in the *review*. And so, the festival is authorised by the Queen Mother, and the acceptance of her challenge to the townspeople is assured by the peace-offering to her from the irascible elder Sintim. Commenting on the significance of Sintim's gift of a white lamb to the Queen Mother's daughter, the postmaster tells Labaran: 'You can always tell the pulse of the town through Sintim. Always. He will make trouble for as long as he is able, but he is always to be found on the winning side of town at the decisive end. What a relief(!)' (62).

The *revival* that results from the REVISION is represented through the success of the plans for the two development projects introduced by Labaran. The lands for the bookshop expansion and for the cassava project are assured; all other preparations are in place. By moving from *review* in the moribund ritual to *revival* in the projects already initiated, Sutherland makes a direct link between the ritual's symbolism and its substantiation in contemporary action plans. The final act representing *revival* of the forefathers' and foremothers' precepts is Sintim's gracious acknowledgement of Labaran's contribution in initiating the two projects, even addressing this 'Northerner', for the first time by his name.

Applying the ritual-assessment paradigm to Werewere Liking's work *Elle Sera de Jaspe et de Corail* introduces the ritual of initiation (in fact, communal initiation) for an entire town. Specifically, Liking envisions a rebirth of African society or, more accurately, the birth of a New Race of Africans, a New Race that will be imbued with new standards, new values. Liking's town of Lunaï is intended as a microcosm of contemporary Africa. Thus, the details of characters and events are to be abstracted to the general African populace. It is, therefore, this entire populace that is in need of ritual initiation. In fact, the structure of the narrative can be analysed in terms of an initiation ritual.

Impelled by the conviction that the language of a society bears much of its cultural content, Liking sees the imperative for a new language, a new discourse through which the New Race of Africans will be represented. The author creates a new language herself, in the naming and in the execution of the text's form: 'chant-novel', and in the naming of the narrator through her neologism *misovire*, which can be rendered roughly as 'male-basher'.

This narrator, a young, perceptive, but disillusioned young African woman – disillusioned by the degeneracy of the social and political state of independent Africa as it has been run by men – *reflects* on the moral and spiritual state of Lunaï while composing in her diary an initiation ritual that will yield the 'New Race'. As an observant, sensitive, intellectual, she is the author's custodian of the initiation, for Liking believes that it is the artist, an individual of particular sensibilities and vision in the community, to whom this responsibility falls. In the complex form of this chant-novel, the REVISITING of the initiation ritual takes place throughout the course of the narrative. That is, the journal-writer's journal of nine sections, called 'pages', is itself a theoretical script for an initiation. Thus, the review of the townspeople's behaviour and social condition that warrant the initiation is conducted at each of the nine stages in the writing of the full-book theoretical initiation script. The final 'page', the ninth, is the text for a complete, REVISED initiation ceremony in itself, yielding a REVISED populace, as it were, the New Race, imbued with the REVISED value system and discourse. With the theory developed over the course of the diary, the final 'page' presents the practice, a REVISION of the ritual that reconciles that traditional form to the reality of contemporary Africa.

It is important to note that the revised values of Liking's New Race incorporate a *revision* of the relations between women and men. Her young woman narrator/journalist/initiation custodian had unwittingly turned into a male-basher only out of the frustration of watching men ruin the new African governments, while excluding women of vision from sharing in the building of their states. And so, with revised standards, the New Race will correct this fault and achieve a proper partnership in the building of the society. By extension, the antagonism that the fault has engendered between the sexes would be mitigated. The resonance here with Efua Sutherland's works is engaging. To call Sutherland's Queen Mother and Foriwa 'male-bashers' would be to miss the mark of their critique in declarations such as '[we are] tired of the empty croak: "We are men. We are men" ', and '…him with whom this new life will be built. He is not here, mother. I don't see him in these empty eyes. I see nothing alive here, mother nothing alive…' (50). However, the social stagnation represented by the local suitors and 'professional' draughtsplayers, on the one hand, and the meaningless exhibitions of 'manliness', on the other, is thrown into relief by the strengths of the 'stranger' who brings the potential productivity of hand and mind. The whole theme of the society's expectations of the marriageable maiden, which Sutherland has adapted from a traditional tale, is revised, in Sutherland's treatment, by the socially minded conditions that determine Foriwa's standards for a partner. Thus, Sutherland, as well as the more militant Liking, draws an intimate link between the true substance of manliness and the partnership of shared vision and action between women and men that progress demands.

Sutherland's formulation, 'parading in the ashes of their grandfathers' glorious deeds', as one critique rituals, befits perfectly the theme of the Senegalese novelist Aminata Sow Fall's *Le Jujubier du Patriarche*. The novel analyses the tenacity of ancestry-based social caste. The illegitimacy of the claim to social superiority, the perversions of social relationships, and the devastation the system wreaks on the lives of those within as well as outside the caste are aspects of this system that the writer critiques. In Sow Fall's text, as in Sutherland's and Liking's, it is through the experience and insight of women that the social contradictions within the traditions are exposed.

At the end of Sow Fall's narrative, the ritual ceremony in question is physically revived after having been extinct for generations. In fact, the *revival* and the REVISITNG coincide. Reflection on the plight of individuals who have suffered through the perverted retention of the divisions in modern times forms part of the saga. Particularly the life of Naarou, a 'poor relative', given at age six to the family of degenerate aristocrats to be reared among them in the position of house girl, and that of Yelli, the patriarch of the degenerate aristocratic family, form the outlines of the contemporary state of the family. It is the news of the decay of the family's tree, the patriarch's *jujube* of the title *Jujubier du Patriarche*, in their ancestral village that motivates a guilt-driven pilgrimage, which in turn gives rise to the re-telling of the clan's legendary history, a communal review of that history and of the current misrepresentation of it by the upper-caste branches of the clan. REVISION of the status of long-dispossessed members and the covenant to resuscitate the family tree – literal and figurative – are the results of the revival of the annual pilgrimage tradition.

If, as Werewere Liking suggests in *Elle Sera de Jaspe et de Corail*, the quintessence of a culture is borne by its language and its social rituals, then the site of any meaningful confrontation between the traditions and new or borrowed practices would obviously be the language and the rituals. Pathfinding Mother Efua Sutherland's writing consciously, deliberately creates such confrontations with the traditions; she composed her works in both Akan and English. Werewere Liking uses basically the French language for her creative expression, but she 'does violence' to the French language (to use Aimé Césaire's conceptualisation) to accommodate her literary imperatives (and in other of her works she has incorporated her Bassa language in rituals that she depicts). Although Aminata Sow Fall, in the novel cited here, has used only French, she achieves a griotic quality in her account of the legend of Yellimané, whether recited by the old practitioner Naani or by Naarou, who excelled as a singer of the legend from the time she was a schoolgirl. This linguistic feature of the text strongly suggests the author's attempt to capture Wolof orature in French. In this very new move for the otherwise stylistically conservative Aminata Sow Fall we find a resonance with Efua Sutherland's written rendering of the Akan storyteller's art in 'New Life at Kyerefaso':

Shall we say,
Shall we put it thus? ...

The challenge to language notwithstanding, the pressure on rituals exerted by modern reality exacts a price that corresponds to the 'structural adjustment' that the texts here demonstrate. The literary potential of this structural concept based on some form of ritual revis(it)ing process has been given impetus by Ghana's Efua Sutherland, from the Akan tradition, and has quite independently found further expression in the Bassa tradition by Werewere Liking and in the Wolof tradition by Aminata Sow Fall. Out of their vision of the socially regenerative power of the traditional rituals, these African writers seek to inspire their societies to 'tighten their cloth', in Sutherland's words – to re-wrap their traditional garments around their bodies, withstanding the tug exerted on them by the cultural 'structural adjustments' inevitable in dynamic societies.

Sandra Richards

Dramatising the Diaspora's Return: Tess Onwueme's *The Missing Face* and Ama Ata Aidoo's *The Dilemma of a Ghost*

In the 1920s African-American poet Countee Cullen wondered 'What is Africa to me?' and thereby gave voice to issues of identity and ambivalence with which those exiled from the continent have been grappling since their historic dispersal. From the nineteenth century colonisation movements, to Marcus Garvey's back-to-Africa plans, to the emergence of independent African nations in the latter half of the twentieth century, Africa-descended peoples in the Americas have dreamed of an escape from racist domination and a return to the warm embrace of the African motherland; their creative literature has participated in that collective dream. For most of this long history, African writers, in contrast, have not demonstrated a similar preoccupation with reconnecting with the descendants of those sold into transatlantic slavery (Gourdine: 16). In a canon of black female playwrights, five women stand out for their representations of the African Diaspora's connections to the continental homeland: In the United States, Shirley Graham and her 1935 opera *Tom Tom*, Lorraine Hansberry and her 1959 *A Raisin in the Sun* and Lynn Nottage and her 1996 drama *Mud, River, Stone*. On the other side of the Atlantic, Ama Ata Aidoo of Ghana and Tess Onwueme of Nigeria – and now the United States locate their Disaporic protagonists on African soil. In the case of the African playwrights in particular, their texts must take on the challenge of speaking simultaneously to two audiences whose life experiences are likely to produce radically different responses to the plays. Additionally, both authors understand the condition of Diaspora as including Africans themselves, such that the texts posit husbands who are alienated from their indigenous culture and thus must make their own journey home to 'authenticity'. This paper functions as an adjunct to my larger research project on performances of the memory of slavery in the Black Atlantic; in the Ghana portion of the project, I have been fascinated by the ways in which the trope of a reunited African family, mobilised on both sides of the Atlantic, operates in interactions between locals and Diasporans at such sites like the slave castle dungeons of Elmina and Cape Coast. Thus, I will pursue a similar line of inquiry here. I argue that though Onwueme's *The Missing Face* may satisfy cultural longing for a return to a pre-lapsarian or Eden-like point of origin, Aidoo's *The Dilemma of a Ghost* is more honest in articulating the difficulties that members of the geographically/

historically far-flung African 'family' face in attempting to re-member them/ourselves as one. For Onwueme, the trope of return is valid; the journey ends in authenticating 'roots' that overwrite history. For Aidoo, the specifics of place – cultural stereotypes, customs, language, and history – structure this return as a space of negotiation and uncertainty. Her travellers and hosts alike must weather the flux and flow of 'routes' that bring new information and perspectives to wash over their sense of identity.

BACKGROUNDS

Of the two women, Ama Ata Aidoo is the senior, for she was born in 1940 in the Central Region of Ghana, where the castle dungeons of Elmina and Cape Coast are the looming, silent metonyms for our traumatic descent into slavery, colonialism, and dependency. A chief's daughter, she grew up in a royal household and matriculated at the University of Ghana, Legon, from which she graduated in 1964. *The Dilemma of a Ghost* is her first play, and it was produced by a student group during her senior year at Legon. She came into young adulthood during the heady days of Kwame Nkrumah's Pan-Africanism, that strove to wrest the continent from colonialism and unite it around a vision of African self-determination (Gourdine: 9-10). From 1964-1966, Aidoo was a Junior Research Fellow at the Institute of African Studies at Legon,[1] where the legendary Dr. Efua Sutherland, pioneer of (contemporary) Ghanaian theatre, was also employed. Though Aidoo did not journey to the United States until the late 1960s, when she had a creative writing fellowship at Stanford University, it is likely that during her student days at Legon, she had met people like her naïve protagonists, Eulalie Rush and Ato Yawson; for as she shared in an interview with Adeola James, 'In Nkrumah's Ghana one met African-Americans and people from the Caribbean' (quoted in Gourdine: 16), and as critic Brenda Berrian notes, intercultural marriages between Ghanaian 'been to' men, educated abroad, and foreign women were at an all-time high during this period.[2] Aidoo's second play *Anowa* addresses the impact of the transatlantic slave trade on nineteenth century Ghanaians. Produced in 1970, it marks her departure from the theatre, for from that time, Aidoo has chosen to write novels and short stories.[3] In the early 1980s, she briefly held the post of Minister of Education, but given her outspokenness on women's rights, ran foul of the Rawlings government and she settled in Harare, Zimbabwe in 1983, where she taught and wrote.[4] She has taught in the United States and now lives between Ghana and teaching in the US.[5]

Tess Onwueme was born in 1955 in an area of Bendel state, Nigeria, where the Igbos are the dominant cultural group. By the time she began her university education at Ife, the dream of Black independence had metamorphosed into a nightmare for many, because Nigeria had already experienced civil war and military dictatorship. Onwueme was awarded an MA in Literature from the University of Ife in 1982, and obtained the Ph.D. from the University of Benin in 1987.[6] A prolific author, who has probably written more plays than any other African woman in the last twenty years, Onwueme also taught at various Nigerian universities throughout the 1980s. Presumably, like Aidoo, she encountered Diasporans from the United States and the Caribbean during her campus years. Since 1989 she has resided in the United States. She published *Legacies* in 1989, seemingly while still in Nigeria, and subsequently rewrote and re-titled it as *The Missing Face* in 1997. It was produced at Henry Street Settlement's Abron Art Centre in New York in 2001. Currently, she is Distinguished Professor of cultural diversity and Professor of English at the University of Wisconsin, Eau Claire.[7]

Having offered an admittedly brief summary of the authors' locations, I would like now to compare their representations of the Diaspora's return. I will reverse the order of the discussion and start with the later play, namely Onwueme's *The Missing Face*, where the power of its theatricality undermines the cultural work that the text proposes to its spectators. Hoping to argue persuasively my perspective in fairly short order, I will then devote more time to Aidoo's *Dilemma of a Ghost*.

THE MISSING FACE

Briefly stated, *The Missing Face* centres around Ida Bee and her teenage son, Amaechi, who have travelled from Milwaukee to the family's reputed birthplace in Idu, Nigeria, in order to 'find [their] place in the world' (4)[8] and to locate themselves in 'a place that can fill the emptiness with kinship and the spirit of our ancestors'. The son is an unwilling traveller who argues that his family and home are back in the United States. They have unwittingly stumbled into the sacred grotto and family compound of Chief Odozi at a point when the community is engaged in ritual cleansing in preparation for a new year. When discovered, Ida cannot state her exact relationship to the several clans of Idu kingdom; she knows only that her father, before abandoning the family in search of work, gave her one-half of an *Ikenga* mask, telling her that one day she would restore the family to wholeness. She also identifies Momah – who is dancing as part of his final rites of initiation into manhood – as Jack, the student who accepted her support and fathered her son during his sojourn in the United States. Angry at having his past revealed, Momah storms off without saying anything; it is left up to the chief and his wife to ascertain the validity of Ida Bee's accusations and, more importantly, to mediate this disturbance so that the community can move forward to a prosperous new year. The elders prove to have an easier task of accepting Ida Bee than do the two men, Momah and Amaechi, in assuming their manhood, that is, in accepting their responsibilities to family and exerting leadership in meeting an unknown future with confidence. Under the power of ritual, father and son claim their true identities; Momah's *ikenga* half is found to match that of Ida Bee; and a newly fashioned bronze *ikenga* that Amaechi willingly wears signifies that the desired unity has been achieved. Surprisingly ignored in the final celebration of this new dawn are the implications of the fact that Momah and Ida Bee, as possessors of the two *ikenga* halves, are in fact brother and sister.

It is important to recognise that Onwueme is a symbolist, more interested in the clash of ideas on a global scale than in the messy detail and nuance with which idealists must necessarily contend in trying to pursue their dreams in a particular locale.[9] In a context where few African writers have addressed the topic of the Diaspora's return, she places the issue before her home(?) or continental audience, and through the Momah character, she occasions reflection about an internal and alienated Diaspora, which, being educated, has responsibility for Africa's welfare. For both Diasporan and Continental, she reassures that the flame of Pan-African unity continues to burn brightly. And, with the spectacle of towering masquerades, adept singers and dancers, and electrifying drumming, she offers an engaging, powerful theatrical experience. Certainly, all these are positive reasons to applaud Tess Onwueme.

Rather than dwell on aspects of Onwueme's dramaturgy that detract from these positives, I want to focus on several moments which, in their scripted and/or performative potential, insinuate the cultural work that this text's spectators must undertake. Ida Bee's conversations, first, with her son and then, with chief Odozi, demonstrate that neither group of returnees and locals is monolithic in its outlook: their different histories and consequent subjectivities shape their understanding of home and belonging. For Amaechi, his lived experience of being 'born black in Milwaukee' (4) and of having relatives who share his reality, determines his identity as an American. For him, the norm includes friends who have no fathers in their homes and students who take guns to school in order to survive black-on-black violence, so that what he terms the 'jungle' of Africa has nothing to teach him about manhood or dignity that is viable for what spectators may regard as the urban jungle of the States. His mother, Ida Bee, is a survivor of racist violence, external to a black community, much like the social activist whose name hers recalls. Her sense of the world, her articulation of identity, as registered in her discourse about masculinity, seems to derive from the Negritude and Black nationalist movements of the 1950s and 1960s, when artists and activists constructed visions of a glorious African past as part of the needed inspiration and mobilisation for the decolonisation process. Thus, she attempts to counter Amaechi's American equation of guns and manhood with this description of the African man who, she contends:

carries the power of his gun in his heart, then walks boldly through the forest of demons with a steady stride, his feet planted firmly on the ground like an elephant, trampling vipers and scorpions that threaten his progress toward the light of the sun (7).

To this vision of a naturally sanctioned agency, Amaechi responds simply: 'I wouldn't know such a man if I saw him' (ibid).

A similar, seemingly unresolvable clash of perspectives occurs when Ida Bee is challenged to state her lineage. From her history and lived experience, such identification is irrelevant; she responds to Odozi's inquiries:

We are the children of Africa...born in the new world. Africa is our land. We do not have to claim any particular land or country because Africa was our nation...before the white man came to divide...disperse us (12).

Laughing dismissively and terming her an *oyibo*, translated as 'stranger' or 'white person', Odozi states the profound threat to his world view that Ida represents. He says, 'Well, my people, in my old age, a stranger has come to tell me that I do not know who I am. She wants to tell me who I am' (13). He follows this comment with the observation that every person, no matter how poor, and every animal (other than bats) has its place in their society. In that Ida Bee and Amaechi are obviously human, they must be part of a *known* social network. This perspective recalls the definition of a slave articulated in Ama Ata Aidoo's *Anowa* , where Anowa describes herself as a 'wayfarer, with no belongings either here or there' (36), and her husband juxtaposes the equivalent term: 'Wayfarer, you? But are you talking about...about...*slaves*?' (36 italics added). Similarly, in Aidoo's *Dilemma of a Ghost*, Ato Yawson's uneducated grandmother cannot understand how 'any human being born from the womb of a woman has no tribe' (47) and wails with shame when she learns that her grandson has married a slave, the distinction between a descendant of a lineage-less person and an actual slave being meaningless for her. For all these traditional, West African people, to be human is to be part of a social unit; to be lineage-less is to be a non-human or slave. For most Diasporans, the old lineage, founded in consanguinity, cannot be reconstructed; location in a new lineage, based on shared experience and imaginative leaps, is what renders us persons.

The psychic investment in identity-construction that each perspective posits is high. '[The] world is turned upside down,' says Odozi (12). Here, art has the ability to offer spectators/readers a non-threatening opportunity to vicariously try on a formulation different from that with which they ordinarily navigate their lives. In Onwueme's *The Missing Face*, these opposing constructions are resolved through re-enactments that are double-voiced and highly dependent on the performers' artistry and the audience's cultural literacy. First, the Idu community onstage and spectators in the auditorium experience Ida Bee's pain through a flashback, in which Momah's belief in African backwardness and his abandonment of his child are re-enacted. Seeing the way in which their son has shamed them, the Idu elders are then moved to re-enact the cord-cutting and naming ceremonies by which Amaechi's kinship is acknowledged, and Nebe mimes with Ida Bee the 'neck cutting' ceremony that transforms a new wife from an outsider into a member of the extended family.[10] Ida Bee and Amaechi's humanity is validated because the child's blood places them within the family. Yet because two cultural scripts are operating simultaneously, the claim that lineage is what one makes of it, that Diasporans are free to claim any and all parts of Africa as home, may be lost in the seduction of the performative moment. These cultural scripts can be mapped, on the one hand, onto a West African population whose centuries-long war against enslavers induced amnesia about the people taken captive and thus rendered lineage-less, and on the other, onto an historically exiled community whose subjectivity is built around a core loss or aporia. One script dictates reading the flashback literally: Amaechi is indeed Momah's son and thus the cutting cord, naming, and neck cutting ceremonies are entirely appropriate. Another script reads this flashback more metaphorically: Momah's abandonment of his son and his belief in Black inferiority in the face of Western white technology constitute a contemporary equivalent of an historical betrayal and of an ongoing racial self-doubt. Within this latter perspective, the incorporative ceremonies perform a fiction that satisfies deeply felt needs to belong; under the influence of skilful performers, we can imagine our own incorporation into an African network. Fed on the artistic fiction that Onwueme and others offer, prompted by the welcoming invitations found in tourist pamphlets and web sites, some of us journey to Africa hoping to enact the homecoming we have vicariously experienced.[11]

DILEMMA OF A GHOST

A generation earlier, in 1965, Ama Ata Aidoo crafted Eulalie Rush, who travelled to the newly independent Ghana inspired by images of '...palm trees, the azure sea, the sun and golden beaches' (Aidoo: 36) proffered in tourist brochures and by stories of the Biblical Ruth who left her family for the embrace of her husband's people. But unlike Ruth or Ida Bee, Eulalie does not find an easy acceptance. Unlike Onwueme, who deploys a quest motif in which the protagonist is guaranteed to find enlightenment by the close of the narrative, Aidoo sets this drama of return within the oral tradition of a dilemma tale. In so doing, she raises moral, ethical, and sociopolitical issues for her audiences to debate and learn from (Bascom; Brown, 132; Odamtten;) she engenders questions as to who exactly is the Diaspora child come 'home' or what social conditions have prompted a ghost's appearance.

In the space allowed me I want to closely examine the prelude in order to demonstrate the cultural work or social issues this text insists we engage. The drama takes place in the courtyard of the newest wing of the Odumna clan house; in the foreground is a path linking the family compound to roads leading to 'the river, the farm, and the market' (31). This new wing has been built to house Ato Yawson, whose family had gone to great expense to send him abroad to receive a Western-style education. Although they know he will spend most of his time in the city pursuing opportunities now available to the new nation, they expect that he will return at festival times, when the stools or symbols of family lineage and authority are washed and renewed. Attached on one side and enclosing the space is the old wing, where most of the family who 'did not hear the school bell when it rang' (47) live. Thus, semiotically, before the play has even begun, the text signals an interest in how the past and present are related and indicates that this relationship has consequences for the world beyond the family compound.

Into this space comes a narrator who introduces herself as 'the Bird of the Wayside' and explains her identity as:

The sudden scampering in the undergrowth,
Or the trunkless head
Of the shadow in the corner (33).

A presence that the audience can see characterises herself as an absence fleetingly apprehended. In the drama that unfolds another absence will take visible form. At the most literal level, Eulalie is the ghost whose life has been forgotten and who now re-appears demanding recognition; she is most clearly the Diaspora person. But Aidoo is careful to dramatise the ways in which Ato Yawson is also a ghost or non-person, because he does not remember the obligations that his rootedness in family entails. Thus, as the drama unfolds, one sees that Ato espouses the Western construction of marriage as a romantic union between 'free' individuals. He has not bothered to inform his family of his marriage; he ignores societal expectations that he will support his mother who has sacrificed on his behalf; he is more interested in parading his knowledge than he is in explaining Eulalie's background in terms that his family might understand. And, most importantly, he fails to explain that the couple are using contraceptive devices, leaving Eulalie open to family anxieties about her possible barrenness. In that the play has recognisable parallels with offstage realities in Ghana, this representation of the 'been-to' educated abroad critiques the class of young professionals who will be critical to the nation's postcolonial development.

But I get ahead of myself. Let us return to the *Bird of the Wayside* who offers clues as to how we spectators/readers may profitably receive the text.

Confident in her ability to tell a story, she says nonetheless, 'the mouth must not tell everything' (33). Instead, she will have the audience work and labels them a 'stranger' outside the perspectives of those characters about to appear onstage. Positioned at a distance – apparently alienated – they must watch attentively, for 'sometimes the eye can see/And the ear should hear'. In other words, reflexivity will be important, because the theatre's multiple sign systems may contradict each other. Indeed, in fairly short order we see the young couple at some unnamed overseas campus on graduation day. Though they profess love for each other through tone and such clichéd endearments as 'sweetie pie' and 'darling', they also argue about cultural differences between African-Americans and Africans. Similarly, before we see Yawson's family, we observe two neighbours who are united in the unending toil they experience as women but divided by their status as mother and motherless. This issue of fertility – and with it, lineage – will soon come centre stage as the family grapples first with Eulalie's identity as a slave (or slave descendent) and later, with her apparent barrenness.

The Bird of the Wayside also makes two other comments important for decoding the text. She recites the clan's moniker or praise song, 'We are of the vanguard/We are running forward, forward. . .' and in describing the new yam festivals Ato is expected to attend, she explains:

The ghosts of the dead ancestors are invoked and there is no discord, only harmony and a restoration of that which needs to be restored. But the Day of Planning is different from the Day of Battle (34).

Thus, in fairly short order, the play presents a number of binarisms: new vs. old; absence vs. presence; African-American vs. African; educated elite vs. traditional peasantry; motherlessness *vs.* motherhood, planning vs. execution. We need remember that Aidoo is fashioning a dilemma story whose objective is not a neat resolution in which the event concludes with the privileging of one side of the binarism; the methodology of this dilemma genre aims for the messiness of community palaver or talk that may stop without validating any position. What is important is the dynamic of discussion that eschews reified positions and keeps the community ever striving towards some consensual equilibrium.

As the drama progresses, the implied opposite of a particular utterance is made manifest; the absent becomes present . Those who boast movement are revealed as immobilised; those who promise peace can also affect discord. Ato recalls in a dream a children's game in which a ghost stands at a junction unable to decide whether to go to Cape Coast or Elmina, and as his relationships to both Eulalie and to the family deteriorate, Ato resembles that ghost stumbling in the dark, unable to find his way. Both Cape Coast and Elmina are linked to the transatlantic Slave Trade, which the Yawsons, though related to prominent Fanti clans living near these castle-dungeons, have cast from memory. As entrepreneurs deeply invested in the slave trade over several centuries, the Fantis – and Ghanaians more generally – have a responsibility to those exported across the Atlantic. Thus, like an *abiku* whose unsettled spirit keeps returning to life and demanding recognition , the orphaned Eulalie comes hoping to find a nurturing family and 'a restoration of that which needs to be restored'. The family that boasts 'we are moving forward' will remain in limbo, not producing a future until it comes to terms with its past in the present. Interestingly, at the play's conclusion, it is the seemingly tradition-bound mother Esi Kom who runs to catch a falling Eulalie and leads her into the old wing of the compound; left in the courtyard, wondering what to do next, is Ato. Given Eulalie's cultural arrogance, given the linguistic barriers that make communication between the women difficult, given Ato's displaced sensibility, *Dilemma of a Ghost* offers no happy ending. Rather, it challenges its multiple-positioned audiences[48] to acknowledge a painful, silenced history, to debate competing claims, and to imagine new constructions of humanness, whereby all the ancestors can be honoured and their stools washed. Though this last sentence has a rhetorical upbeat ring to it, reality is something yet again. The dilemma that Aidoo posed some fifty years ago is still being debated today, as Diaspora tourists – or pilgrims – travel 'home', as some descendants seek the same rights as Ghanaian citizens, as northerners demand that their stories of pillage, rape, and enslavement be told; and as a more recent Diaspora resident both in the nation's cities and overseas seeks to define development in the twenty-first century.

John Lemly

Hesitant Homecomings in Hansberry's and Aidoo's First Plays

Once in a while I catch myself wondering whether I would have found the courage to write if I had not started to write when I was too young to know what was good for me. — Ama Ata Aidoo[1]

In a secular and contingent world, homes are always provisional. Borders and barriers which enclose us within the safety of familiar territory, can also become prisons, and are often defended beyond reason or necessity. Exiles cross borders, break barriers of thought and experience. — Edward Said[2]

When, as a university student in her early twenties, Ama Ata Aidoo first dared to be a woman playwright, there were few models anywhere in the world. And even fewer if she looked among the daughters of Africa. But two pioneering examples did point the way. One, of course, was Efua Sutherland, head of the Drama Studio in Accra, founder of the National Theatre Movement, who had just joined Legon's new Institute of African Studies. And there was also an African-American dramatist who had recently broken the barriers of colour and gender that long had left the theatre dominated by white male writers. An unknown from Chicago's Southside, only twenty-eight, had written the Broadway hit of 1959, taking the Drama Critics Circle award away from such venerable men as Tennessee Williams and Eugene O'Neill. *A Raisin in the Sun* sky-rocketed Lorraine Hansberry into international prominence. Within a few years it was widely translated, read and performed around the world. In 1963 it played at the Ghana Playhouse in Accra; a few months later, Aidoo's first play — *Dilemma of a Ghost* — was staged at Legon's Commonwealth Hall.[3]

The affinities between these young playwrights' first plays are illuminating. *Dilemma* extends *Raisin's* subplot in which Beneatha Younger is tempted by her Nigerian suitor Asagai to accompany him to Africa. Hansberry leaves their romance in limbo as the play's climax turns on the family's courageous defiance of suburban segregationists. Aidoo shows what might have happened had the African-American woman followed her student husband back home. Reading the plays in dialogue with each other reveals how remarkably Aidoo critiques Hansberry's hopeful vision of determined amelioration. Indeed, the troubled ending of *Dilemma* suggests the less optimistic, more radical developments in Hansberry's later work – as well as in Africa and in America – during the brief years between her Broadway debut and death from cancer in 1965.

* * * * * *

In form, *A Raisin in the Sun* is a comedy, celebrating the Younger family's indomitable will to seize an American 'dream deferred'.[4] The lone white character on stage, a racist functionary, is banal, soft-spoken, a cardboard villain more Walter Mitty than Bull Connors. Privileged daughter of upper-class parents, Hansberry had nevertheless known firsthand the terrors of American apartheid. Her father fought in the courts for years to overcome residential restrictive covenants that sanctioned segregation in Northern cities. Her mother had kept guard with a loaded pistol while a mob terrorised their house in a 'white neighbourhood'. But the play only hints at that reality. The script's most explicit allusions to 'coloured homes' being bombed were cut from the original production, the Hollywood film, and early editions. Theatre-goers were spared such vivid reminders of racism, even as the nation's struggles for Civil Rights were about to erupt. Instead, the play concludes with the prospect that the African-American family will overcome, will gain their rightful place in the suburbs, even as this young, gifted, black woman had enjoyed unprecedented success in the mainstream theatre.

It has been easy, then and later, to misread the hope expressed in *A Raisin in the Sun*. Early on, as the Black Arts movement took off, some critics dismissed it as bourgeois irrelevance:

> ...the aspirations of the new, rising Negro mercantile class to own colour TV, refrigerators that have two doors, sports cars, split-level homes, central heating, self-wiping dishes and air-conditioning. In short, it is not a play about human dignity, but how to invest wisely.[5]

Responding to such reductive misreading, Hansberry did not apologise; she vehemently answered such charges of 'fuzzy-headed notions of idealism'.

> I absolutely plead guilty to the charge of idealism. But simple idealism. You see, our people don't really have a choice. We must come out of the ghettoes of America, because the ghettoes are killing us; not only our dreams, as Mama says, our very bodies. It is not an abstraction to us that the average American Negro has a life expectancy of five to ten years less than the average white. You see . . . that is murder (YGB 117).

In the play it is Asagai, Hansberry's 'favourite character',[6] who most fully and literally articulates that determined idealism. Renouncing her own dreams as 'a child's way of seeing things', Beneatha turns on Asagai: 'All your talk and dreams

– 123 –

about Africa!' (III: 133) New black leaders, she argues, will simply exploit their people as their colonial masters did before them.

> Don't you see there isn't any real progress, Asagai; there is only one large circle that we march in, around and around, each of us with our own little picture in front of us – our own little mirage that we think is the future.

> ASAGAI: That is the mistake. . . . It isn't a circle – it is simply a long line . . . that reaches into infinity. And because we cannot see the end – we also cannot see how it changes. And it is very odd but those who see the changes – who dream, who will not give up – are called idealists . . . and those who see only the circle – we call *them* the 'realists' (III: 134).[7]

Asagai's bold prophecy of the changes 'that make history leap into the future' expounds on Hansberry's conviction 'that the ultimate destiny and aspirations of the African people and twenty million American Negroes are inextricably and magnificently bound up together forever'.[8]

His speech here typifies what Julius Lester has called Hansberry's 'real sense of what was to come. . . . a remarkable element of prognostication in her plays'(LB 19-20). Within two years of the opening night, Lumumba would be dead, almost exactly as Asagai grimly envisions his own possible fate: 'Perhaps I will be a great man . . . . and find my way always with the right course. . . and perhaps for it I will be butchered . . . some night by the servants of empire'(135). And America's struggle for equal rights grew more bloody and became entangled in the atrocity of Viet Nam, even while the heady dawn of African independence quickly clouded over. Hansberry's 'simple idealism' grew complicated, equivocal. All along she had rejected 'happy endings or clichés of affirmation' (YGB 227), had aspired to 'the depth of art it requires to render the infinite varieties of the human spirit – which invariably hangs *between* despair and joy'. In her final plays that balance would tilt toward despair, but even *A Raisin* is informed by her belief that 'We are all surrounded by the elements of profound tragedy in contemporary life, no less than were Shakespeare and the Greeks' (YGB 119-20).[9]

This unsentimental insistence on a tragic world-view makes the play's 'African' sub-plot much more than mere tender romance or comic relief. At the moment when Walter Lee has squandered their father's legacy, Asagai offers Beneatha marriage and emigration to Africa as an alternative way out of the ghetto. He gives her back her dreams, not by glib romantic promises of postcard Africa, but by his steadfast embrace of the future. In an interview with Studs Terkel, Hansberry called him 'the true intellectual . . . so absolutely confident in his understanding and his perception of the world that he has no need for any of the façade of pseudo-intellectuality, for any of the pretence and the nonsense'(41). He locates himself unequivocally in the midst of history, whatever may happen to him and his people. Unlike his counterpart in Aidoo's play, Asagai is not undone by the dilemmas he confronts.

Playful and assured, Asagai lures Beneatha back home: 'Three hundred years later the African Prince rose up out of the seas and swept the maiden back across the middle passage over which her ancestors had come . . . and, in time, we will pretend that – (*very softly*) – you have only been away for a day' (137). Hansberry herself never literally got back to Africa, but in the few years left to her she was coming home, on a trajectory that had begun in childhood. Niece of the pre-eminent Africanist William Leo Hansberry and later student of W. E. B. Du Bois, she studied her heritage long before African Studies entered the curriculum or *dashikis* and *kente* were commonplace among Black Americans. In a fictionalised autobiography she records how 'Africa claimed her':

> . . . she had spent hours of her younger years poring over maps of the African continent. Postulating and fantasising: *Ibo, Mandingo, Hausa, Yoruba, Ashanti, Dahomean.* Who? Who were they?! In her emotions she was sprung from the Southern Zulu and the Central Pygmy, the Eastern Watusi and treacherous slave-trading Western Ashanti themselves. She was Kikuyu and Masai, ancient cousins of hers had made the exquisite forged sculpture at Benin, while surely even more ancient relatives sat upon the throne at Abu Simbel watching over the Nile (YGB 50).

Hansberry's writing put her among the first African-American artists to make what Kofi Anyidoho has called this 'journey back to memory . . . to ancestral time and place' and ahead into the uncertain future of post-colonial Africa. Produced posthumously, her last play *Les Blancs* enacts the reluctant homecoming of another 'been-to', one not so sanguine and self-confident as Asagai, caught up in violent revolution from which there seems ultimately no turning away. Having spent his youth 'waltzing around the world', having 'sold [him]self to Europe' (LB 88: 148), he hesitates to join the bloody rebellion engulfing his Kenya-like homeland and pitting brother against brother. In apocalyptic carnage, the play closes with its would-be non-hero reduced to an animal-like cry of anguish. It is the fire next time, an ending far removed from *A Raisin's* final glimpse of Beneatha's dreams of Africa and Walter Lee's apotheosis: 'He finally came into his manhood today, didn't he? Kind of like a rainbow after the rain' (III: 151). In the distance between these two endings is some measure of the range of Hansberry's vision of Africa and of 'man's defeat *and* triumph in the face of absurdity' (YGB 176).

Less masterful, but even more precocious in many respects, Ama Ata Aidoo's first play picks up where *Raisin* leaves off. *Dilemma* opens on an American campus as the protagonists are already conceding that a tourist brochure – 'the palm trees, the azure sea, the sun and golden beaches' – does not depict the reality awaiting them (Prelude: 9).[10] Although not yet having visited America, the young playwright steadily deconstructs any facile dream that a piece of land – whether Chicago suburb or former Gold Coast – is there for the taking, that love and determination suffice for one 'to belong to somewhere again'(9). At his homecoming to Ghana, the young graduate Ato Yawson becomes increasingly unable to know and choose what he wants, because as Vincent Odamtten has argued: 'He refuses to confront his and our history honestly'; 'the representative of the neocolonial intellectual is paralysed . . . unable to decide about his role in the struggles that have arisen as an inevitable consequence of the antagonistic contradictions during the immediate post-independence era.'[11] In this essential respect he differs from Asagai, or rather perhaps, such self-assurance notwithstanding, few would be able to unravel the inevitable dilemmas awaiting Hansberry's character back home. Despite promises to his African-American bride that 'all my people [will be] your people', he is unable to mediate between them (9). An amphibious education in both languages and cultures has not prepared him to say what is required. His characteristic stammering is anticipated earlier by his grandmother's anguish at joining the ancestors.

My spirit Mother ought to have come for me earlier.
Now what shall I tell them who are gone? The daughter
Of slaves who come from the white man's land.
Someone should advise me on how to tell my story.
My children, I am dreading my arrival there
Where they will ask me news of home.
Shall I tell them or shall I not?
Someone should lend me a tongue
Light enough with which to tell
My Royal Dead
That one of their stock
Has gone away and brought to their sacred precincts
The wayfarer (I: 19).

The questioning is like the dilemma song itself: 'I don't know/I can't tell' (III: 28). Her aphasia is triggered by his. Only a wise, articulate grandson could 'lend a tongue' to resolve her own predicament, but Ato throughout is peculiarly tongue-tied. Repeatedly, as one stage direction puts it, he *makes more futile attempts to speak'* (V: 52).[12] Ato's mother, reminiscent of Walter Younger's, is strong enough to make up for his failure of manhood, by speaking in his stead, by knowing what to tell. Thus at the end she welcomes and shelters her orphaned daughter-in-law, appearing to fulfil the opening plea that 'your Ma be sort of my Ma too' (9). But Ato is left not knowing where to turn, where to go, what to tell, the epitome of what Du Bois calls 'the world-wandering of a soul in search of itself'.[13] If he cannot go home again, indeed most likely neither can his wife. In a brilliant study of the Orpheus trope in Aidoo's work, Therese Migraine-George argues that this fleeting ending 'may in fact highlight its very impossibility....Ato probably knows that the coke-drinking, smoking, and urbanised Eulalie, stigmatised by Ato's family members as the "wayfarer" (19), "this black-white woman/a stranger and a slave" (22), can never become part of a community from which he himself feels irrevocably alienated because of his Western experience.'[14] The play questions not so much their marriage,[15] but whether a cosmopolitan elite can reconnect with the new nation's essential village culture and folk wisdom. And Ato warrants the sort of contempt expressed toward African émigré men in Aidoo's other works, such as *Our Sister Killjoy* (120-21ff.), or in "Everything Counts":

> . . . she was thinking of how right the boys had been. She would have liked to run to where they were to tell them so. To ask to forgive her for having dared to contradict them. They had been so very right. Her brothers, lovers and husbands. But nearly all of them were still abroad. In Europe. America, or some place else. They used to tell her that they found the thought of returning home frightening. They would be frustrated.
>
> Others were still studying for one or two more degrees. A Master's here. A Doctorate there. . . That was the other thing about the revolution.[16]

Men's nationalist revolutionary rhetoric too often cloaks their hypocrisy. In a provocative exchange with Dingwaney Needham, Aidoo ponders whether 'the better term for me to use is Pan-Africanism rather than African nationalism'; that: 'Part of the reason nationalism is inadequate is because women were excluded from its definition, its scope. . . If this is what nationalism means, or has come to mean, then I realise I cannot touch this term. And yet I still think we need an African identification for there surely are an African people.'[17] Like so much of her later work, Aidoo's first play anticipates these essential questions of an African woman's place in or between societies which are hard to call home.

The young Hansberry encountered much less difficulty in creating credible men, who like Walter grow strong, or like Asagai represent 'the emergence of an articulate and deeply conscious intelligentsia in the world' (Terkel 41). In a lengthy comment on the Nigerian student, she elaborates how much he typifies a rising middle class of colonial peoples:

> Intellect: warm and free and confident...They generally have the magnificence of actively insurgent peoples along with the sophisticated ease

of those who are preoccupied with the eventual possession of the future. Despair cannot afflict this man in these years; he has ascertained the nature of political despotism and seen in it not the occasion for cynicism – but an ever growing sense of how the new will never cease to replace the old. He thinks man and history are marvellous on account of this view. Finally, it is my own view.[18]

Ato's travels and studies, by contrast, have unmanned him, left him spooked by ghosts and 'afternoon dreams, horrid, disgusting, enigmatic dreams' (III: 29). He is no man of the people, not even of his own incredulous clan. He has no clue how to confront the future.

Ato is not Asagai, and *Dilemma* not a sequel to *Raisin*. Ama Ata Aidoo had already written a draft of the play before Hansberry's drama was performed in Accra in 1963. In a 1994 interview, she recounted to me vague memories of having seen that production, particularly of the last scene 'as the family's belongings and furniture are being moved out'. Pointedly, when Asagai enters, then he confesses to 'like the look of packing crates! A household in preparation for a journey! . . . Movement, progress. It makes me think of Africa' (III: 132). For better and for worse, such a nomadic life has been the lot of many an African intellectual, Aidoo included, in the decades since Independence.

It is less likely that *A Raisin* was an actual influence on Aidoo's play, than that these two prescient young artists across the Atlantic shared a deeply congruent sense of their moment in history. Reading the two plays together, however, reveals more than parallels of situation; rather, nearly simultaneously they afford a look at the ties and tensions between African-Americans and Africans in the early 60s, turning or returning home. Together they testify to Aidoo's claim that 'the historical connection between Africans in Africa and the Diaspora. . . holds one of the keys to our future.'[19]

Both these plays explore Said's contention that 'Homes are always provisional'. Ato and Eulalie, it seems, most probably have not and cannot come home again, and even the Youngers, like Moses, haven't yet reached their promised land. [Hansberry laughed off one critic: 'If he thinks *that's* a happy ending, I invite him to come live in one of the communities where the Youngers are going!' (Terkel: 41). Each of these young playwrights conveys a deeply intuitive sense of longing, an aching expressed by the German *Heimweh*, that is not easily and never fully met. And for each the theatre itself also proved to be an imperfect and impermanent home. [In the mid-1990s] I interviewed Efua Sutherland about the National Theatre Movement and the Drama Studio, which had only recently been pulled down, replaced by the modern National Theatre building. She said to me: 'If nothing else, it should have been kept as a living monument to a remarkable moment in our history . . . a time to be challenged . . . [it was] a symbol of our people's awakening . . . to assert our cultural rights.'[20]

Then she handed me a typescript of Aidoo's poem, 'In Memoriam: The Ghana Drama Studio'.[21] That elegy is all about rootlessness, what one feels returning and 'defining Home'. With unusual economy, the poem condenses a vast etymological history, concluding in resilient and derisive resignation:

> The Ancients had said that
> Home
> Is where your shrines flourish . . .
>
>   the sacred duty
> to feel at home anywhere in Africa,
> and love every little bit of this
> battered and bartered continent which
> I still, perhaps, naively call my own . . .
>
> 'Home'
> can also be any place anywhere
> where someone or other
> is not trying to
>
> fry your mind,
> roast your arse, or
> waste you and yours altogether.
> Hm???

The 'Ghana Drama Studio had been my shrine . . . of sorts', a home. Conceptually and architecturally Efua Sutherland never lost sight of that essential domestic setting, the very scene of Aidoo's play. The design for both theatres Sutherland built in the 1960s – in Accra and Atwia – was like a Ghanaian courtyard, 'because everything that happens dramatically in life in this country usually happens in the courtyard . . . of an ordinary house'. People could 'identify with it. The actors . . . and the audience would walk into this place and feel at home'.[22] That is the central question of both these plays, as in the theatre building itself: where and whether one can meet this fundamental need, as Eulalie says, 'to belong to somewhere again'. As a young woman Aidoo was drawn to the stages that Efua Sutherland helped give the people of Ghana. About the same time, noting 'a new affirmative political and social mood in our country', Hansberry had had a remarkably similar impulse: 'I'd like to see a parallel movement in our country . . . a national theatre and other art programmes . . . so that kids all over the United States can go see Shakespeare . . . Or Eugene O'Neill. Or Lorraine Hansberry!' (Terkel: 41) But her genius was soon silenced. And so too was Aidoo's promise as a dramatist.

Somehow I never got over it really, that I couldn't see a production of the play [*Anowa*] before it became a book. Somehow I was so traumatised, I literally stopped. I made a conscious decision not to write plays anymore unless I had access to a theatre or at least an acting group. And since then my life has not been stable enough for me to have such a resource, and so I haven't written. I haven't thought about it before this way. Hansberry unfortunately died, and though I have lived, I deliberately killed that aspect of me. I didn't want to allow myself to think about it in these terms.[23]

Had fate been kinder, the recent history of Africanist drama would surely have been different, more glorious. Because of life's vagaries, these three women pioneers of Pan-African theatre could not bring their respective visions to full fruition, but their work lives on nearly a half century later. In their gift is much solace: ' "Home" can also be any place anywhere.'

Margaret Busby

Introducing Daughters of Africa

This essay is extracted from Margaret Busby's introduction to her epoch-making anthology
Daughters of Africa – An International Anthology of Words and Writings by
Women of African Descent from the Ancient Egyptian to the Present (1992).
*The editors have, with the approval of the author, edited the piece to make it independent of the
anthology, specifically for the present collection of essays. Margaret Busby adds: 'Although
much has changed in the years since it was first published – sadly, some of the wonderful
contributors have died, publishers have come and gone with the significant transformations there
have been in the literary climate, while many talented new writers have emerged and exciting new
works been produced – Daughters of Africa stands as a historical marker of where we were in
the early 1990s. I hope to be able to bring us up to date in a new edition.'*

Introduction

To Black Women

Sisters,
where there is cold silence –
no hallelujahs, no hurrahs at all, no handshakes,
no neon red or blue, no smiling faces –
prevail.
Prevail across the editors of the world!
who are obsessed, self-honeying and self-crowned
in the seduced arena,

It has been a
hard trudge, with fainting, bandaging and death.
There have been startling confrontations.
There have been tramplings. Tramplings
of monarchs and of other men.

But there remain large countries in your eyes.
Shrewd sun.
The civil balance.
The listening secrets.

And you create and train your flowers still.
                                                    – Gwendolyn Brooks

'O, ye daughters of Africa, awake! awake! arise! no longer sleep nor slumber, but distinguish yourselves. Show forth to the world that ye are endowed with noble and exalted faculties.'

– Maria W. Stewart, *Productions of Mrs. W. Stewart* (1835)

Imagine a thirsty traveller trying to catch a flowing river in a calabash and you may have some idea of the impossible task facing a compiler of an anthology of this sort. The source may be known, the direction clear, but inevitably much spills out, leaving only a taste of those precious waters. The thirst for literature with personal relevance has inspired many Black women's creativity – Toni Morrison has explained that what she writes are the kind of books she wants to read, a sentiment endorsed by Alice Walker: 'I write all the things *I should have been able to read*',[1] as well as by Zimbabwean novelist Tsitsi Dangarembga who has said: 'I'd try to look for myself in the books that I read, but I didn't find me.' Similarly, perhaps the first reason for the contents of this anthology is subjective: it is the sort of anthology I wish I had had access to years ago but which did not exist.

So it should be understood that in this way my selection is personal, and not meant to limit recognition of excellence to only those women included. In addition, my aim was to show the immense range, in terms of genre, country of origin and style, that a category such as 'women writers of African descent' encompasses. Without doubt I, or anyone else, could compile a similar volume that would include a completely different selection and still leave out many women who deserve to be read and to be better known. It would be misleading to call this a definitive work, implying that everything excluded merits lesser consideration. I prefer to see it as a contribution to the cause of reclaiming for women of African descent a place in literary history. If its effect is to spur others on to do better, it will have achieved its purpose.

As Filomina Chioma Steady acknowledged, '...the black woman, within a cross-cultural perspective, represents much diversity in terms of nationality, class affiliation, generational differences, and particular historical experiences'.[2] On the most obvious level, we come in every possible skin shade, from deepest ebony to palest cream, and society and circumstance have in the past created, and sometimes still perpetuate, a hierarchy of tone that has exerted tyrannical sway over our lives. The whole question of terminology is a complex one, fraught with pitfalls and ever-changing with the rise and fall of political and cultural ideologies...Maybe eventually we will, in the words of Gwendolyn Brooks, Poet Laureate of Illinois and the first Black writer awarded a Pulitzer Prize in 1950, 'Prevail across the editors of the world!'

Clearly, African women have always played a central role as storytellers within their communities. However, as Lauretta Ngcobo has written:

Oral tales are inclusive and in a variety of ways reach out to as many people as possible, so that ultimately they become the common property of the majority. Writing, on the other hand, is designed for a select class, those who can read. Essentially, therefore, it is exclusive, intended from the outset to reach only the eyes of those who have achieved literacy: the script itself automatically excludes those who do not have it.[3]

The fact that recent decades show a greater spread of printed material than previous centuries is linked to not just literacy problems but access to publishing. . .

Only comparatively recently have Black women begun to find receptive outlets and wider distribution for their work through mainstream publishing houses in the metropolitan West; nevertheless, it is commercial fashion that has usually dictated the agenda. Aside from the valiant efforts of academic publishers (notably Howard University Press, and Heinemann Educational Books, who published in 1966 the first work by Flora Nwapa, pioneer African woman novelist), it has been left to autonomous Black companies (including, in the USA, Third World Press, Broadside Press, Harlem River Press and Africa World Press; in Britain, New Beacon Books, Jessica Huntley's Bogle L'Ouverture Publications, Karnak House, Akira Press and Karia Press; in Canada, Anne Wallace's Williams-Wallace), and to small general presses (for example, Three Continents Press, Thunder's Mouth, Pluto, Zed Press or Allison & Busby) to demonstrate a consistent commitment to Black writing presented outside possibly ghettoising series. The setting up since the mid-1970s of feminist imprints (in Britain: Virago, The Women's Press, Sheba Feminist Publishers, Pandora, Onlywomen; in the USA, Naiad, Shameless Hussy, Spinsters Ink) has enabled more Black women's voices to be heard. Rarest of all are thriving ventures run by/for Black women, such as Kitchen Table: Women of Color Press, or the British-based Black Womantalk and Urban Fox Press, all founded since the 1980s. Crucial to the proliferation of the writings of Black women, and their right to the critical attention they deserve, is the continuing existence of publishers such as these – and above all the encouragement of Black women to enter the publishing industry to build on the efforts of those brave women (among them New York literary agent Marie Dutton Brown, and Toni Morrison in her role as a senior editor for Random House) who have stood the storm.

Beginning *Daughters of Africa* with a selection of anonymous songs and poetry from Africa – often dealing with the universal theme of love relationships – underlines the oral tradition that runs throughout the Diaspora and highlights the fact that African women's creativity has roots that extend beyond written records. In West African countries such as Senegal and The Gambia it was the duty of professional musicians known as *griots* to preserve and sing the history of a particular family or tribe going back several generations, as well as to improvise on current affairs – a facility echoed by calypsonians in the Caribbean. (That the oral tradition is closely linked with music makes it natural that the expression of Black female pain and joy are epitomised in the blues and songs of African-American artists such as Bessie Smith, Billie Holiday, Dinah Washington, Josephine Baker, Aretha Franklin, Nina Simone). 'Orature', the term coined by the late Ugandan literary critic Pio Zirimu, encompasses both the tradition of unwritten creativity and verbal transmission of that creativity. In the absence of literacy in many African societies, folk tales and stories – many featuring 'trickster' figures such as the spider (Ananse, in Ghana), the tortoise or the hare – functioned both as entertainment and instruction, passed down from generation to generation, resurfacing in the New World in the guise of the 'Uncle Remus' stories in the USA or Anancy stories in the Caribbean. The linguistic versatility demonstrated by people of Africa and the African Diaspora is in itself a remarkable testament to survival of vicissitude in a history that has weathered subjugation and colonisation by the powers of Europe. Those Africans transported to the New World in the course of the slave trade were forbidden to speak in their own native tongues, whether Yoruba or Asante Twi:

> What these languages had to do, however, was to submerge themselves, because officially the conquering people – the Spaniards, the English, the French and the Dutch – insisted that the language of public discourse and conversation, of obedience, command and conception, should be English, French, Spanish or Dutch.[4]

Thus, Diaspora Africans draw both on an official 'educated' language – in which, since the time the young slave Phillis Wheatley began to compose poetry in the eighteenth century, they have demonstrated literary skills beyond mere imitation – and on those submerged African retentions. Nor is it unusual in Africa itself for people to be multilingual – conversant with one or more of their own indigenous languages as well as with an imported European language, which may also have evolved a creolised or pidgin form (incorporated, for instance, in the work of Nigerian Adaora Lily Ulasi). The modern creative use of patois or dialect, or lately, 'dub poetry' in which reggae music forms a counterpoint to the words (see, for example, the poems of Jamaicans Louise Bennett, Valerie Bloom or Jean Binta Breeze), show an uninhibited departure from the received standard language in favour of what Edward Kamau Brathwaite calls *nation language*, the kind of English spoken by those brought to the Caribbean as slaves and labourers:

> I use the term in contrast to *dialect*. The word 'dialect' has been bandied about for a long time, and it carried very pejorative overtones. Dialect is thought of as 'bad English'. Dialect is 'inferior English'. Dialect is the language used

when you want to make fun of someone. Caricature speaks in dialect. Dialect has a long history coming from the plantation where people's dignity is distorted through their language and the descriptions which the dialect gave to them. Nation language, on the other hand, is the *submerged* area of that dialect which is much more closely allied to the African aspect of experience in the Caribbean. It may be in English: but often it is in an English which is like a howl, or a shout or a machine-gun or the wind or a wave. It is also like the blues. And sometimes it is English and African at the same time.[5]

Orthography and syntax may be used unconventionally to refreshing effect, as in the work of Ntozake Shange, who explains her style thus: 'The spellings result from the way I talk or the way the character talks, or the way I heard something said. Basically the spellings reflect language as I hear it.'[6] Informing her work is a refusal to conform to the norms of an imposed 'educated' culture, in preference to 'popular culture' or 'vernacular culture':

We do not have to refer continually to European art as the standard. That's absolutely absurd and racist, and I won't participate in that utter lie. My work is one of the few ways I can preserve the elements of our culture that need to be remembered and absolutely revered.[7]

Arguing for the legitimacy of Black English within the educational system, June Jordan wrote tellingly in a 1972 essay:

Both Black and white youngsters are compelled to attend school. Once inside this system, the white child is rewarded for mastery of his standard, white English: the language he learned at his mother's white and standard knee. But the Black child is punished for mastery of his non-standard, Black English: for the ruling elite of America have decided that *non*-standard is *sub*-standard, and even dangerous, and must be eradicated.[8]

She concluded: 'If we lose our fluency in our language, we may irreversibly forsake elements of the spirit that have provided for our survival.'[9]

Tradition and history are nurturing spirits for women of African descent. For without an understanding of where we have come from, we are less likely to be able to make sense of where we are going. But awareness of past trials and tribulations must not bow us, rather strengthen us for whatever the future holds. 'Only history plants consciousness', asserts Lourdes Teodoro in her poem 'The Generation of Fear'. The legacy of the slave trade with Africa confronts us daily in the very existence of the Diaspora. In the course of the commercial system that was the Atlantic slave trade, together with the slave trades of the trans-Sahara and East Africa, over a period of some four hundred years from the mid-

1400s, 15 to 20 million Africans were against their will shipped to the Americas and Europe. Portugal, Britain, Denmark, France, Holland, Spain and other European countries, as well as America, were all implicated. To rehearse again the traumatic facts is not to wallow in victimhood but to ensure an understanding of what our foremothers had to survive.

During the Middle Passage, the journey from Africa to the Americas (Cuban Nancy Morejón's poem 'Black Woman' imagines some of the emotions that voyage may have engendered), female captives were subject to seamen's advances. According to one former slave-ship captain:

> When the women and girls are taken on board a ship, naked, trembling, terrified, perhaps almost exhausted with cold, fatigue, and hunger, they are often exposed to the wanton rudeness of white savages. The poor creatures cannot understand the language they hear, but the looks and manner of the speakers are sufficiently intelligible. In imagination, the prey is divided, upon the spot, and only reserved till opportunity offers. Where resistance or refusal would be utterly in vain, even the solicitation of consent is seldom thought of.[10]

Brought naked from the ship's hold to the auction block, they were assessed for breeding potential, a scene recreated in 'The Slave Auction' by the popular poet Frances Ellen Watkins Harper (1825-1911), who wrote and spoke out forthrightly about the wrongs of enslavement:

> The slave began – young girls were there,
> Defenseless in their wretchedness,
> Whose stifled sobs of deep despair
> Revealed their anguish and distress.
>
> And mothers stood with streaming eyes,
> And saw their dearest children sold;
> Unheeded rose their cries,
> While tyrants bartered them for gold...

Brutalised and sexually exploited – and stereotyped – by white slaveholders, Black women bore mulatto offspring for their masters, or were forced to conceive babies for economic gain:

> She was to be had for the taking. Boys on and about the plantation inevitably learned to use her, and having acquired the habit, often continued it into manhood and after marriage. For she was natural and could give herself up to passion in a way impossible to wives inhibited by puritanical training.[11]

Then there was the pain of separation when children and mothers were sold to different masters; first-hand testimony of one such parting was given by Louisa Picquet, who recalls being sold away from her mother at the age of fourteen:

When I was going away I heard someone cryin' and prayin' the Lord to go with her only daughter, and protect me. I felt pretty bad then, but hadn't no time only to say goodbye...it seems fresh in my memory when I think of it – no longer than yesterday. Mother was right on her knees, with her hands up, prayin' to the Lord for me. She didn't care who saw her: the people all lookin' at her. I often thought her prayers followed me, for I could never forget her....
Q – Have you ever seen her since?
A – No, never since that time. I went to New Orleans, and she went to Texas. So I understood.[12]
. . .

Some emancipated slaves, including Henrietta Fullor, were able to make the return journey back to Africa, to settlements in Liberia and Sierra Leone (unlike the speaker in Louise Bennett's 'Back to Africa'). The earliest published African-American poet is Lucy Terry, born in about 1730 in Africa, from where she was kidnapped and brought to New England as a slave. Her historical position is guaranteed by only one poem, 'Bars Fight' written in about 1746. More substantial evidence of poetic skill is found in the work of Phillis Wheatley born in Senegal in about 1753, and taken as a seven-year-old slave to the USA. A child prodigy, she was reading and writing and learning Latin within sixteen months, and at the age of thirteen began writing poems of classical accomplishment, one of her earliest entitled 'On being brought from Africa to America'. Despite achieving celebrity, both in America and in Britain, where she travelled with her mistress, and being the first Black and only the second woman (after Anne Bradstreet) to publish a book of poetry in the USA, she died in poverty aged barely thirty.

The trauma of enslavement, the instinct to resist and escape, the striving for freedom, would have been material enough for many more volumes of testimony by nineteenth-century Black women that have in recent years been rediscovered and reprinted (notably in the 1988 Schomburg Library of Nineteenth-Century Black Women Writers' series, under the general editorship of Henry Louis Gates, Jr). Sometimes these 'slave narratives' were dictated to amanuenses sympathetic to the abolitionist cause; often they were published with the aim of raising funds for personal welfare or education:

A new variable constrained the telling of these stories, for these women had to sell their intimate memories and to sort out the property rights to their lives. The act of recording their lives, ironically, recorded their financial distress.[13]

From accounts that survive, such as those by 'Old Elizabeth', Mary Prince, Mattie Jackson, Annie Burton, Ann Drumgoold and Bethany Veney, comes remarkable insight into the women's own efforts to rise above their unfortunate circumstances. Many of those African-American women who published work in the nineteenth century found sustenance in religion and undertook preaching tours, as did Zilpha Elaw, who published her memoirs in 1840 at the end of a five-year mission to Britain. Occasionally they earned platforms as moving orators, speaking out against oppression by race and sex. Maria Stewart – whose exhortation to Black women to strive for education and political rights furnished the title for this anthology – became the first American-born woman to lecture in public in 1832. The passion of Sojourner Truth's renowned address to the 1852 National Women's Suffrage Convention echoes down the generations:

Ain't I a woman?
Look at me
Look at my arm!
I have plowed and planted
and gathered into barns
and no man could head me...
And ain't I a woman?
I could work as much
And eat as much as a man –
When I could get it –
And bear the lash as well
and ain't I a woman?
I have born thirteen children
and seen most all sold into slavery
and when I cried out a mother's grief
none but Jesus heard me...
and ain't I a woman?...
If the first woman God ever made
was strong enough to turn the world
upside down, all alone
together women ought to be able to turn it
rightside up again.

A Narrative of the Life and Travels of Mrs Nancy Prince (1853), recording the author's travels in Russia and the West Indies, is an example of the fact that nineteenth-century Black women's experiences and concerns extended far beyond the confines of enslavement. Mary Seacole, who was born in Jamaica twenty-five years before the abolition of slavery and died in London in 1881, was incontrovertible proof that in freedom Black women could undertake major roles in setting the wider world to rights. Her *Wonderful Adventures of Mrs Seacole in Many Lands* – a success on its publication in 1857 but largely forgotten until it was reprinted in the 1980s – tells of her life of adventure and dedication that culminated in her becoming as notable a figure in the Crimean War as Florence Nightingale. Comparably revealing are Susie King Taylor's 1902 reminiscences of her life as laundress, teacher and nurse to the Union army during the US civil war.

The history of Black women in the United Kingdom since slavery days is inextricably linked with the economic needs of others, of Britain and British interests in the West Indies and Africa. The act of emancipation whereby slavery was 'utterly and forever abolished and declared unlawful throughout the British Colonies' as passed in 1833, taking effect the next year. But under colonialism Black people in Africa and the Caribbean still had to endure domination by Whites. In the West Indies the plantation system that lasted into the twentieth century, providing commodities such as sugar, cotton and cocoa for the British economy, depended on cheap labour, but with the growing reluctance of ex-slaves to continue to be exploited, indentured labourers were brought in from India, and even from China, to increase competition for work and so reduce wages. In the depression of the 1920s and 1930s, poverty and unemployment led some to emigrate to the American mainland where farm and factory work was available. (Coping with the societal differences involved with migration is a theme of works such as Joan Cambridge's *Clarise Cumberbatch Want to Go Home*, 1987; and US-based writers such as Rosa Guy and Louise Meriwether have Caribbean origins, as does the generation that includes Dionne Brand and Marlene Nourbese Philip, who settled in Canada). During the Second World War, recruits from the British colonies contributed unstintingly to the war effort, coming to Britain to work as civilians or in the armed forces. After the war many West Indians were encouraged to emigrate to a Britain that needed assistance in rebuilding an economy that was short of labour. When on 22 June 1948 the *Empire Windrush* docked at Tilbury carrying 492 Jamaicans, some of whom were returning to 'the Motherland' where they had seen war service, the headline of the London *Evening Standard* was 'WELCOME HOME'. Peter Fryer writes:

> In some industries the demand for labour was so great that members of the reserve army of black workers were actively recruited in their home countries. In April 1956 London Transport began recruiting staff in Barbados, and within 12 years a total of 3,787 Barbadians had been taken on.

They were lent their fares to Britain, and the loans were repaid gradually from their wages....And a Tory health minister by the name of Enoch Powell welcomed West Indian nurses to Britain.[14]

The jobs these Black immigrants came to fill, jobs in which they still predominate – driving tube trains, collecting bus fares, emptying hospital patients' bed-pans – were invariably the unglamorous ones at the lower end of the labour force:

Black women were faced with no other prospect than to fill the jobs which the indigenous workforce were no longer willing to do, in the servicing, semi-skilled and unskilled sectors. Service work was little more than institutionalised housework, as night and daytime cleaners, canteen workers, laundry workers and chambermaids – an extension of the work we had done under colonialism in the Caribbean.[15]

Yet, the indigenous British workforce felt threatened; nor was their irrational worry a new one. The Black presence in London in 1764, when the capital's total population was 676,250, had prompted *The Gentleman's Magazine* to comment:

The practice of importing Negro servants into these kingdoms is said to be already a grievance that requires a remedy, and yet it is every day encouraged, insomuch that the number in this metropolis only, is supposed to be near 20,000; the main objections to their importation is, that they cease to consider themselves as slaves in this free country, nor will they put up with an inequality of treatment, nor more willingly perform the laborious offices of servitude than our own people, and if put to do it, are generally sullen, spiteful, treacherous, and revengeful. It is therefore highly impolitic to introduce them as servants here, where that rigour and severity is impracticable which is absolutely necessary to make them useful.[16]

The 1962 Commonwealth Immigration Act was introduced whose effect was to regulate the numbers of Black people entering Britain, institutionalising the prejudice experienced as racist attacks and police brutality against Blacks. The inflammatory speech in April 1968 of Enoch Powell, a senior Conservative Member of Parliament, with its talk of rivers foaming with blood unless immigration was further curbed and 're-emigration' encouraged, was to bring race relations in Britain to a low ebb. Children left behind in the Caribbean were sent for, lest they be excluded for ever. (Iiola Ashundie's short memoir 'Mother of Mine' and Joan Riley's 1985 novel *The Unbelonging* give two aspects of the reactions of those offspring who came later.) The US Civil Rights

Movement, and high-profile participants such as Angela Davis, provided inspiration. In the early 1970s Black women in Britain began to organise within their own groups, most notably the Organisation of Women of Asian and African Descent (OWAAD), which flourished between 1978 and 1983, holding annual conferences. A generation of young women since then – including Maud Sulter, Jackie Kay, Dinah Anuli Butler – has rallied to the challenge of exploring the British Black condition, with its particular ramifications according to race, class and gender.

Although women such as Maria Stewart, Sojourner Truth and Anna J. Cooper – who in her 1892 book *A Voice from the South by a Black Woman of the South* discussed from a feminist viewpoint the situation of Black women, seeing their progress as key to the advancement of the whole race, since 'a stream cannot rise higher than its source' – were speaking out early against oppression by racism and sexism, it was not until the 1970s that Frances Beale used the term 'double jeopardy' to characterise the condition of being Black and female.[17] The poor social and economic conditions affecting a majority of Black women constitute a further oppression by class. The urgent need remains to surmount these oppressions. Far from complying with the passive, acquiescing stereotype, Black women through the centuries have been formidable leaders (like Queen Hatshepsut, whose magnificent obelisk at Luxor still stands as a monument to her defiant reign in the Egyptian eighteenth dynasty, and Makeda, Queen of Sheba), occupying central positions in the history of liberation struggles. Queen Nzinga in Angola in the 1630s and 1640s tried to coordinate resistance to Portuguese slave-traders; Nanny (celebrated in a poem by Lorna Goodison) leader of the Jamaican Maroons – runaway slaves – fought a guerrilla war against the British in 1733; Harriet Tubman became known as the Moses of her people for organising in the 1850s an 'Underground Railroad' that helped hundreds of slaves to escape; Ida Wells Barnett from the end of the nineteenth century waged a tireless crusade against lynchings and racial injustice; Rosa Parks's defiant refusal to move to a seat allocated for Blacks on a segregated bus in 1955 ignited the Civil Rights movement. Deborah K. King has written: 'Through the necessity of confronting and surviving racial oppression, black women have assumed responsibilities atypical of those assigned to white women under Western patriarchy.'[18] King further argues that 'a black feminist ideology presumes an image of black women as powerful, independent subjects. By concentrating on our multiple oppressions, scholarly descriptions have confounded our ability to discover and appreciate the ways in which black women are not victim'.[19]

The concept of feminism is an uncomfortable one for many Black women who perceive the Western women's liberation movement as tainted by the racism evident in society as a whole. (Angela Davis, writing on the empowerment of Afro-American women in her 1987 essay 'Let Us All Rise

Together: Radical Perspectives on Empowerment for Afro-American Women', recalls that in 1895 Black women organised their own Club Movement, 'having been repeatedly shunned by the racially homogenous women's rights movement'.) Many prefer instead to espouse Alice Walker's theory of *womanism*, as defined in the front of *In Search of Our Mother's Gardens*: a womanist is 'committed to the survival and wholeness of entire people, male *and* female...Womanist is to feminist as purple to lavender'.[20] Yet whatever the labels, it is an incontrovertible fact that for over a century Black women have been vocal in resisting sexism both within and outside their own communities. Amy Jacques Garvey, writing in 1925 in an editorial in *The Negro World*, served notice on Black men that any further vacillation on their part would force Black women to take over the sole lead in the struggle. Notwithstanding Christine Craig's tribute to her grandmothers and their mothers for keeping their silence 'to compost up their strength' – 'It must be known now how that silent legacy/nourished and infused such a line/such a close linked chain/to hold us until we could speak/until we could speak out/loud enough to hear ourselves/and believe our own words' ('The Chain'). bell hooks [*sic*], a rare example of a Black woman whose writings have always embraced feminism, sees it not as a means to emerge from silence into speech, nor even to hold onto speech, 'but to change the nature and direction of our speech, to make a speech that compels listeners, one that is heard'.

Michele Wallace, in her controversial book *Black Macho and the Myth of the Superwoman*, wrote in 1978 of the intricate web of mythology that surrounds the Black woman, according to which: 'Less of a woman in that she is less 'feminine' and helpless, she is really *more* of a woman in that she is the embodiment of Mother Earth, the quintessential mother with infinite sexual, life-giving, and nurturing reserves.' Indeed, the image of Black women as superhuman towers of strength and survivors of whatever misfortunes life has thrown at them is not always borne out by the facts. The success and critical acclaim accorded to Pulitzer prizewinners Toni Morrison (for her superb *Beloved* in 1987) and Alice Walker, or the fortitude that enabled Buchi Emecheta to salvage a successful writing career from the jaws of adversity, are offset by the plight of other fine writers – among them Phillis Wheatley, Nella Larsen, Zora Neale Hurston, Bessie Head – who died in differing degrees of obscurity and penury, unfulfilled or in tragic circumstances.

When the toil and drudgery of slavery was done, Black women frequently could find work as domestics in white households. Claudia Jones (1915-64), Trinidadian-born journalist and activist, wrote in 1930: 'Following the emancipation, and persisting to the present day, a large percentage of Negro women – married as well as single – were forced to work for a living. But despite the shift in employment of Negro women from rural to urban areas, Negro women are still generally confined to the lowest-paying jobs....The low scale of earning of Negro women is directly related to her almost complete exclusion from virtually all fields of work except the most menial and underpaid, namely, domestic service.' In 1978 Jeanne Noble could still observe: 'While it is true that the members of black female domestics are diminishing...the image of the black domestic is still woven in the very fabric of America, especially in the South, where the role was perfected.'[21] The image of the Black woman as domestic haunts works such as Ann Petry's *The Street* (1946, the first novel by a Black woman to sell over a million copies) and Lorraine Hansberry's all-Black Broadway success *A Raisin in the Sun*. It is interesting to compare the way writers such as Alice Childress's *Like One of the Family* and Barbara Makhalisa's 'Different Values', writing respectively about domestics in North American and South African contexts, use humour subversively.

Satire, polemic, fantasy – the moods and styles of expression vary and shift continuously. This anthology has aimed to give an idea of the wide range of genres explored by women of African descent: historical fiction (for example, Valerie Belgrave and Sherley Anne Williams), science fiction (Octavia Butler), literary novels, short stories, poetry, essays, journalism, oral history, memoirs, diaries, letters, essays, plays, folklore...(The magical and supernatural as a part of ordinary life is a hallmark, as in Myriam Warner-Vieyra's *As the Sorcerer Said...*(1980), and acceptance of the inevitability of things: 'The river does not wash away what is meant for you.' The significance of fiction for Black people was a belief held strongly by Pauline Hopkins, who wrote in the preface to her novel *Contending Forces* (1900):

> It is a record of growth and development from generation to generation. No one will do this for us: we must develop the men and women who will faithfully portray the innermost thoughts and feelings of the Negro with all the fire and romance which lie dormant in our history.

A predilection for autobiographical writing in one form or another is perhaps unsurprising, given the need to correct the misconceived images of the Black women that have proliferated through the ages in fact and fiction, generated by those who are not Black and female. As Mary Helen Washington has put it: 'People other than the black woman herself try to define who she is, what she is supposed to look like, act like, and sound like. And most of these creations bear very little resemblance to real, live black women.'[22] Washington further says: 'If there is a single distinguishing feature of the literature of black women – and this accounts for their lack of recognition – it is this: their literature is about black women; it takes the trouble to record the thoughts, words, feelings, and deeds of black women.'[23]

Through oral history and autobiography come memorable pictures of Black women's rites of passage and daily life: a young girl's arranged marriage, in *Nisa:*

The Life and Words of a !Kung Woman (1981); the initiation of a Liberian girl in Alice Perry Johnson's 'The Beginning of a Kpelle Woman'; Jane Tapsubei Creider's glimpse of life among her Nandi people in *Two Lives: My Spirit and I* (1986); the vivid sights and smells of the Brazilian shantytown recorded in the diary of Carolina Maria de Jesús, who despite the diurnal grind of foraging for herself and her children can still write at the end of the day: 'The book is man's best invention yet.' In creative writing too there are elements that seem precisely to capture the atmosphere of the societies that inspired them: Caribbean childhoods conjured up in Grace Nichols's *Whole of a Morning Sky* (1986), Zee Edgell's *Beka Lamb* (1982), Merle Collins's 'The Walk' (from her 1990 collection of stories *Rain Darling*), or Jamaica Kincaid's *Annie John* (1985); Elean Thomas's sensitive drawing of Josina, 'everybody's woman and yet nobody's woman' (in *Word Rhythms from the Life of a Woman*, 1986); Somali writer Saida Herzi's gruelling dramatisation of the ordeal of female infibulation *Against the Pleasure Principle*.' Perspectives on Southern Africa include Joyce Sikakane's prison experiences, *A Window on Soweto*, 1977, Zoë Wicomb's honest depiction of the underside of romance across the colour bar, *You Can't Get Lost in Cape Town*, 1987, Dulcie September's unvarnished look at urban life, *A Split Society – Fast Sounds on the Horizon*, Bessie Head's perceptive vignettes of 1970s' Botswana village life, *The Collector of Treasures* and *Tales of Tenderness and Power*; and Ellen Kuzwayo's unsentimental description of the realities of polygamy as they affect two ordinary women; *Sit Down and Listen: Stories from South Africa*, 1990.

The inescapable fact of polygamy in Africa is treated in a variety of illuminating ways – from Mabel Segun's cynical article 'Polygamy – Ancient and Modern', to Buchi Emecheta's poignant chapter from her 1979 novel *The Joys of Motherhood*, 'A Man Needs Many Wives', to the deft touch of Mabel Dove-Danquah's short story *Anticipation*. And the unquestioning acceptance of custom and ritual – as indicated in Efua Sutherland's *New Life at Kyerefaso* – contrasts with the necessary adjustment that follows contact with Western education and society – typified by Noni Jabavu's account of her return to South Africa after many years abroad, (*The Ochre People: Scenes from a South African Life* 1963); Tsitsi Dangarembga's fictional treatment of the effects for a young girl in Zimbabwe of learning new values through missionary schooling (*Nervous Conditions* 1988); or Mariama Bâ's epistolary picture of a Muslim woman liberated from 'the bog of tradition, superstition and custom' (*So Long a Letter* 1981). The emergence of a younger generation of high-calibre women writers in Africa, including Tsitsi Dangarembga, is an encouraging sign; so too is the commitment of African women, such as Abena Busia, Molara Ogundipe-Leslie and Ife Amadiume, who are combining imaginative writing with literary criticism and other forms of non-fiction. But their number remains small and the prejudices and obstacles they face – for instance, being ignored by male critics – are great. Adeola James in her illuminating book of interviews, *In Their Own Voices: African Women Writers*

Talk, draws attention to the particular situation of women writers in Africa today, who 'in the twenty-five years since they started being published, have made a significant contribution, which until recently, has been only grudgingly acknowledged'.[24]

The development of streetwise instincts to staunch the debilitating drain of poverty is a defence mechanism discovered by Rosa Guy's protagonist Dorrie in *A Measure of Time*. From another tributary flows the privileged angst of being born into genteel middle-class mores, clearly seen in Marita Bonner's essay 'On Being Young – a Woman – and Coloured', or Dorothy West's portrait of Boston's Black intelligentsia after the First World War (*The Living is Easy*).

The 'tragic mulatto' figure widespread in American literature finds echoes in the work of writers such as Jessie Fauset (*Plum Bun*) and Nella Larsen, who in her novels, explores the syndrome of light-skinned Blacks 'passing' for white in order to achieve social advantage, a self-denial that Frances Harper's Iola Leroy eschews. As interracial relationships become more common throughout the Diaspora, problems of cultural identity surface – for Jenneba Sie Jalloh in connection with her Irish heritage (*Across the Water: Irish Women's Lives in Britain* 1988); for Ayse Bircan, a Turkish Black woman married to a Kurdish man, in connection with her son's complexes; and for the Afro-German women Abena Adomako, Julia Berger, Angelika Eisenbrandt and May Opitz who [narrate] their frank personal stories. For yet others, something of a comedy of errors has evolved, when the problem – 'the bequest of confusion' Dinah Anuli Butler writes about in her poem to her father – is external and in the eye of the beholder. The ultimate solution for Pauline Melville (author of the prize-winning 1991 short-story collection *Shapeshifter* that defies categorisation) is to choose to take as her 'tutelary spirits Legba, Exu and Hermes, the gods of boundaries.'

Occasionally the meeting of social and personal frustrations produces situations of unique poignancy, with characters for whom fulfilment seems impossible; as with the abandoned romantic heroine in Cuban Marta Rojas's *Rey Spencer's Swing* (1990); or Claire, the 39-year-old unmarried narrator of Haitian Marie Chauvet's novel, *Amour, colère et folie: 1968*, desperately in love with her brother-in-law, who describes the background that has shaped her:

I was born in 1900. A time when prejudice was at its height in this little province. Three separate groups had formed and these three groups were as divided as enemies: the 'aristocrats', to whom we belonged, the petits bourgeois and the common people. Torn apart by the ambiguity of a particularly delicate situation, I began to suffer from a very early age because of my dark skin, whose mahogany colour, inherited from some distant ancestor, stood out glaringly in the close circle of whites and light-skinned mulattos with whom my parents mixed. But all that is in the past, and for the moment at least, I don't feel inclined to turn towards what is over and done with.

Affirmation of self-image, or erosion of it, in the confrontation with white western concepts of beauty – usually in terms of skin shade and hair texture, often associated with their appeal to the opposite sex – feature as issues in many of the selections. The hairdressing salon, spotlighted by Marsha Prescod in 'Auntie Vida's Hair Salon' – which might be someone's front parlour – has always been a crucial meeting place for Black women, and talk of hair often figures large. Lucinda Roy, in her celebratory poem 'If You Know Black Hair', sees it is a prized symbol of indomitability; Gwendolyn Brooks's eponymous heroine in *Maud Martha* (1953) is resigned to the knowledge that her father prefers her sister Helen's hair to her own because it 'impressed him, not with its length and body, but simply with its apparent untameableness [sic]'; while Una Marson's 'Kinky Hair Blues' epitomises the paradox of our love/hate relationship with our unreconstructed appearance:

...I like me black face
And me kinky hair,
I like me black face
And me kinky hair.
But nobody loves dem,
I jes don't tink it's fair.

Now I's gwine press me hair
And bleach me skin,
I's gwine press me hair
And bleach me skin.
What won't a gal do
Some kind of man to win.

Relationships between the sexes are another source of abundant subject matter, and though different generations have different mores, some ideas remain the same although they cannot always be taken at face value. Compare the advice on [acquiescent] wifely duties given by [the Zanzibari mother] Mwana Kupona Msham to her daughter in the nineteenth century ['Utende wa Mwana Kupona'] with the Bemba girls' initiation song ('The man is the peak of the house.../It is women who make the pinnacle/On top of the roof'). Again, consider the attitude of Kristina Rungano's long-suffering wife in her subversively wry poem, 'The Woman', published in 1984. Whatever grievances she bears towards her man, however onerous and unreasonable his demands, she says:

Yet tomorrow I shall again wake up to you,
Milk the cow, plough the land and cook your food;
You shall again be my lord,
For isn't it right that woman should obey,
Love, serve and honour her man?
For are you not the fruit of the land?

Iyamidé Hazeley's poem 'Political Union' (1987) takes a more modern view of male-female relationships within the context of social and political liberation. Yet the ultimate aim is that we may be all on 'The Same Side of the Canoe', in the title words of Alda do Espírito Santo's poem. At times, conflict results from interracial alliances, pointed out by Baby Palatine's disapproval of Joy's dating of a white boy in Marsha Hunt's novel (*Joy* 1990), or as unfolds in Louise Meriwether's short story 'A Happening in Barbados' or Maya Angleou's 'The Reunion'. Even more problematically received can be relationships between women.

'Yet women-identified women – those who sought their own destinies and attempted to execute them in the absence of male support – have been around in all of our communities for a long time', as Audre Lorde has pointed out.[25] Red Jordan Arobateau's perceived dilemma of being a light-skinned Black woman is compounded by her sexual orientation: 'My psychiatrist informs me: 'You are white.' (He also tells me it's wrong to be a lesbian. He is white. And not homosexual. This is brainwashing). Other sisterly relationships are revealed, for example, in short stories such as Ama Ata Aidoo's, "Two Sisters," Sandi Russell's, "Sister", and Baba of Karo's collection of special girlhood friendships.

Woman-headed households are commonly depicted, in families where the man is absent possibly as a consequence of the realities of economic and social pressures. In line with the familiar phenomenon of 'my mother who fathered me', portraits of strong mother-daughter, grandmother-granddaughter relationships abound both in creative writing and in memoirs (the inclusion of both Adelaide and Gladys Casely-Hayford provides a rare opportunity to observe generational differences in themes and concerns. Old women, in fact and in fiction, inspire some of the most tender writing. In Beryl Gilroy's *Frangipani House* (1986), set in an old people's home, Mama King tries to come to terms with being deprived of 'her faithful friends, work and hardship'. Erna Brodber's Granny Tucker prays with her granddaughters Jane and Louisa (*Jane and Louisa Will Soon Come Home* 1980). Jewelle Gomez remembers nostalgically a swimming lesson with her 'Dahomean queen' grandmother in her story, 'A Swimming Lesson'. Astrid Roemer tentatively unravels the psychology of a mother and grandmother (in her novel *A Name for Love* 1987). Naomi Long Madgett compassionately senses the 'heavy years' borne by a woman she observes, who 'coaxes her fat in front of her like a loaded market basket with defective wheels' (in the poem 'New Day'). An 84-year-old woman imparts the wisdom of her years in Sonia Sanchez's, 'Just Don't Never Give Up On Love' (*Homegirls and Handgrenades* 1984). Paule Marshall pays an affectionate tribute to her grandmother in 'To Da-Duh, In Memoriam' (from *Reena and Other Stories* 1983). Yet there is also at times a feeling of regret for the loss of old values, the old ways – Mĩcere Mũgo's poem asks "Where Are Those Songs?" Similarly, Margaret Walker, whose popular poem "For My People" speaks of 'the gone years and the now years and the maybe years', wonders in "Lineage": 'My grandmothers were strong....They were full of sturdiness and singing....Why am I not as they?'

If we should ever falter in our confidence of our power eventually to overcome, Hattie Gossett's poem 'World View' gives a timely reminder that:

> theres more poor that nonpoor
> theres more coloured than noncoloured
> theres more women than men

> All over the world the poor woman of colour is the mainstay of the little daddy-centred family which is the bottom line of big daddy's industrial civilisation.

Contemporary issues of global importance and scope are boldly and explicitly tackled in the work of writers such as Jayne Cortez and June Jordan (acknowledging in 1976, in 'Declaration of an Independence I Would Just as Soon Not Have', her own awareness that political change will not come about through lone activity, that only through connecting herself with liberation struggles in the Black Movement, in the Third World Movement and in the Women's Movement will she be free to be who she is, Black and female) and are in various ways implicit in that of many others.

Abena Busia's poem 'Liberation' speaks uncompromisingly of that 'fire within us':

> of powerful women
> whose spirits are so angry
> we can laugh beauty into life
> and still make you taste
> the salt tears of our knowledge –
> For we are not tortured
> anymore;
> we have seen beyond your lies and disguises,
> and *we* have mastered the language of words,
> we have mastered speech.

And know
we have also seen ourselves.
We have stripped ourselves raw
and naked piece by piece until our flesh lies flayed
with blood on our *own* hands.
What terrible thing can you do us
which we have not done to ourselves?...

Throughout these women's words runs the awareness of connectedness to a wider flow of history, to the precursors, our foremothers. Our collective strength, like that of a chain, derives from maintaining the links.

James Gibbs

Selected Bibliography on Efua Sutherland[1]

I. SELECTED POEMS

"Mumunde My Mumunde," "An Ashanti Story," "Little Wild Flowers," "It Happened." In *An Anthology of West African Verse*. Olumbe Bessir ed. Ibadan: Ibadan University Press, 1957: 7, 13-16, 22-23, 42-47.

"The Redeemed," "Once Upon a Time," "The Dedication," "Song of the Fishing Ghosts." In *Messages: Poems from Ghana*. Kofi Awoonor and G. Adalai-Mortty ed. London: Heinemann, 158-169.

II. SHORT STORIES

"New Life at Kyerefaso." In *An African Treasury*. Langston Hughes ed. New York: Crown, 1960: 111-117. Frequently anthologized

Obaatan Kesewa. Accra: Bureau of Ghanaian Languages, 1967: 11 pages.

"Samantaase." *Okyeame* 1 (1) 1961: 53-58.

III. LETTERS, ESSAYS, ARTICLES

"Letter from Homerton College" as Theodora Morgue. August 1949. In *S. Monica Calling*, a pamphlet produced by the Order of the Holy Paraclete, c. 1949: 25-26.

"Proposal for a Historical Drama Festival at Cape Coast." Discussion Paper, 1980.

"Theatre in Ghana." In *Ghana Welcomes You*. Janice Nebill ed. Accra: Orientation to Ghana Committee, 1969: 83-87.

"The Drama of Ghanaian Life." In *Drum* February, 1962.

"The Playwright's Opportunity in Drama for Our Children." Presented at a Seminar on Writing and Production of Literature for Children. Institute of African Studies, University of Ghana, Legon. Cited by Esi Sutherland-Addy 2004.

"The Second Phase: A Review of the National Theatre Movement in Ghana." Legon: Institute of African Studies, 1965. Also In *FonTomFrom: Contemporary Ghanaian Literature, Theatre and Film, Matatu*. Amsterdam, Atlanta 21-22 2000: 45-57. See Anyidoho, Kofi and Gibbs, James eds.

"Venture into Theatre." *Okyeame*. Accra 1 (1) 1961: 47-48.

IV. BOOKLETS

Kusum Agoromba Presentations. Legon: Institute of African Studies, 1968. Brochure on productions may have involved ES.

Playtime in Africa. With photographs by Willis E. Bell. London: Brown, Knight and Truscott, 1960; New York: Atheneum, 1962: 62 pages.

The Original Bob — The Story of Bob Johnson: Ghana's Ace Comedian., Accra: Anowuo, 1970.

The Roadmakers. Accra: Ghana Information Service, 1960. London: Newman Neame, 1963. (A pictorial essay for children). Extract in Esi Sutherland-Addy and Aminata Diaw eds. *Women Writing Africa: West Africa and the Sahel*. New York: Feminist of the City University of New York. 2005: 219-220.

V. PLAYS

Children of the Man-Made Lake. In *FonTomFrom: Contemporary Ghanaian Literature, Theatre and Film, Matatu*. Amsterdam, Atlanta 21-22 2000: 95 –115.

Edufa. London: Longmans, 1967: 62 pages. An extract had appeared in *Okyeame* 3 (1) December 1966:47-49. Full text in *Plays from Black Africa*. Frederic M. Litto ed. New York: Hill and Wang, 1968:209-72, and *Crosswinds: An Anthology of Black Dramatists*. William B. Branch ed. Bloomington: Indiana University Press, 1993, Premiere December 1962.

Foriwa. Tema: Ghana Publishing Corporation, 1971: 67 pages. Premiere of Akan version, March 1962. Extract in Esi Sutherland-Addy and Aminata Diaw eds. *Women Writing Africa: West Africa and the Sahel*. New York: Feminist of the City University of New York, 2005: 220-224.

Tahinta! A Rhythm Play for Children. Edmund Opare, Illustrator. Accra: Afram Publications, 2000.

The Marriage of Anansewa. London: Longman, 1975. With *Edufa* Harlow: Longman, 1987. Several productions of versions before publication. Audio tape of radio drama and study guide, directed by Akua E. Kychura, produced by Africa Media Productions. Study guide by Yvonne J. Blake, 2003.

Voice in the Forest, Ralph Sutherland, Illustrator, Accra: Afram Publications 2006.

Vulture! Vulture! : Two Rhythm Plays. Accra: Ghana Publishing House, 1968: 32 pages. Cassette version released.

You Swore an Oath. A One-Act Play Sub-titled *Anansegoro*. *Presence Africaine* Paris, 22, 50 (1964): 231-247.

A. Recordings of Productions (Audio/Video/DVD)

Ananse and the Dwarf Brigade. Video and DVD directed by Sandy Arkhurst, and Performed by National Theatre Players and Mmofra Foundation Language Club. Produced by Film Africa, 2006.

Tahinta! A Rhythm Play for Children. Audio Cassette and CD narration by Amowi Sutherland Phillips, Performed by Mmofra Foundation Language Club, 2000.

Voice in the Forest. Audio CD read by Abena Busia, with Music by Takashi, 2006.

B. Unpublished plays, some adaptations, include the following:

Ananse and the Dwarf Brigade.

Nyamekye.

Odasani (adaptation of *Everyman*).

The Pineapple Child.

Tweedledum and Tweedledee.

Wohyee Me Bo.

VI. TRANSLATIONS

"Apetepirew," "The Tree-felling Knife," "Good-hearted Drunk, I'm Suffering." Translations of Poems by Kwa Mensah in *Okyeame* 4 (2), June 1986: 49-51.

"Nyankora," "Nea Ohwehwe Annya." Translations of Poems by Patience Addo in *Okyeame* 4 (1) 1986: 17 and 19.

"Poem in Praise of Osei Tutu from Traditional Apaee." In *Okyeame,* 2 (1) 1964: 21-22.

VII. EDITORIAL ACTIVITIES

With Awoonor-Williams, George and Others. *Okyeame* 2 (1) 1965 and subsequent issues.

With Sangster, Ellen Greer and Others. *Talent for Tomorrow: An Anthology of Creative Writing from the Training Colleges and Secondary Schools of Ghana.* Tema: Ghana Publishing House, 1966. Others in series dropped "Training Colleges"from titles 1968, 1970, 1971, 1972.

VIII. FILM

"Araba: The Village Story."1967.

IX. INTERVIEWS

Lautré, Maxine. "Interviewed by Maxine Lautré." *Cultural Events in Africa* 42 1968: I-IV. Interview reproduced in Dennis Duerden and Cosmo Pieterse eds. *African Writers Talking.* London: Heinemann, 1972: 183-195.

Nichols, Lee. Interviewed by Lee Nichols." *Conversations with African Writers.* Washington D.C.: Voice of America, 1981: 278-287. See also, "Interviewed by Lee Nichols." Lee Nichols. *African Writers at the Microphone*. Washington: Three Continents Press, 1983.

Okyere, Suzie. "Interviewed by Suzie Okyere." "The Commission on Children." *Mirror*. Accra, 26 November 1983.

Woode, Kwesi. "Interviewed by Kwesi Woode." *Annual Writers' Congress*. Accra, Ghana, Association of Writers, 1973:16-18.

SECONDARY SOURCES

Biographical, Critical And Background Studies

(Anonymous first in chronological order)

Anon. *Longman Anthology of World Literature by Women 1875-1975*. Marian Arkin and Barbara Sholler ed. New York: Longman, 1989: 696.

Anon. "Efua Sutherland." In *Black Writers: A Selection of Sketches from Contemporary Authors*. Linda Metzger ed. Detroit: Gale, 1988: 536-7.

Anon."Tribute to Mrs Efua Theodora Sutherland." In *Weekly Spectator*, 3 February 1996: 5. One of the many obituaries that appeared in the Ghanaian and British daily press.

Anon. "Studrafest in Cape Coast Today" in *Weekly Spectator*, 29 May 1999, 6.

Anon. "Efua Sutherland Remembered." In *(GRI) Ghana Review International* 22 January, 2001.

Abarry, Abu Shardow. "The Significance of Names in Ghanaian Drama. "In *Journal of Black Studies* 22 1991: 157-67.

Adams, Anne V. "Revis(it)ing Ritual: The Challenge to the Virility of Tradition in Works by Efua Sutherland and Other African Writers." In *FonTomFrom: Contemporary Ghanaian Literature, Theatre and Film, Matatu*. Amsterdam, Atlanta 21-22 2000: 85-94.

Akyea. E. Ofori, "The Atwia-Ekumfi Kodzidan – An Experimental African Theatre." In *Okyeame* 4 (1) December 1968: 82-84.

Amankulor, J. N.. "An Interpretation and Analysis of *The Marriage of Anansewa*." In *Okike Educational Supplement* 1 1980: 149 – 171.

Angelou, Maya. *All God's Children Need Travelling Shoes*. London: Virago, 1987.

Angmor, Charles. *Contemporary Literature in Ghana 1911-1978: A Critical Evaluation*. Accra: Woeli Publishing Services, 1996 .

—. "Drama in Ghana." In *Theatre in Africa*. Oyin Ogunba and Abiola Irele eds. Ibadan: Ibadan University Press, 1978: 55-72. See also Richard K. Priebe. *Ghanaian Literatures*. New York: Greenwood 1988: 171-186.

Ankumah, Adaku T. "Efua Theodora Sutherland." In *Postcolonial African Writers: A Bio-Biographical Critical Sourcebook*. Pushpa Naidu Parekh and Siga Fatima eds. Jagne, Westport: Greenwood, 1998.

Anyidoho, Kofi, *et al. Tributes to Efua Theodora Sutherland*, 1996. This volume of funeral tributes includes essays by members of Efua Sutherland's family and friends. Bill Sutherland and Maya Angelou are among those who contributed.

Anyidoho, Kofi. "Auntie Efua: We cannot Forget." *Glendora*. Lagos 1/3 5-6. [See also *ALA Bulletin*. Richmond. 22 (3) Summer 1996: 9-12, and *Panafest Official Souvenir Brochure*, 1999: 16, 20].

Anyidoho, Kofi. "National Identity and the Language of Metaphor." *FonTomFrom: Contemporary Ghanaian Literature, Theatre and Film* in *Matatu*. Amsterdam, Atlanta 21-22 2000: 1-22.

Anyidoho, Kofi. "Dr Efua Sutherland: A Biographical Sketch." In *FonTomFrom: Contemporary Ghanaian Literature, Theatre and Film, Matatu*. Amsterdam, Atlanta. 21-22 2000: 77-82. Reprint.

Anyidoho, Kofi and Gibbs, James, eds. *FonTomFrom: Contemporary Ghanaian Literature, Theatre and Film* in *Matatu*. Amsterdam, Atlanta 21-22 2000: volume dedicated to Efua Sutherland.

Asagba, Austin O."Storytelling as Experimental Drama: A Study of Efua Sutherland's *The Marriage of Anansewa*." In *Lore and Language* Sheffield 8 (2) 1989: 43-50.

Asgill, Edmondson J. "African Adaptations of Greek Tragedies." In *African Literature Today* 11 1980: 175-189.

Asiedu, Awo Mana. *West African Theatre Audiences: A Study of Ghanaian and Nigerian Audiences of Literary Theatre in English*. Ph.D Thesis: University of Birmingham, January 2003.

Aworele, Yinka. *Critical Notes with Questions and Answers on "The Marriage of Anansewa."* Ilesha: Fatiregun, 1979.

Baker, Donald. "African Theatre and the West." In *Comparative Drama* 11 1977: 227-251.

Bailey, Marlon M. "The Last Visitor's Note."In *Glendora* Lagos 2, 3 and 4 1998: 14-18. Longer version with title, "Reflections on a Conversation with Efua Sutherland," available on www.southernct.edu/projects/ctreview/essays/spring98essays/bailey.htm accessed 2004-06-03.

Banham, Martin. *African Theatre Today*. London: Pitman, 1976.

Ben-Abdallah, Mohammed. "Interviewed." In *Talking with African Writers*. Jane Wilkinson. London, James Currey, 1992: 32-46.

Berrian, Brenda F. "Bibliographies of Nine Female African Writers." In *Research in African Literatures* 12 1981: 214-236. The excellent section on Sutherland includes reviews and a variety of other items that are not included here.

Brown, Lloyd W. "African Woman as Writer." In *Canadian Journal of African Studies* 9 1975: 493-501.

—. *Women Writers in Black Africa*. Westport, CT and London: Greenwood, 1981, 61-83.

Carpenter, Peter. "Theatre in East and West Africa." In *Drama* 68 1963: 30-32.

Crane, Louise. In *Profiles of Modern African Women* .Philadelphia: Lippincott, 1973: 36-56.

Crow, Brian. *Studying Drama*. London: Longman, 1983.

de Graft, Joe. "Dramatic Questions." In *Writers in East Africa*. Andrew Gurr and Angus Calder eds. Nairobi: East African Literature Bureau, 1974: 33-67.

Davies, Carole Boyce. "Wrapping One's Self in Mother's Akatado Clothes: Mother-Daughter Relationships in the Works of African Women Writers."In *SAGE: A Scholarly Journal on Black Women* 4 (2): 1987: 11-19.

Deandrea, Pietro. *Fertile Crossings: Metamorphosis of Genre in Anglophone West African Literature*. Rodopi: Amsterdam 2002.

Dibba, Ebou. *Efua T. Sutherland: "The Marriage of Anansewa."* London: Longman, 1978.

Djisenu, John K. "The Art of Narrative Drama." In *FonTomFrom: Contemporary Ghanaian Literature, Theatre and Film, Matatu*. Amsterdam, Atlanta 21-22 2000: 37-43.

Drachler, Jacob ed.. *Black Homeland, Black Diaspora: Cross Currents of the African Relationship*. Port Washington NY: National University Publishers, 1975. Editorial introduction to interview with William Sutherland listed below.

Dseagu, S. Amanor. *A Definition of African Tragedy*. Legon: English Department, 1984.

Etherton, Michael. "Efua Sutherland. "In *The Cambridge Guide to World Theatre*. Martin Banham ed. Cambridge: Cambridge University Press, 1988: 933. See also entry in *The Cambridge Guide to African and Caribbean Theatre*. Martin Banham, Errol Hill and George Woodyard eds. Cambridge: Cambridge University Press, 1994: 41.

—. "Review of *Foriwa*." In *Books Abroad*. Spring 1969: 305.

—. *The Development of African Theatre*. London: Hutchinson, 1982.

Gibbs, James. "A Team Player Passes On: Efua Theodora Sutherland: 24 April 1924 -21 January 1996." In *West Africa* London 5-11 February: 181.

—. "Efua Theodora Sutherland." In *African Writers Volume II* . Brian C. Cox ed. New York: Scribner's, 1997: 833-850.

—. "Efua Theodora Sutherland: A Bibliography of Primary Materials, With a Checklist of Secondary Sources." In *FonTomFrom: Contemporary Ghanaian Literature, Theatre and Film, Matatu*. Amsterdam, Atlanta. 21-22 2000: 117-123.

—. "Ghana." In *A History of Theatre in Africa*. Martin Banham ed. Cambridge: Cambridge University Press, 2004: 159-170.

—. "Theatre of the Villages." In *West Africa* London 19-25 February 1996: 278-279.

Graham-White, Anthony. *The Drama of Black Africa*. New York: French, 1974.

Hagan, John C. "Influence of Folklore on *The Marriage of Anansewa*: A Folkloristic Approach." In *Okike* 27-28 1988: 19-30.

Jones-Quartey, K. A. B. "Tragedy and the African Audience." In *Okyeame* 3 (1) 1966: 50-55.

July, Robert W. *An African Voice: The Role of the Humanities in African Independence*, Durham NC: Duke University Press, 1987: 73-81.

Kedjani, John. "Observations of Spectator-Performer Arrangements for some Traditional Ghanaian Performances." *In Research Review*" Legon 2 (3) 1966: 61-66.

Kerr, David. *African Popular Theatre*. Oxford: James Currey, 1995.

Killam, Doug and Ruth Rowe. *The Companion to African Literature*. Oxford: James Currey; Bloomington: Indiana U P, 2000.

Kwaku, Rosemary. "Festac 77 / Cover Story." In *Ghana Review*, 2 (3) 1977: 19-23.

Lindfors, Bernth ed. *Africa Talks Back*. Trenton: Africa World Press, 2002: 69-88. See interview with Joe de Graft.

Lokko, Sophia. "Theatre Space: A Historical Overview of the Theatre Movement in Ghana." In *Modern Drama* 23 1980: 309-19.

MacRae, Suzanne H. "Efua Sutherland's Cultural Stagecraft: *Marriage of Anansewa*." Paper presented at the ALA Conference University of Arkansas, Fayetteville, April 2004.

McHardy, Cecile. "The Performing Arts in Ghana." In *African Forum*. 1 (1) Summer 1965: 113-117.

Mclean Amissah, G., *Reminiscences of Adisadel: A Short Historical Sketch of Adisadel College*. Accra: Afram, 1980.

Morriseau-Leroy, Felix. "The Ghana Theatre Movement." In *Ghana Cultural Review* 1 (1) July-Sept 1965: 10 and 14.

Muhindi, K. "L'apport d'Efua Theodora Sutherland à la Dramaturgie Contemporaine." *Presence Africaine* Paris 133-134 1985: 75-85.

Nketia, J. H. Kwabena. *Ghana – Music and Drama, A Review of the Performing Arts*, Legon IAS, 1965.

Nwahunanya, Chinyere. "The Playwright as Preacher: Contemporary Morality in Three Ghanaian Plays." In *Literary Endeavour* 10 1-4 1988-89: 25-44.

Okafor, Chinyere. "A Woman is not a Stone but a Human Being: Vision of Woman in the Plays of Aidoo and Sutherland." In *Medium and Message*, Ernest Emenyonu *et al* eds. Calabar: Department of English and Literary Studies, 1981: 165-77.

—. "Parallelism Versus Influence in African Literature: The Case of Efua Sutherland's *Edufa*." In *Kiabàrà* Port Harcourt 3, 1 Harmattan, 1980: 113-131.

Onukwufor, Chika C. "*The Marriage of Anansewa*: A Modern West African Drama for the WAESC Candidate." In *Muse* 11 1979: 55-58.

Pearce, Adetokunbo. "The Didactic Essence of Efua Sutherland's Plays." In *African Literature Today* 15 1987: 71-81.

Rockefeller Foundation Archives, Record Group 1. 2, 496R. Ghana Experimental Theatre. 1958-61.

Schipper, Mineke. *Theatre and Society in Africa*. Johannesburg: Ravan, 1982.

Schmidt, Nancy J. "African Women Writers of Literature for Children."In *World Literature Written in English* 17, 1 1978: 7-21.

—. "Children's Books by Well-Known African Authors." In *World Literature Written in English* 18 1979: 114-123.

Sutherland-Addy, Esi. "Drama in Her Life." Interview with Adeline Ama Buabeng."In *African Theatre Women*. Jane Plastow ed. Oxford: James Currey, 2002: 66-82

Sutherland-Addy, Esi, Headnote for "New Life" in Esi Sutherland-Addy and Aminata Diaw (eds.), *Women Writing Africa: West Africa and the Sahel*, New York: Feminist of the City University of New York, 2005 (217-219).

Sutherland-Addy, Esi. "Creating for and with Children in Ghana – Efua Sutherland: A Retrospective" in *African Theatre* vol. 6 (2006), 1-15.

Sutherland, William. "Interviewed by Ernest Dunbar." In *Black Homeland, Black Diaspora: Cross-Currents of the African relationship*. Jacob Drachler ed. Port Washington, N Y: National University Publications, 1975.

Sofola, Zulu. "Efua Sutherland, 1924 – " in *Encyclopedia of Post-Colonial Literature in English*, Ed., Eugene Benson and L.W. Connolly, London: Routledge, 1994, 1458.

Talbert, Linda Lee, "*Alcestis* and *Edufa*: The Transitional Individual" in *World Literature Written in English*, 22 (1983), 183-90.

Tanzer, Joshua, "Not Enough Drama in Ghana." In www.offoff.com/theatre/2001/edufaphp3. Dated 22 February 2001.

Thies-Torkornoo, Susanne. "Die Rolle der Frau in der afrikanischen Gesellschaft: Eine Betrachtung von Ama Ata Aidoos *Anowa* and Efua T. Sutherland's *Foriwa*. In *Matatu* 1 1987: 53-67.

Uka, Kalu. "Beyond the Catharsis: The Communal Perspective of Dramatic Appeal." In *Nigerian Journal of the Humanities* 1(1) 1977: 77-90.

Vavilov, V. N., "A Talented Poetess"in *Midwest Weekly*, 2, 42 (1965), 22-23.

Vieta, Kojo T, Dr. (Mrs) Efua Theodora Sutherland, (1924-96) in *The Flagbearers of Ghana*, Accra: Ena, 1999, 472-9.

Wetmore, Kevin J. *The Athenian Sun in an African Sky: Modern African Adaptations of Classical Greek Tragedy*. Jefferson, NC: MacFarland, 2002.

Wilentz, Gay. *Binding Cultures: Black Women Writers in Africa and the Diaspora*. Bloomington: Indiana University Press, 1992.

—. "Writing for the Children: Orature, Tradition and Community in Efua Sutherland's *Foriwa*." In *Research in African Literatures* 19(2) 1988: 182-196.

Zell, Hans, and Helen Silver. *A Reader's Guide to African Literature*. London: Heinemann, Revised Edition 1983: 493-495.

Websites

http://connection.ebscohost.com/content/article/1024156762.html

http://72.14.253.104/search?q=cache:01IEOCtyiLwJ:www.brunel.ac.uk/4042/entertext4.2/dasilva.pdf+Efua+Sutherland&hl=en&ct=clnk&cd=79&gl=us&client=firefox-a

http://sounds.bl.uk/View.aspx?item=024M-C0134X0202XX-0100V0.xml

http://search.barnesandnoble.com/booksearch/isbnInquiry.asp?z=y&endeca=1
&isbn=0786410930&itm=1

http://www.howard.edu/bellerson/afwmcin_pjt/afwmcin/timlne-afwc.html

http://dubois.fas.harvard.edu/news_events/ghana_symposium.html

http://catalog.socialstudies.com/c/efua.html?s@MIc5nIJGBPZhE

http://en.wikipedia.org/wiki/Efua_Sutherland

http://www.doollee.com/PlaywrightsS/sutherland-efua.html

http://www.britannica.com/eb/article-9070507/Efua-Sutherland

http://www.geocities.com/infohumanities/humanitiessample.html?9783526013
86

http://tomraworth.com/25may05.html

http://www.southernct.edu/projects/ctreview/essays/spring98essays/bailey.htm
ml

http://people.africadatabase.org/en/profile/16101.html

PART II

EFUA SUTHERLAND AND CULTURAL ACTIVISM

Robert July

'Here, Then, is Efua':
Sutherland and the Drama Studio

Some years ago while in the process of gathering material for a book dealing with the arts in Africa, I was able to talk at length with Efua about her work. In particular she spoke about those days during the 1950s and early 1960s, describing her hopes, her plans, and eventually her accomplishments in creating a modern theatre in Ghana. At the time that we talked we recorded our conversation, and the tapes have remained among my papers for now some 35 years. When asked to contribute a piece for the volume on Efua's influence, I wondered what I could offer, then remembered the tapes and replayed them. The memories came back, a rush of great vividness, hearing Efua again, the music of her speech, her enthusiasm, her determination, her gaiety and humour. It occurred to me that what I could best provide was not my own recollections and judgements, but the real thing. I could reconstruct on paper Efua herself, in her own words, relating what she was doing and thinking, particularly back in the heady days of Ghana's independence, when she herself did so much to liberate her own people from a cultural colonialism to parallel the political independence of the day.

Here then is Efua.

I was interested in theatre...because of my background at school and at college...I went to schools in Cape Coast and Asante-Mampong. They were run by nuns. They were actually very good about introducing us to literature...I performed a lot when I was at school and college... Also in Cape Coast where I grew up there was a secondary school, and they used to put on in Cape Coast an annual Greek tragedy, as a school performance...the staff and students. My uncle went to that school,[1] which was probably why I got to attend those plays where he performed. And I remember seeing Robert Gardner...yes, as Creon in Antigone, when I was a child, as a young girl. Antigone, Agamemnon...I loved it...I understood what was going on ...I read a lot of the Greek tragedies. And when I was teaching at training college, Asante-Mampong, I produced some of these plays myself. I produced the *Medea*. I produced Antigone, I produced the *Alcestis*...I tried to write some plays myself. Christmas plays and things like that. But I was playing at the time. Just interest...

Deciding to do it seriously was the outcome of my starting the Ghana Writers Society...after independence ...September 1957. I started that all of a sudden because I felt that a newly independent country needed a force of creative writers. My experience in teaching had led me...I am basically an educationist...And I feared [for] children, training college students...

comparing the material they were using here with what I had seen kids using in England saddened me a bit. I knew it was wrong. So I started writing as a result of my training college teaching experience...Suddenly in 1951 I started writing, I started creative writing seriously. I was writing poetry at the time. I suppose everyone starts writing poetry, they think they are great poets...It was just that I wanted to write. It wasn't until 1957...I said, oh, I see! ...Independence...etcetera, etcetera, etcetera. Let's get on with this business of writing for ourselves.

I remember, J. B. Danquah had heard about me when I started writing and getting published. I remember once I came from Asante-Mampong where I was teaching at the training college...to Accra, and he had me come to his place...and he was really very interested in my writing. I went back to the college and there was something in the mail...it was a gift from J. B. Danquah...Wasn't that nice?!...By 1957 I suppose I was ready to take the step. So I wrote letters to J. B. Danquah, Busia...Kofi Busia...Michael Dei-Anang. I told them I wanted us to have a meeting because I had an idea and I wanted to consult them. I wrote to them and they had a meeting, they came...and we met...and I told them I wanted to form the Ghana Society of Writers. So they encouraged me to go ahead...which I did...And we had our meetings...and before I knew it I was heading a delegation to go to the festival at Tashkent...the Afro-Asian Writers' Conference...That was in 1957...So I went to that conference and I saw things that pushed me. Children's books in schools which I objected to...I didn't like what was going on...

And then independence itself. I was terribly excited about independence. I had been excited about it for two or three years...and then it actually happened. At the day it happened there were a lot of people at that time, including Martin Luther King; he and Coretta King came. I actually was with them on the night of the transition. We went to the midnight parliament, the first parliament they put together. Then we came out...And, I remember very clearly in the streets outside with Nkrumah and all those people saying "Ghana is free forever"...We watched the Ghana flag go up and British flag come down...Very, very exciting times...I'm not surprised that that moved...with that inspiration and that excitement and he [Martin Luther King], he was moved too...Actually I heard him say, 'Free at last', that night ...in that street, that early morning...he echoed the 'free at last' statement... at that moment...

Tashkent...what moved me there was to see a huge exhibition of books from all other countries that were represented, and see the African area...the few shelves...That hit me...I said to myself then that I would help to fill those shelves...

So I came back and the writers' movement was going on...we had started the idea of a magazine...I came back more resolved that this thing shall work, and suddenly saw the problem about dramatic literature, the creating of dramatic literature....We needed a programme to develop playwriting and I starting the thought that led to the beginning of the theatre, the experimental theatre, the Ghana Experimental Theatre, I called it. And then in 1959 to 1960, we started building the Drama Studio...that comprised the programme...the idea of the programme...and we opened it and we were away...in October of 1961...

I knew that it was through that means that we would begin to create forms and styles of dramas, of theatrical expression that would stand as Ghanaian...Between 1961 and 1963 was a very creative period for the Ghana Studio. And we were doing two things at once. We were finding talent and getting them involved in practical theatre work... and also developing an audience... Except in the rainy season, we used to have regular productions throughout the year. When the production was on, there were regular weekly productions...We started at small audiences and then the audiences began to grow, and began to widen in scope; different kinds of Ghanaians learned to come to the Studio, the Studio productions...It was very important that it [the Studio] was in town...

The Drama Studio came as a sudden answer to a problem I had been having, starting the theatre programme. I looked at all the empty rooms and buildings I could find around the Ministry area. Up and down the Ministry steps, talking to people, saying I needed a place. I wanted to start a programme in drama. Eventually I talked with the Scouts people...It was in 1958 exactly. Right down the beach across from the Scouts headquarters there was this aluminium shed, and I asked about it. They said it was the Sea Scouts' den; that they used it only occasionally. So I said, 'Could I have it?' They eventually relieved me of my problem by letting me use it for a little fee. I moved the group I got together into that place and used it as a regular programme building. Every day... working day...So then about 1960 I was ready with a programme. Then the Rockefeller Foundation fund helped us coming along...And then I said, 'Oh, that's what I need. I need a place.'

There was an Englishman in the Ministry of Town Planning...when I was looking for a place. I had spoken with him. He said 'Look, there is a place there that we want to preserve. We don't want people to rush in and build on this place. We want to preserve that land as a park area. So why don't you come and look at it.' So he took me to see the Ghana Studio land. And I said, 'Can I have it?' He said, 'Sure, you can have it.' [It was] government land. So he said, 'Go and get the papers.' So I went to the Land Department. The man who was there at that time really annoyed me. He said, 'Oh, You want to do what with it?' I said, 'I want to put a studio on it. I am doing a theatre programme.' He got up from behind his desk and started throwing his legs about and said, 'Oh, you want girls on the stage?' My goodness! I was cross with that fellow!

I needed [a place] at that time not just to provide us with a space for the programme, but also to stand as a symbol of the programme...Something tangible that people could point their fingers at and say, 'That's a place where African drama, experimental African drama is going on.' It was quite important to do that. So the Drama Studio as a building is really very important, because it helped to make this whole idea gel for people...I designed it as a Ghanaian courtyard. Once again the importance of people being able to identify with it. The audience...they could walk into this place and just feel at home. You could have just called it a theatre and got a design from a book, a design, you know, one of these model theatres...I didn't want to do that. It was terribly important that the building itself is pertinent to the idea...So, as a Ghanaian courtyard, because everything that happens dramatically in life in this country usually happens in the courtyard. The naming ceremonies, the puberty rites, all these things...The courtyard is the setting of a house, of an ordinary house, for many often dramatic events. That is why it would be familiar.

The programme was at the beginning to root a modern theatre programme in the dramatic traditions of this country. That was the starting point. Find out what the forms of traditional drama that exist can do for modern theatre. I started with the story-telling tradition, and did that because it was a familiar form. It was very dramatic; it had all sorts of wonderful material. And so I thought, well, a lot of people now living in towns, [have] been to school, don't come to the village base and participate in it. So what do you do in modern theatre to use those resources? Create a form out of those resources. That's what I did. Between 1958 and 1959 I was working on this experiment, evolving a form from a theatrical tradition that used to be a part of [everyone]...

There have been phases of work. That was the first phase. I was satisfied we were evolving. The drama was played out to audiences and the response was excellent. I said, 'Okay, that will work. We'll go onto the next.' In 1958, 1959, I was ready to move on and I set myself a problem. The problem had to do with school education, the familiarity...Everybody has been to school with the English tradition of theatre. Shakespeare...the European...Shakespeare, Molière...all those things. So I said, 'All right! Now what do I do first about the idea of giving both the actors and the audience something new although it would be based in something they knew about?' How does one introduce some form of originality? So it occurred to me to think about Ghanaian interest in matters religious, and I chose to work on *Everyman*; first because of its Christian connection and because that offered opportunities to Ghanaians in terms of what was precious to them because of their religious interest. So I started working on this...and developed a play in which you had very Ghanaian characters and every man's problems, about living carelessly and then finding out what complications there would be at the end...So it was a very interesting experiment and we were working on that and on other types of training scenarios...

In 1960 I moved out of the shed into the Drama Studio area...in the grounds that had been leased to me. I moved the group…By the time the building was ready, the production of *Everyman* was complete and that was the inaugural play…Nkrumah came…

The Ghanaian interest in religion was one of the things I was interested in as subject matter…I started with one group in the shed. The group was very carefully selected. I just went round to a place like the Public Works Department in town, and I would meet workers at lunch break and talk with them, that I want to start a programme. I am looking for people who have creativity and so on, who like music, who have been to see concert party shows and understand stage work. They have had experience with this older tradition, the concert party tradition of theatre in Ghana. When I talked this way I would get a response. I would get two or three people from that group. I went to the army barracks…and looked around, and asked, "Are there any people here who are interested in 'this kind of thing'?" I was able to pick up from there two excellent actors, very talented people. I found one… he might have been somebody's steward or batman or something like that, because he was pressing clothes when I was introduced to him. He really turned out to be a stupendous actor…There were about forty people… [They did] everything. I started from the beginning to train the group to be self-sufficient, managing everything…

I think I might add one brief postscript, if Amowi is willing. It is an excerpt from a letter I wrote her shortly after seeing her at the Schomberg memorial in 1996:

I always thought that there was something almost childlike in [Efua's] manner, as if she were the embodiment of all the children she loved so well. I remember one time, some years ago when I was in the midst of one of my African junkets, I was in Ghana and it was Independence Day. Efua and I were together somewhere in downtown Accra on one of the streets leading to the stadium where they held the independence ceremonies. There was a parade of assorted groups, mostly children from various schools, as I remember, but at one point the entourage of a chief came into view. There was probably more to it than this, but I remember in particular a little man marching along solemnly bearing the chiefly stool on his head. Right behind the stool came the chief himself, borne along high on a litter, beautifully bedecked in his cloth and crown, and gold, gold everywhere — gold rings and bracelets, a heavenly firmament of spangles and glitter. It was an impressive performance and the chief was having a marvellous time waving regally to the enthusiastic plaudits of the crowd. Efua was standing beside me, and I turned to see how she was taking it all in. Nothing blasé. Not a bit. She was literally dancing up and down, clapping her hands like a ten year old, her face beaming, her eyes glistening with pleasure. She was charming, and I rather think this was the essential Efua. Great enthusiasm, simple, direct, almost childlike. Very beautiful.

Sandy Arkhurst

Kodzidan

INTRODUCTION

Ghana's rich, deep and complex traditional culture has, over the years been greatly enhanced by the variety of its ethnic groups, with their different cosmologies, religions, customs, histories and artistic traditions complementing one another. This traditional culture was immensely intriguing to early European colonialists, administrators and researchers/scholars in its potency for group motivation. For example they were quick to realise how the people would attend a royal call by a court crier with a gong-gong (double bell), and dare not refuse under sacred oath, while even the threat of torture could not induce them to a meeting with white overlords to discuss tax or land tenure.

In modern times, the continuous potency of indigenous cultural values in the dynamics of people-based development has been acknowledged with deep conviction. As a result, many aspects of traditional cultural practices and precepts still draw relevance and functionality in contemporary Ghana, centuries of colonial and foreign influence and exploitation notwithstanding. Yet it cannot be denied that many Western political, economic, religious and social systems have been adopted by/imposed upon Ghana, creating an ambivalent situation and precarious balance between our ethnic cultures and diverse world perspectives.

Many problems relating to development and the improvement in quality of life for all people of Ghana have plagued successive governments and formal institutions. The dilemma of how to provide basic necessities and education for Ghanaians while not destroying traditional cultural norms and institutions is not an easy one to solve. It has always been a riddle, akin to the proverbial *Santrofi anoma* in Akan myth, for if you catch this mythical bird you have caught calamity and yet if you leave it to go free, you have deprived yourself of a blessing.

Developmental issues in Ghana, as elsewhere in Africa, are many and varied in scope and immediacy. They include concerns like mass-illiteracy, teenage pregnancy, drug misuse and abuse, sanitation, political/civic ignorance, lack of motivation and empowerment. These problems demand a critical examination of the cultural and societal forces behind them, leading to a repudiation of destructive attitudes and a purposeful promotion of functional and relevant community animation, through culture, for positive change. The problem remains as to how best to accomplish these goals and exchange the necessary information. The impetus for development projects comes sometimes from the governmental organisations and at other times from local and community initiative.

HUMBLE BEGINNINGS

It is very difficult to imagine this article unfolding in anything but a disjointed manner despite an outline I have arranged. My ideas about *Kodzidan* are simply too many and I feel I could write a journal of considerable length and still manage to relate only a fraction of what I have learnt and experienced. Nonetheless, the challenge is on and my intentions lie in tracing the tendencies of my expectations, attitudes, and realisations throughout the many stages of the *Kodzidan* or 'house of stories' experiment spearheaded by Mrs. Efua Sutherland.

Mrs. Efua Sutherland taught me at the School of Music and Drama (now School of Performing Arts) at the University of Ghana, Legon. After my studies she identified me and asked me to assist in a programme she was organising at the village of Ekumfi Atwia. From the moment I set foot in Atwia to the time the *Kodzidan* or 'house of stories' was physically built, I managed to find some new lessons and change of perspective. I was able to tap into creative endeavours and develop wider appreciation for so many things. The time I spent on stage with local performers and in assisting with the programme added an entirely unique dimension to my experience.

I would like first to think about my initial expectations which were formulated as a response to the formal drama and theatrical education I had been through. I must admit I made a few elitist assumptions which later proved only natural. I imagined our tackling issues of general concern much like Acting Technique, Directing, Playwriting and Scene Design. My vision was an ill-formed University graduate's version of a village community's plight. Here I thought, was a chance to teach the villagers all I had learnt about drama and theatre. It is quite obvious, in retrospect, that I had carried with me images of Western theatre technique, biased opinions of what dramatisation ought to do, and a superiority complex.

The first few meetings at the village brought with it some humbling realizsations which worked to reshape my thinking and helped me to evaluate the mistakes I had made. Ideas of traditional theatre in Ghana were being presented to me as was an entirely new conceptualisation of dramatic possibilities. Suddenly I was made aware of my misconceptions and was forced to leave behind me the theatre I worked in for some years, the performances which had moulded my perspective and the familiarity of Western techniques on stage. I began to conceptualise audience participation and the lack of dichotomy between performers and audience. I began to think about improvisation and its effects as well as differences to be found between theatre and drama. A picture began to take shape and I began to turn my focus in this new direction. My enthusiasm was no longer for professional theatre, but was being channelled towards my evolving role in the Atwia programme. It was not long before I realised my role to be that of a drama graduate learning what was unknown. With this realisation came a decision to relinquish my 'I-am-here-to-teach-you-drama' mind-frame and to seek earnestly new ideas relative to what had been presented to me in university class discussions. I began by considering the foundation on which the programme was being built. I began analysing concepts I had previously taken for granted. I realised I had never before tried to understand what dramatisation involved. I also began to ask myself questions like: 'What does theatre mean/do to me?' and 'What do I want to do with theatre?' A lot of self-analysing took place at all stages of the programme and I can honestly say that I learnt the answers to questions that I had not even begun to formulate.

COMMUNICATION AND THEATRE

My feelings about media for effective communication ran a deep course as I began thinking of mentally retarded children, the deaf, the dumb, and the blind. The Atwia *Kodzidan* programme gave rise to a plethora of new ideas with respect to theatre for communication, and all of these realisations had me looking toward a very rewarding future.

The type of media used in developmental projects is a strong indicator of what effect they will ultimately have on the people. Any media which is a novelty and an influence in itself, such as film, television, or video, may detract considerably from the educational message which it is attempting to convey. In addition, these are largely uni-directional methods, which dictate rather than communicate, not allowing the audience to ask questions of the information given. Of course, the specific needs of the development project and the people it is aimed at will influence the choice of media used. The needs of people in a rural village or a congested urban centre are completely different and must be taken into account. But whenever an educational or awareness-raising message needs to be put out, it must be in the local language; it must be community based and relevant to the people, it must be delivered by spokes-persons to whom the people can relate. It should also be in a form which facilitates dialogue between members of the community and educational workers. These needs and requirements point to theatre as a very effective medium for development communication. Its successes are well documented, and a strong precedence and acceptance exist in many communities for it.

Because of this strong precedence and acceptance, several governments, educational institutions, Arts Councils, and other organisations in Ghana have been paying attention to cultural development programmes by promoting drama and festivals. These programmes are as exciting as they are challenging. Lack of sufficiently trained manpower in the area of directing and theatre management and the lack of adequate theatre facilities are usually the major obstacles to the realisation of the noble objectives of the cultural programmes. The country has come out with a clearly laid out cultural policy that should help to harmonise the various cultural activities throughout the country. Such a coherent policy should hopefully make it possible to commission the building of theatres that are truly indigenous. Most of the theatre structures we have cannot accommodate most of our traditional performances such as the masquerades, festivals, dances and story-telling which require non-formalised use of space.

COMMUNITY DEVELOPMENT AND THEATRE

The Ekumfi Atwia House of Stories (popularly known as *Kodzidan*) was built to provide the right model for a national indigenous theatre. But an indigenous theatre must always be functional. It takes a visionary to spearhead an indigenous cultural revolution in the face of a more popular foreign and domineering culture. The brain behind the *Kodzidan*, Mrs. Efua Sutherland, (popularly known everywhere and by everybody as Auntie Efua), realised that in the face of poverty, environmental degradation, lack of sanitation and resources, and the fading influence of indigenous cultural values, developing countries needed a means for motivating the people to help themselves. After several years of colonial rule and a long period of relatively unsuccessful development plans that had neglected average citizens and had only served to benefit the urban few, she believed it was natural that development at the community level would be the most beneficial and would guarantee more returns than development on the larger scale. Community development was to rely upon the extent to which the people could work to better themselves and to help their own community. She had observed that when people relied on outside assistance, little got accomplished and communities became immobilised, not taking matters into their own hands.

How did Auntie Efua go about realising her dream of helping people to develop themselves and their communities? She realised it much earlier than many other development agents in Developing World countries that one cannot develop people. One can only motivate people to develop themselves.

Auntie Efua had this conviction before Paulo Freire and Augusto Boal started their pioneering work in Latin America. The economic problems of the nation, Ghana, were taking their toll on the rural population. The rural dwellers had lost faith in their leaders, the educated people and the city-dwellers. They had been cheated for far too long and therefore had lost faith in themselves as people and had become suspicious of any development agent who would want to help. After trying to work with other communities, Auntie Efua finally settled on Atwia, because the village was prepared to give her a chance to try. Even here the very first day Auntie Efua arrived in Atwia to begin her work, the writer, who was with her, overheard a peasant lady say, 'Na ewuraba feefew yi rohwehwe ebenadze wo hen ekurase ha? Iyi nkye Nkran na owo de otsena O?' ('What does this beautiful and well-dressed lady want in our village? Her place should be in Accra'). The import of this comment became clear to the writer a year later, after about fifty visits when at a forum the villagers confessed that they were going to be more cooperative with Auntie Efua because they had then realised she meant well. Up until then, they had fed the team that travelled a little over 100 kilometres from Legon with half truths while working with them two afternoons a week!

EKUMFI ATWIA

Atwia is located only a few kilometres from the Central Regional capital of Cape Coast, about six kilometres off the Accra-Takoradi highway. In the 1960s several sections of the regional capital had been built to impress and to provide comfort. The streets were wide and clean. Modern architecture, well-kept lawns and hedges, constant power-supply and ever-flowing water taps, several educational institutions and shopping centres were the hallmarks of Cape Coast.

Taking one's self away from this town and heading towards Atwia, the contrast was as sharp as day and night. The buildings were close to each other, haphazardly arranged, and interspaced with gullies caused by erosion, creating an unsightly artificial drainage system under some houses with the threats of sudden collapse of the walls. A rocky dirt road led to and around the village. The houses had roofs made of a combination of thatch, debris and rotting roofing sheets. A very insignificant percentage of children in the village had access to formal education in a school a few kilometres from the village.

The primary occupation of the constituents had historically been subsistence farming, as there was no market in the village. Residents travelled to Mankesim, the nearest market town on given market days to buy their needs and to sell the little they produced from their farms. Their land supported pineapple growing but fetched low prices from the fruit processing factory at Nsawam that had encouraged them to go into that business. The only source of water was a stream several metres away from the village. Lack of easily accessible running water was a great inconvenience to the people. Fetching water took much of their time and energy that could be used to help the village develop.

There was no modern health facility but only drug peddlers hanging around. The nearest health institution was the Saltpond Government Hospital which is about forty kilometres away. Sanitation was poor as there were no proper waste disposal systems. As a result many uncontrolled private dumps and unauthorised sanitary sites existed, creating a high risk of rodent infestation and disease outbreak.

Entering the village one would come across several sheep and goats, inside and out, with droppings all over, waiting to be washed into the nearby stream by rain. Small bathrooms were seen with house drains developing into virtually stagnant, meandering offensive pools which were left to breed mosquitoes. The description of Ekumfi Atwia could be a scenario for almost any village in Ghana. Something had to be done to ensure the total well-being of the rural dwellers. What had to be done was to constitute a realistic and wholly beneficial reflection of integrated development. The need for a truly balanced and self-sustaining development process in rural communities must now, as then, be underscored.

APPROACHES TO INTEGRATED DEVELOPMENT

Identified interest groups may pursue integrated development at a high risk. These groups may give disproportionate emphasis to some aspects of development and ignore other related issues; for example, concentrating on population control programme and neglecting health programmes, emphasizing infrastructural development to the detriment of human and environmental considerations. It is easy for one to overlook the myriad natural, social and human problems such development brings in its wake. It is easy to see the glitter of electric light, high-rise buildings, industrial areas and new and urban townships as worthwhile indicators of progress and development. Auntie Efua, however, embarked on channelling development efforts through natural and well-balanced routes, taking care to concentrate on what should rightly be the central consideration for all development effort – the human factor. Such natural channels for development could not be reached without communication that was rooted in the people's own culture.

Kodzidan then became more than just a place for performance. It was developed to become an instrument of mobilisation and to create communal solidarity. In the context of crisis the place became a court room, a mini-parliament to take decisions concerning the village, and a durbar ground on festive occasions. It was, as it were, a classroom for informal education for the different generational groups. *Kodzidan* was a concept which encouraged **education** of the residents to create the desired awareness and motivation for them to want to do things for themselves. It gave them the opportunity to be **organised** in their programmes for success, and provide the necessary discipline for the sustenance of the community projects. Information distribution and sharing formed a solid base for the Atwia programme. The education, organisation and the discipline of the people helped them to tap whatever potential and resources, human and material, in their environment for the benefit of that society. Conventional practices have concentrated on education and are doing far less business with organisation and discipline. The use of community theatre for development, however, ensured community involvement and problem management thereby giving equal value to all the three crucial pre-requisites for development. Through community involvement, the residents were encouraged to generate development from among the people. To a remarkable extent, all development projects and efforts attempted during the period had been culture based.

A considerable amount of time was spent on needs assessment. Often times Auntie Efua would put a break on the assistants because we would be anxious to see the product of our efforts. She kept reminding us 'the process is more important than the product'. It was necessary to spend time to identify the real needs of the community, not the wants, and apply the appropriate technique, and of course relying on the indigenous resources and the cultural backgrounds. With this kind of strategy, symptoms of community problems could be treated while attacking the root causes. It would be wrong to say Auntie Efua would have succeeded in achieving the high level of communal spirit, discipline and dedication with a perpetually dependent and passive community.

There was a great demand on her to first create the necessary awareness. She made sure it wasn't a matter of 'feeding' and 'withdrawal'. Her problem was not with the peasant farmers alone. She had to convert the facilitators and get them to, as it were, become assimilated into the organism of the community, so that our blended potentials could lead to coherent internal organisation and discipline. The conscious involvement of the community throughout the processes gave them the opportunity to ask questions, make suggestions, argue and in fact participate in every way so as to ingrain their own beliefs, values, priorities, problems and goals into the development effort. Thus Auntie Efua identified the cultural structures of the community and used them as tools to carry development messages, encouraging mass participation in all the processes for development. A few sessions of interactions with the community revealed who the residents were, how they lived, what they knew, what they did and what they wanted. The special expertise in this community was in storytelling. Their rich language was full of proverbs, and their games and songs were a delight to watch and listen to. The oral performance media provided commentary upon and critiqued the development process. Stories they had told over and over and had heard often as entertainment to while away time were beginning to have significance and new meaning giving deeper insight. Residents were beginning to relate incidents and situations in the stories to their own lives. From then, the stories ceased to be remote sounding information about the problems of *Obi-krom* 'someone else's town' and became the focus on issues in *henkrom* 'our town'. The oral tradition that had been accepted in the community for generations became channels to convey development information to the people. Self help became a major component of improving standards of living. Traditional leadership was strengthened to mobilise the people and encourage them to undertake communal labour.

The *Kodzidan* was largely built through communal labour and it became the rallying point for every community activity. It becomes obvious that by using the powerful, exciting and popular medium of African theatrical forms for educating the community, Auntie Efua was acknowledging the potency of the authentic indigenous forms which draw their intensity and uniqueness from (a) their use of familiar symbols, local images, intellectual values and linguistic registers; (b) their compelling aesthetic quality in terms of humour, wit and subtle modes of rendition; (c) their people-based, communal-participation facility, and (d) their adaptive and flexible form. These basic qualities have, to a great extent, facilitated the process of transmutation and ensured the survival and continued relevance of indigenous forms like *Anansesem*, instrumental (musical) and lyrical formulas and dances/dance-drama like *adowa*, *agbekor* and cult dances like the hunters' dance. The growth of social development was seen as the basis for promoting economic growth. Programmes undertaken at the *Kodzidan* sought to focus on clarifying the underlying values and beliefs in all activities as a prerequisite to behavioural change. The prime unit of intervention was the whole community, understanding their traditional values, their leadership patterns and roles, and the communication channels and flows of influence amongst these elements. These elements were adopted and modified for sustained development. Recognising the potential, the communities had enabled the programme to introduce new knowledge, attitude and skills within the existing framework.

The identifying characteristics of the Programme at the *Kodzidan* include the fact that no activity or performance was 'manufactured' in someone's private study and dished out to a passive audience. But essentially, it was made from about and by the people themselves. All activities were aimed at creating a platform for communal participation through theatre, in all stages of integrated development; from problem identification, through theatrical presentation of such problems, to collective discussion and, finally, action leading to growth. The element of efficient research, then, was very central to this programme. It employed participatory research which is a vital preparatory and illuminating tool for social transformation.

The programme then constituted an inexhaustible chain of quest and interaction, using the dramatic media, and employing effective indigenous artistic media like drums and gong-gongs, lyrics, symbols, social organs like

Asafo, puppetry, storytelling and artifacts, as the source material. Quite often the people's circumstances became the dramatic source material. Art produced this way becomes a communal property, or more exactly a communal utility used by all in the same way. Drama of this category is most meaningful in a communal society, and it allows the advantage of an almost unlimited field for imaginative creation. Projects undertaken by *Kodzidan* were done in conjunction with other re-enforcing approaches. For example, they promoted literacy with attendant reading materials as well as skill training provided. Furthermore opportunities were provided for the utilisation of what had been learned.

The *Kodzidan* programme should not be seen as having been capable of solving the social and economic problems of Atwia. It should be seen as a forum for the rural population to discuss issues and try to understand their complexities. The critical analysis would lead to awareness and the desire for change. The programme introduced a new method of discussion through the practice of theatre and encouraged the use of this new method by the people themselves.

The general theory for the overall design of this flexible theatre building was to show that a modern community theatre building unit with new requirements could be built to incorporate all the popular acting areas: proscenium, theatre-in-the-round, and end-stage, and that this could be provided quickly and cheaply. This experiment demonstrated several possibilities in the use of the acting areas and their relationship with the audiences. It also enabled ways in which theatre influences the kind of programme run, and how each presentation determines how the theatre could be used. In other words, form and function are always totally integrated.

KODZIDAN AS FLEXIBLE PLAYING PLACE

Careful planning and thought had gone into making the *Kodzidan* flexible and suited to the needs of a modern village theatre and more specially to the needs of a developing theatre. The perimeter walls serve to contain the audience and keep away goats and sheep. They also restrict the size of the audience. The backstage room with two doors provides a backstage where actors can prepare themselves for performance. The doors are used as entrances and exits and on occasions serve as inner rooms. The dressing room also serves as office and storage for properties and items of costume. The performance areas, acoustics and sight-lines at the *Kodzidan* are so appropriate and significant that the audiences are brought remarkably close to the performers – so close that they could merge with the drama either verbally or actively. They come so close that comments that they may wish to make reinforce the intimacy of the performance. In other words the structure of this theatre deliberately encourages audience participation in any given production. The architecture, the building itself, the walls, the nearby trees and shrine, have become the setting which has extended to embrace the whole audience. Not only the audiences, but also the performers, the directors and facilitators have had to come to terms with this.

Kodzidan has generated a particular form of drama which allows an 'audience' of actors in role to mediate the drama for the real audience. This is not the technique of 'planting' members of the cast in the audience, but something much more clearly defined: a character or characters moving in and out of secondary characterisation in order to objectify and comment critically upon certain events and relationship. This has been adapted by Efua Sutherland in her play *The Marriage of Anansewa* through the role of the Story Teller. Thus a model for more formalised exchange between actors and audience is established. This both derives from and extends the storytelling form of performance.

Kodzidan will always be cheap to build and to maintain. If it is not working in the way it should, parts of it can be knocked down and rebuilt more appropriately. It can be modified in its form to suit developing drama and contemporary realities. Because of the success of the Atwia *Kodzidan*, it is very important to extend the concept by establishing new *Kodzidan* (or its local nominal equivalents elsewhere) in the various communities in Ghana. Almost inevitably a *Kodzidan* in a fishing community in Southern Ghana and another one in a farming community in the North would represent different trends. The traditional forms would be dictated by the different social relations which obtain in the two areas. However, the facilitators who would work in the various community theatres should be encouraged to let the traditional forms interact with forms that mirror the wider Ghanaian experience. This interaction would reveal the tensions and contradictions within Ghanaian society which should be very educative for the communities.

Comfort Caulley Hanson

The Ghana National Commission on Children

In 1959, the UN General Assembly proclaimed the Rights of the Child. It followed this declaration in 1976 by designating 1979 as the International Year of the Child, and called upon parents, men and women as individuals, and upon voluntary organizations, local authorities and national governments to recognise, protect and preserve the rights of the child.

Ghana's response to the UN Declaration of the Rights of the Child was to set up in May, 1977, an Ad Hoc Committee on the International Year of the Child. Mrs. Efua T. Sutherland was a member of that Committee. The Ad Hoc Committee was charged, among other objectives, to take stock of the then extant policies and programmes which had been formulated and were being implemented for the benefit of children; to consider measures to be taken to extend and strengthen those benefits; and to specifically prepare a programme for the celebration of the International Year of the Child.

The Ad Hoc Committee discharged its duties with credit. On 31st December, 1978, through the intervention of Mrs. Efua Sutherland the then Head of State ratified the proclamation of the UN General Assembly on the rights of the child and commissioned a week-long celebration of the International Year of the Child from 22nd to 29th January 1979. Finally, in completing its assignment, the Ad Hoc Committee recommended the setting up of a permanent Commission on Children to serve as an umbrella administrative/executive machinery for the formulation of appropriate policies to promote and preserve the rights of children.

The recommendation was eventually accepted, but only after intensive pursuit by Mrs. Efua Sutherland. The then Government passed AFRC Decree 66 on 29th August 1979 to establish a National Commission on Children in Ghana and charged it with the numerous functions stated in the Decree. Mrs. Sutherland, however, declined to chair the Commission when asked to do so after its inauguration, saying, 'I have a lot more to do for the Commission behind the scenes, so get somebody else.' Mrs. Alberta Ollenu, a renowned Ghanaian educationist became the next choice to serve as the first Chairperson of the Ghana National Commission on Children.

Thus, for the first time ever in Ghana, there was a national body to oversee the affairs of children: a national voice for children. The first Commission members, which included Mrs. Sutherland, had nothing by way of programmes and projects to start on except the recommendations made by the Ad Hoc

Committee. It became apparent, therefore, that for the Commission to be able to play its assigned role and achieve the objectives adumbrated in the Decree that set it up, its foundation members would have to be both imaginative and innovative. First, they would have to evolve new programmes and plan new projects to help to promote the statutory functions of existing institutions already dealing with children's concerns in health, education, social services, recreation etc and, second, to redefine their objectives and then, thirdly, to deepen the awareness of the institutions themselves and of the general public of the needs of children. The Commission members proved equal to the stupendous task set for them in the Decree.

The Commission, under the leadership of the two able women (Mrs. Ollennu, 1979–1983; Mrs. Sutherland, 1983–1990) was able to initiate and carry through a number of ground-breaking and dynamic children-based programmes and projects. Under their able leadership the National Commission took the following initiatives:

- Organised a national Workshop on the status of women and their role in better childcare, with special emphasis on the encouragement of mothers of infants to breast-feed their children in preference to artificially manufactured baby foods and other preparations. The nutrition programme of the Ministry of Health, especially in the rural areas, was influenced to a very large extent by the findings of the Workshop; and there has been a positive response in the search for suitable infant food substitutes manufactured from locally available resources, as testified by products on the local market like Weanimix, Cerevita etc.
- Started a Holiday Camp Programme for children between the ages of 7 – 13, which was intended to bring together at one place children from all the ten Regions of Ghana to facilitate the forging of friendship among the children and the sharing of knowledge and experiences of their individual Regions, cultures and customary practices and thereby promote national integration among children in the early stages of their lives.
- Organised a Seminar on Pre-school Services, by which it was able to get all parties involved in this important area of child development to accept the recommendation that sectors responsible for the pre-school programme should retain their programme responsibility but work under the Commission as a coordinating body.
- Established the Park-Library Complex Project which was a unique example of an integrated non-formal education programme. This Project was the brain child of Mrs. Sutherland. She thought it through and gradually led the Commission to appreciate its significance and impact on the learning process of the child. Young architects and landscapers were invited to form a design colloquium to design model parks which use the cultural

background of Ghanaian children as guidance. The project sought to awaken in children their urge to explore and discover their latent God-given qualities and creative abilities within the context of their physical and social environment, and to encourage them to use their leisure time to unfold their creativity in art, crafts, dance etc.

It is gratifying to note that by 1990 the largest Park-Library Complex, at Amakom, Kumasi, the Village Complex at Kyekyewere, the District Complex at Gomoa Assin and the Neighbourhood Complex at Teshie/Nungua near Accra had been completed and were functioning exactly as intended by the National Commission as a focal, converging spot for children of all backgrounds to meet to play and learn from one another.

Furthermore under the leadership of Efua Sutherland, the Commission initiated a Child Literacy Programme focusing on children within the age range of 6 to 15 years, who had either missed entry into schools or had dropped out of school by reason of their parents not being able, because of economic hardship, to enroll and maintain them in school. To mobilise funds in support of the Child Literacy programme the Commission set up the Child Education Fund and appointed trustees whose major functions included the mobilisation of funds from local as well as external sources to fund the purchasing of books and other learning aids for literacy centres for children to be set up in all the ten Regions of the country. Monies from the Child Education Fund were also to be used to support local effort in the construction of classroom blocks in the rural areas of Ghana.

The Commission under the chairpersonship of Mrs. Efua Sutherland, also established a Sociology and Child Research group, based at the University of Ghana, Legon. The group on behalf of the National Commission undertook various pieces of research, for example, into the plight of children serving as maids in homes and those employed as porters in markets and elsewhere, and submitted reports. These research results not only enrich the library of books and writings on Ghanaian children but also serve as aids to further research and policy formulation for Government and NGO institutions carrying out functions which impinge on the rights and welfare of children.

There is no gainsaying the fact that under the leadership of Mrs. Sutherland, known to her other colleagues on the Commission simply as 'Auntie Efua', the work of the Commission on Children reached a watershed. Regional committees of the Commission were set up at the ten Regional Capitals and were chaired with the promotion and implementation at the regional levels of the National Commission's various programmes and projects. The country's journalists were encouraged to write feature articles focusing on the rights and problems of children of Ghana in particular. Through their writings journalists acted as important catalysts to the work of the Commission by constantly advertising in the pages of their newspapers and magazines the Commission's activities on behalf of Ghanaian children.

Thus, by the rather abrupt end of the Commission's stewardship under Auntie Efua's leadership in March 1990, the Commission's public image had been raised very high and the awareness of its work both locally and internationally had begun to yield dividends by way of donations in cash which flowed in to support the Commission's programmes and projects.

H. N. A. Wellington

Architecture: Spatial Deployment for Community Experience (Encounter with Efua T. Sutherland)

Writing an essay for a volume encompassing the *oeuvre* of a known academic colleague is quite involving, and does pose a varied number of challenges. On one hand there is the obvious challenge of pursuit of excellence for a scholarly effort in such an exercise. On the other hand, there is a more complex challenge that involves both the mind and the heart. In that case, while attempting by such an essay, to explore some aspects of the thought and works of the colleague, one is confronted with the necessity, for the purpose of inspiration, to simultaneously fall back on the emotional contact one has with the colleague.

Experience shows that, notwithstanding the immensity of the challenges involved, such a task may be more easily taken on, if one can directly access the subject of the volume for support. In this particular instance, the subject of the volume, Dr. (Mrs.) Efua Theodora Sutherland was no more at the time of writing and, therefore, a readily available direct support was non-existent. This had been a handicap while preparing my contribution. Nevertheless, my response to the challenge to write had been accompanied with a certain amount of euphoria. Without doubt, undertaking to contribute to the volume, did bring happy memories, and at the same time, a unique opportunity to document some of the profound impressions emanating from my close relationship and interactions with the late colleague.

As it were, rummaging the recesses of my mind to glean insights and ideas to assist in writing on the social dimensions of architecture was certainly an arduous task.[1] Nevertheless, there was a continuous flow of energy available to sustain the ardour for the task, supplied from the memory of the long but stimulating discourses which took place between Auntie Efua, as she was affectionately known, and myself. These discourses were held on several occasions, as we visited together either in her welcoming house nestled within the well landscaped idyllic and almost rustic environment at Dzorwulu, or at the offices of her brain-child, the Ghana National Commission on Children in Accra, or strolling together on the rolling lawns of the Asanteman Children's Park in Kumasi.

One of the most moving, and indeed, the last of such discussions we had, was in the simple but sensitively furnished parlour in her home, a couple of weeks before her transition. Amongst the various issues discussed, the focus was on the Asanteman Children's Park in Kumasi. While reminiscing in her usual poetic and philosophical style, the objectives and conception of the Park Library Complex Projects came up. She went on to retrospect the anticipated role of these projects (designed during her tenure as chair of the Ghana National Commission on Children) in the enhancement of the development process of Ghanaian children, for whose primary use and enjoyment the projects were to be realised. In the midst of this retrospection Efua T. Sutherland made a remarkable request.

The request was addressed to the Asantehene, Nana Otumfuo Opoku Ware II. She wanted to have conveyed to him her wish that Nana adopt the Asanteman Children's Park for his royal patronage and care. Her verbal appeal, as she passionately expressed it to me, was couched in a language of a mother, whose child had been neglected by the father and was pleading with a worthy relative for assistance. The powerful sentiment expressed was as a result of the then poor state of maintenance of the facilities and apparent lack of official commitment to the programmes which were to take place at the Park. On my arrival back in Kumasi, I requested an appointment and was received in a full court of the Asantehene to present Efua T. Sutherland's appeal. Upon hearing the remarkable appeal, Otumfuo responded positively to it. However, he asked for the appeal to be presented in writing by way of confirmation. As it turned out, fate would not allow this passionate appeal addressed to Nana Opoku Ware to be documented. She died before I could bring Nana's response back to her.

Strangely enough, Efua T. Sutherland, who in her life-time communicated her ideas and thoughts so effectively by writing, alas, was unable to express this singular wish of hers in writing. As an honoured courier of such a noble request from such a distinguished scholar and a social-cultural activist, I deem myself duty-bound to write on her behalf in this regard. My contribution to the volume devoted to her cultural activism, therefore, epitomises this particular aspiration of hers to place the care and management of the Asanteman Children's Park under the royal patronage of the Asantehene, Nana Otumfuo Opoku Ware II.

SPACE AND ARCHITECTURE: A POINT OF INTEREST FOR EFUA SUTHERLAND

An exposition on the subject 'Architecture: spatial deployment for community experience' in a volume encompassing the work of a personality such as Efua T. Sutherland, a distinguished literary scholar and an accomplished dramatist/poet, is not inappropriate. This subject, essentially dealing with social and community architecture, was very close to her heart.

As a profoundly creative person and at the same time, a strong social-cultural activist, she saw in architecture (a discipline she never formally studied), the potential to impact society, similar to what she found in her own chosen field of specialisation viz. drama and writing. As Patrick Nuttgens says in his introduction to his essay on 'The Nature of Architecture', for Efua Sutherland: 'Architecture is not just an activity or an event or collection of artifacts. It is not even simply an art. Architecture is fundamental to all human affairs; it stands at the very beginning of civilisation, for without it there would be no possibility of civilisation or culture' (Ben Farmer and Hentie Louw 1993:4).

The practice of comprising literature for dramatic performances certainly engages one's attention for architecture and architectural matters, due to the spatial, acoustic and visual elements amongst the parameters which one usually has to consider for management of stage performance of a piece. No doubt, a regular and persistent engagement of Efua T. Sutherland's attention in this regard as a playwright might have resulted in honing her sensibilities for the built-environment, and thus consequently causing some of her intellectual energies to be directed towards the field of architecture. Over and above that, her then-active involvement both as a client and advisor in the development of the now-razed Drama Studio in Accra could have initially sealed her deep interest in the subject (Refer Diagram Nos. 1 and 2).

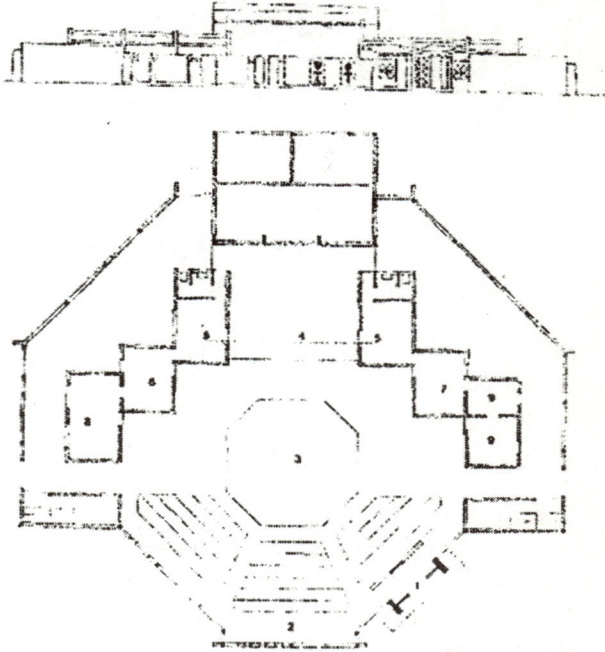

Diagram 1:
Elevation and Floor Plan of Old Drama Studio

Diagram 2:
Pictures of rebuilt Drama Studio, University of Ghana, Legon.

Piloted by these personal experiences and her own extensive observation, she might have probably discovered the fact that, indeed, architecture was fundamental to all human affairs and that it transcended the mundane provision of accommodation for human activities. The insight might have come to her that architecture, as a creative human activity, was naturally imbued, as it were, with an inbuilt capacity for sensitivity in enhancing the spirit of humankind. With this insight she passionately sought, as a lay-person, to challenge architects to release this tremendous potential of architecture to flow into their architectural designs.[2] Her conviction in this regard was seen to have been informed, consciously or unconsciously, by the fact of the notional affinity between architecture and space.

'Space', as a phenomenon, known also as 'void', is observable to be one of the basic endowments of the human as a created being and, for that matter, of all living creatures. It is provable that humans are biologically equipped with a sense of space and as Labelle Prussin expresses in her discussion of nomadic aesthetics, 'critical to our sense of emotional well being is the sense of space' (Labelle Prussin, 1993:190). This phenomenon of space, the Bible informs us, existed at the time of creation of humankind and was, in effect, the stage on which the drama of creation was performed (Book of Genesis, Chapter One, verse one). Since then, the spatial dimension of our existence on earth has been fundamental to our cultural development and advancement and the spatial influence has been pervasive in most human activities. As it were, we do subsist in 'Space' (Lewis Mumford 1961: 282).

The experience of this apparently imperceptible reality—space, described also as the 'charged void' (Paul Shepheard 1995: 63), impinges upon the human existence in the form of a continuum. It begins inside the uterus, during the phase of the foetal existence and extends far beyond into the universe which inhabits all the response-creating elements such as the environment, the atmosphere, the stratosphere, the biosphere and further on to the fringes of the continuum, known as 'outer space'. These two extreme ends of the space continuum appear to fall outside the field of human creative activity. Nevertheless, we have the instinctive capacity to experience what may be termed 'the biological space' while inside the uterus. In the universe at large, we are also endowed with the intellectual capacity to experience the 'cosmological space'. Between the biological space (finite) and the cosmological space (infinite), the individual does experience various categories of space. Some of these are: 'Conceptual space (the space we see or visualise), physical space (geometrically describable and measurable space), behavioural space (the space available for us after structural, circulation or other obstructive influences are accounted for)' (Ben Farmer and Hentie Louw, ibid: 333). These categories of space can either be notional, such as 'personal space', which exists only in the minds of individuals, or can be tangible, such as the 'architectural space', which is objective and sensuously perceivable.[3]

Architecture, as a matter of fact, is a tiny bite, with human teeth (energy – technology) and human taste (spirit – culture), into this awesome phenomenon of the space continuum, pursued with the attempt to enclose a bit of the charged void directly available to man (conditioning of space). In response to the complex factors associated with human needs, the mere conversion of a unit of the continuum into a useable space becomes, as Nuttgens observes, 'an expression of human experience' (Patrick Nuttgens 1993: 5) thus making the space-driven venture a cultural phenomenon.[4]

Indeed, the attempt of the human being to carve out a component from the continuum, (a habit, not exclusive to the human race),[5] has been manifested in all cultures and civilisations, as has been noted by art historians and other scholars (L. Prussin, ibid: xvi). In response to the challenge to relate to the immense physical space available, humans began to learn how to devise a means to use it 'as a prefabricated kit of parts with which to fracture and reset parcels of space instantly, as occasion demanded' (Herbert Muschamp 1974: 15). Since then, the habit has developed into a tradition of creative activity, invariably consisting of intuitive and rational endeavours to configure, modulate and articulate space to a human scale for the use and pleasure of humankind.[6]

In places where there has been a vigorous pursuit of these space-driven endeavours, the related creative activities have been associated with four significant issues: namely where to utilise space (location issue); how to utilise space (form issue); by what means to utilise space (materials issue); and why utilise space (meaning and purpose issue)? Addressing these issues in the various geographical and cultural milieus of the world has eventually led this creative spatial activity of man to evolve from a previous spontaneous, collective folk-action into the philosophy, art and science of shelter development, known by the nomenclature, 'architecture'. As a result of this genesis, space has remained *sine qua non* in architecture (Farmer and Louw, ibid: 359).

This characteristic feature of architecture, profoundly influenced Efua Sutherland in her understanding and appreciation of all works of architecture, be they those she simply admired as an informed observer or those she was directly connected with, owing to her vested interest in them as physical facilities. Therefore, she regarded architecture essentially as a spatial deployment, i.e. a careful and calculated, as well as a sensitive enclosure of a component of the God-given space continuum for a community experience. In her view, a human activity associated with the intention to utilise space, was almost an inviolable event, which should not be undertaken capriciously. This attitude of mind towards use of space is well expressed in an insightful letter she wrote in September, 1972, to the then Registrar of the University of Ghana to inform him of her decision to transfer her bona fide land title on the site of the demolished Drama Studio to the University. In this letter, she advocated the need for sensitivity towards the site, by writing: 'Kindly permit me to add that it has always been the aim to create an INSPIRING architectural presence on this important site in the capital, and that I hope the University will protect that ideal without compromise' (emphasis in original).

This profound perception of architecture by Efua Sutherland was given a strong hue by both her social-cultural activism and her artistic nature, which energised all her lifetime endeavours.[7] In this regard, action to deploy space began for her at the level of the megaspace – the socio-geographical context in which the spirit of the place (*genius loci*), i.e. the site and all that it embraced, could be clearly identified and empathised with.[8] Empathising with the site meant responding appropriately to how its utilisation was determined by, and made to fit, its location, together with its 'nature pre-existing hierarchies' (Ben Farmer and Hentie Louw, ibid: 83). Space thus enclosed should harmonise naturally with corresponding social activities, organized appropriately to express community need.

The resulting enclosures, consisting not only of brick and mortar but also of landscape, must be a distinct built-environment with a manifested aesthetic integrity. Consequently, Efua Sutherland thought of the creation of the built-environment for community experience, to be more than a bald spatial deployment. Creation of the built-environment must of necessity consist also in a spatial configuration, sensitively construed to respond positively to the sensibilities of the users who would participate in the related social activities.

The keen interest she had in architecture and spatial issues caused her to be a very responsive client and a well informed lay-critic of professional architects as observed by those who related to her on the projects in which they collaborated with her. Consequently, amongst practitioners who did not attempt to understand her untrained passion for architecture, she was regarded as a romanticist with poetic and simplistic architectural ideas and views which could not be subjected to rigorous application on construction sites.

Nonetheless, in her lifetime Efua Sutherland sustained her interest in contemporary Ghanaian architecture and furthermore expressed unabashed respect and admiration for a number of Ghanaian traditional architectural values as alluded to at times in some of her writings[9] and eloquently expressed occasionally in both her public statements and private conversations.[10] She esteemed these traditional architectural values because she experienced, in her life as an ordinary Ghanaian citizen as well as a professional playwright, traditional buildings which were imbued with the spatial integrity that supported and promoted a vibrant and a fulfilling community life.

She often referred to the Adinkra icon known as *fihankra* in her conversations to draw attention to the indigenous acknowledgement of the need for spatial integrity in Ghanaian traditional architecture. She alluded to this icon (see Diagram No.3), because for her, *fihankra* did not only mean 'the circular or complete house, signifying safety or security in a home' (Ablade Glover 1993), but she interpreted it to be an expression of an architecture that displayed integrity of spatial deployment for a wholesome community experience with both social and aesthetic dimensions.

Diagram 3:
Adinkra Icon, FIHANKRA

Indeed, Efua Sutherland's interest for the art and science of creating shelter might have been galvanised by her profound admiration for these spatial and social-aesthetic dimensions of traditional architecture. This mind-set prompted her acute social consciousness and her artistic nature to release an unrelenting personal fascination for harnessing and celebrating space for social activities and events for the purpose of community transformation and advancement. Guided by her intellectual inclinations as a literary scholar while pursuing this fascination of hers, her three loves – love for poetry, love for drama and love for children – blended into a composite impulse to inspire her to evolve a remarkable space-related educational concept in the eighties, when she served as the premiere Chairperson for the Ghana National Commission on Children.

Via this concept, spaces could be creatively deployed to function as community environmental nodes, and these, irrespective of their physical location in the country or geographical position in any human settlement in Ghana, were to create stimulating and informal physical milieus for integrating playing and learning, especially for children. The physical milieu was to provide facility for non-formal educational activities within a context of playing. Playing was emphasised because, as she opined in her paper for a seminar on writing and production of literature for children: 'Play in its purest connotation is a gift programmed into child existence…Playing is the child's natural means of exploring the human and natural environment of his existence, of learning how to exist with and within them, and for resolving the problems he encounters in the process'…(Efua T. Sutherland 1976: 3).

The concept materialised eventually into what she herself christened as the 'Park Library Complex', to become an essential component of the development programmes of the Commission (Wellington 1988: 4-7). The Park Library Complex (PLC) was officially designated as a 'resource centre that promotes guided child development and enables the child to explore and discover both (i) his inherent God-given qualities and creative abilities and (ii) his physical and social environments' (GNCC 1987: 11-24). The resulting projects which were thus executed to install the PLC facilities in some of the rural and urban communities, engaged her personal attention. She ensured that consultants and contractors associated with these projects had a firm commitment to the achievement of fine quality work in the structures they erected.

The developed Park Library Complexes, such as the Fontomfrom PLC at Kyekyewere, PLC at Gomoa Brofoyedru, the Asanteman Children's Park and the National Children's Park at the Ridge in Accra, began to beam with life as the Commission organised activities for children and other local community members began to utilise the facilities which had been provided. Besides the daily activities which took place at the various PLCs, such as reading at the literature resource centre, story telling and drama performance at the amphitheatre, creative work at the pavilions, and active playing with the cognitive-development play equipment, the Commission also organised national and regional events such as the mobile science workshops and the Head of State parties for children of all ages (refer to Diagram No. 4).

Diagram 4:
Pictures of the interiors of the Literature Resource Centre at the Asanteman children's park.

Notwithstanding the emerging positive impact of the PLCs on the action-oriented programmes of the Commission (M. Z. Majodina 1988: 2-3), an apparent change in policy with the departure of Efua Sutherland from the office of the Chairperson, got the focus of the Commission on employing the PLCs as a system by which 'programme-organisers can operate programme-packages to enrich the developmental horizons of the child for a fulfilling future' (Wellington 1988: 15) tragically blurred. With this changed corporate attitude, the Commission became less active in integrating the PLCs into its programmes and consequently divested itself of responsibility towards them.

The Park Library Complexes have, therefore, come under the management of local stakeholders, and some are functioning actively as community resource facilities with high popularity profile amongst both children and parents. In this capacity, they continue to demonstrate their merits as fine examples of social architecture, being both environmentally stimulating and socially germane architectural values which were close to the heart, and foremost in the mind of Efua Sutherland.

THE ASANTEMAN CHILDREN'S PARK: AN ARCHITECTURAL
INTERPRETATION OF A SPATIAL DREAM

One of such Park Library Complexes is the Asanteman Children's Park located in Kumasi. Having considered this particular PLC as a model one for further development of other PLCs, Efua T. Sutherland invested tremendous interest in its development and made herself a patron-saint for its evolution as an idea. This led to a close and stimulating collaboration between her and the architect for the project[11] while the Asanteman Children's Park Project was travelling through the gestation and project execution phases. The design of the Park, which, became a journey into and an exploration of the nuances of her ideas and ideals for spatial deployment for community, is consequently an expression of architectural interpretation of one of the spatial dreams Efua T. Sutherland cherished (see Diagram No. 5). The Amakom site, a disused city park, was selected by the GNCC for its locational properties and inherent *genius loci*. On the verge of the Kumasi Central Business District and next to a group of schools, surrounded by major residential enclaves, the site is safely and conveniently accessible to a large number of children with their families. The almost idyllic settings (a grove of a variety of mature exotic and local trees), created by a natural rolling topography with a spring and a well-landscaped environment, provided an ideal space to be deployed for such a community use as against its former function as a neglected and foreboding den for drug abusers and petty criminals.

Having defined the extent of the available space to be configured for the PLC facilities and fitted with a functional and aesthetically appropriate protection fencing system, a celebrated entrance, located on the highest point

Diagram 5:
Pictures of a section of the Asanteman children's park.

at the site, was conceived to equip the Park with a sense of place. Beyond this entrance, a serpentine circulation space takes visitors through the wooded sections to the various units, clustered into major activity zones, serving as multi-purpose hall (museum and art gallery), library-cum-story-telling/drama amphitheatre, cognitive play area, hands-on work pavilion and arboretum.

The cluster of multi-purpose hall and library-cum-story-telling/drama amphitheatre has been configured into an irregular geometric form in natural terra- cotta colours. The entrance to this cluster is articulated with a statue of a nursing Ghanaian mother, breast-feeding her baby in a typical traditional manner. This affectionate concrete statue draws the child-visitor into the recesses of the cluster with its variety of interior spaces, modulated to affect the user's cognitive and imaginative abilities. This has been achieved by means of applying textures and elements of *Adinkra* symbolism, together with subtle colours on the floors and walls. To emphasise a 'caring environment' (Appleyard 1979: 275), a detailing system has been integrated into the space articulation media. This system consists of a filigree of both wooden and mild-steel security arrangements, depicting floral forms, geometrical shapes and traditional *Adinkra* symbols, placed on window and door openings (see Diagram No. 6).

Diagram 6:
Picture of Performing Court and Library, Asanteman Children's Park

The cognitive play-equipment (almost in ruins now due to neglect) was set up in a landscaped space, enveloped by the surrounding verdant and salubrious park environment. In juxtaposition to this space is the octagonal-shaped pavilion, conceived as a mother's kitchen and erected in brick and roofed with green alu-chromed aluminium sheets to serve as a facility for hands-on creative activities (see Diagram No. 7).

Diagram 7:
Picture of the Work/Play Pavilion, Asanteman Children's Park

In addition to the employment of the aforementioned detailing system to complement the space articulation, the interior of the pavilion has been dramatised by an encircling belt of inscribed *Adinkra* symbols bas-relief plinth, together with a spider-like form imprint in the finished washed terrazzo floor slab. As a counter-point to this spatial effect created at the lower visual level, the web-like roof structure is exposed at the ceiling level to offer the child-user, who enters the pavilion's arched doorway, the opportunity to exercise the imagination to see the mythical 'Ananse', the spiderman, ascending the roof from his position in the floor imprint.

All the architectural entities which configure to provide the required facilities for the Park, nestle in a floral milieu that consists of vegetal species such as cassia auriahfomis, terminalia catapa and flowering shrubs such as jasmine and lady of the night. This milieu thus creates a reposeful and tranquil effect within the Park, to attract other visitors, other than the children and their parents, questing for rest and solitude, especially at weekends (see Diagram No. 8).

Diagram 8:
Picture of a statue of a mother breastfeeding her child, Asanteman Children's Park.

Notwithstanding its abrogation from the list of legacies bequeathed to the GNCC, the Asanteman Children's Park, is certainly an excellent example of a 'conditioned space', and as has been discussed, it is potently functioning as a popular community environmental node. As such, it demonstrates distinct social-architectural values which happily coincide with Efua T. Sutherland's dream of a spatial deployment that brings the community to experience a purposeful and a profitable environment.

In this vein, the Park, together with the other Park Library Complexes located in some Ghanaian rural and urban communities, will continue, insofar as they remain under proper care and good maintenance, to be virtual realities of her ideas and ideals of space. As such, unobtrusively the PLCs do serve as one of the prominent contemporary beacons of orientation for thought and practice in the field of architecture in Ghana. By this fact, it can be asserted that the spatial dreams of Efua T. Sutherland have indirectly become a legacy for the architectural profession in Ghana.

Furthermore, the design philosophy, together with the architectural theoretical considerations that underpin the development of the Park Library Complexes, may continue to wield a strong influence on the training of future generations of Ghanaian architects, while the Park Library Complex concept remains popular with students of the Kwame Nkrumah University of Science and Technology School of Architecture in the course of their studies. In this light, such a seminal contribution from a non-architectural mind that has become a landmark in architectural education as well as child-development studies in Ghana, will forever be treasured and highly appreciated.

Vivian Windley

Pan-African Partnership on Children's Literature: Reminiscences of a Diaspora Educator

It's been more than thirty years since my first visit to Ghana. My interest in Africa had begun many years before as a fantasy woven during my early childhood. But I wanted my experience to be more than a visit to Africa for two or three weeks as a tourist. I wanted to live, interact with the people, and immerse myself in African culture. In 1974, on my first sabbatical leave from the City College of New York, my dream finally came to be a reality. It was not so common to visit Africa in 1974 as now, when thousands of tourists descend upon Accra and the other tourist sites. Even though I would later learn of African-Americans who had emigrated to Ghana soon after Independence in 1957, Africa was in 1974 still uncharted territory for a visitor interested in acquainting herself with the people and culture.

For the next 30 years, I would return to Ghana for 6 months to a year, each time trying to get a glimpse into a culture steeped in tradition while also taking on various educational assignments: (1) teaching at the University of Ghana as Affiliate Visiting Scholar in the Institute of African Studies; (2) guest lecturing, conducting workshops at teacher training colleges, and producing a seven-part radio interview series on education for teachers throughout the country; (3) conducting a research project in the village of Apirede; (4) travelling to different areas of the country; and (5) most important, having passionate dialogue and observations of Efua Sutherland's work with children in the field of children's literature, the building of Park Library Complexes and a 'House of Stories'.

My focus in this article is the contribution of children's literature to the child's natural development of the arts of language: listening, speaking, reading and writing. This account, in part a memoir of our very special friendship, will be interwoven with the work of Efua Sutherland and her contributions to children.

My acquaintance with Efua Sutherland arose from my admiration of this brilliant, regal woman whom I came to know at the Institute for African Studies at the University of Ghana, Legon. Her attention to and respect for me were stimulated by accounts of my involvement in the adoption of the John Teye Memorial Institute, located just outside Accra, by a group of African-American educators with which I was actively involved, known as the African-American Educational Associates. Learning of my teaching experience as professor of

Children's Literature at the City College of New York and authorship in the Houghton Mifflin Publishers' Reading Programme, Efua Sutherland recognised that we had much in common. Over a period of years, our acquaintance became strengthened by mutual professional respect and admiration, developing into a loving friendship between 'sisters'.

EFUA SUTHERLAND'S CONTRIBUTION TO GHANAIAN CHILDREN'S WORLD OF LITERATURE

Efua and I spent long hours in conversation about her work with children during my visits to Ghana and on her visits to New York. Her eyes would light up and she would become highly animated with excitement as she talked about her plans for children. Her discussion was always intellectually succinct, lucid and direct. As the Fantes say, her 'language flowed like water'. Always a teacher at heart, she knew that books for children do more than entertain them. Her special mission was to work for the development of all the arts of language: listening, speaking or oral language, reading and writing, in addition to drama. She told me about her efforts in starting the Writers' Society to encourage people to write for children.

BOOKS FOR CHILDREN TO ENRICH LANGUAGE DEVELOPMENT

'Libraries are not just the province of cities,' Efua told me, 'I want every child, children in small remote villages throughout the country to have access to books and experience the joy of reading.' And to this end, as founding Chairperson of the National Commission on Children, she set out to accomplish this goal. Among its programmes was a Child Literacy programme as well as the building of park and library complexes for children throughout the country. The commission's office was located on the periphery of one of the park spaces that Efua had worked to have set aside for children. Our children, she said, need beautiful parks in which to play. Perhaps her idea of parks was sparked by her book, *Playtime in Africa*, which combined photographs and text to show children happily engaged in wonderful play activities. Although Efua's plan to develop a park as she had envisioned it, unfortunately, never materialised, this park in Accra was posthumously named in her honour.

Efua told me about the Children's Park-Library Complexes in Accra, Kumasi, Gomoa Assin and Kyekyewere. When I returned home, I solicited the help of Rev. Calvin Butts, pastor of the renowned Abyssinian Baptist Church in Harlem, New York, and members of the African-American Educational Associates. Rev. Butts asked each of his parishioners to purchase and donate a book. AAEA members also made contributions. Two critical considerations were brought to our attention by Una Mulzac, owner of the Liberation

Bookstore in Harlem, who, though knowledgeable about children's books, needed help in categorising the books according to ages and developmental stages. We found AAEA members who were teachers at various grade levels, one librarian, and one professor of Children's Literature. First, this committee wanted to make sure that the books represented a balanced choice that included (1) works by outstanding authors and illustrators, e.g. Leo and Diane Dillon, Tom Feelings, Eloise Greenfield, Virginia Hamilton, or Maurice Sendak; and (2) a representative sampling of recipients of children's literature awards such as the Caldecott, Newbery, Coretta Scott King, and Carter G. Woodson awards. Further, we wanted to make sure that the books were categorised, labelled and boxed according to the ages and stages of children's development:

Preschool and Kindergarten, ages 3, 4, and 5: Rhyming books, nonsense books, finger play, picture books with and without words, participation books, story books about pets, playthings, home and immediate environment, everyday experiences, imaginative play, books to be read aloud.

Primary, ages 6 and 7: Books for continued expansion of language, wordless books and folk tales that encourage storytelling, information books; books about the child's own world; poetry and play on words, books about concepts of time, fantasy, humour, poetic justice and gender differences.

Middle Elementary, ages 8 and 9: Books to be read on one's own, peer group acceptance, development of empathy, tall tales, folk tales, adventure, slapstick humour, problem solving books, 'how to' books, puzzles, books about sports and games, books on collecting, series books, poetry-alliteration, onamatopoiea.

Later Elementary, ages 10 and 11: Books on sex and gender differences, family life, siblings, career books, biographies, myths, fables, hobbies, adventure, science fiction, mysteries, prose and poetry.

Middle School, ages 12, 13, and 14: Books that give insight into feelings, friends and family, insights into self, mysteries, adventure, biographies, science fiction, sports, metaphor, imagery and more complex stories.

High School, ages 15-18: books on careers, competitive sports, discovering the self, novels, realistic and non-realistic fiction, high adventure, biographies, peer relationships, more complex stories.

On my return trip to Ghana, Efua was brimming over with delight. She had received the books and invited me to join her on one of her visits to some of the libraries. 'The children would love to have you read to them,' she assured me.

Our first trip was to the Gomoa Assin Park Library Complex, about an hour's drive from Accra in a very small village situated in the hills commanding a breathtaking view. This aesthetically beautiful library was designed by Efua's son

Ralph, an architect, who, like his mother, was sensitive to the beauty of the natural environment. His design was an extension of the landscape. The park library complex was built and landscaped by National Service personnel. They literally carved the complex out of an expanse of lush green tree-covered rolling hills. Huge, twelve-foot-high boulders stood adjacent to the library. As you walked along the walkway, there were arbours, flowering plants and patterns of blocks and green grass to enjoy. 'Some of these children live in dismal conditions. I want them to be exposed to beauty,' Efua said. She proudly pointed out the books that were donated by the Abyssinian Baptist Church and African-American Educational Associates. I talked and read to children and a few parents who were there. With an air of excitement, they told me how happy and proud they were to have this library and asked me to thank the people in New York.

Sometime later Efua took me to see the park library complex at Kyekyewere, located much closer to Accra. The physical setting was less aesthetically exciting than Gomoa Assin, but the complex was larger and there was much more activity with adults working with older children and books in a more structured, interactive group and individual approach to reading. Some children were engaged in creative writing. They wrote their own stories and illustrated them. Efua was very pleased with the integration of reading, writing, and art. She reminded me of her earlier effort in 1957, when she started the Writers' Society to get more people interested in writing primarily for children.

Efua was convinced that children should be encouraged to write their own stories and poetry at an early age. Much earlier on, Efua had been disturbed about a problem very common in Anglophone African countries. Children's books used in the schools were about English history. Illustrations in those books depicted English children, their families and experiences. This was a very serious matter that Efua was determined to correct. To this end, she set up Afram Publications in Accra, for the publication of children's books written and published in Ghana. These books would mirror the life, experiences, and culture of Ghanaian children. In 1992, the concept of a foundation, *Mmofra* (children), dedicated to Ghana's children was founded by Efua to plan programmes to support children's social, cultural, artistic and educational growth. Her focus was always on children.

STORYTELLING AS A COMMUNITY EXPERIENCE

Recognising storytelling as a vehicle for passing on the history and culture of a people, Efua saw the natural transition of the oral tradition to the written tradition. She insisted that I should see the 'House of Stories' which she had built in the village of Atwia, about 78 miles from Accra in the Ekumfi traditional state. This was one of her greatest contributions to the development of children's language – storytelling in the oral tradition.

The village of Atwia was unique in two very special ways. First, the Chief, Nana Okoampah VI, was a dynamo of a woman – a very energetic and forceful person, who commanded respect and admiration from those who knew her as Chief of Atwia and as an accomplished story-teller. And leave it to Efua to find such a woman, the Chief of the village, where she would build her 'House of Stories'! Second, I think it is safe to say that Atwia has the only 'House of Stories' of its kind in Ghana, or perhaps the world. Efua used part of a Research Grant from the Ford Foundation to build this cultural edifice – an impressive open structure constructed in the round in an African traditional style. The design was a collaborative effort between Efua and Willis Bell, an exceptionally talented photographer and builder, but the entire community contributed to the labour. The 'House of Stories' sits in the centre of the village as a monument to the distinctive story-telling tradition of Ghana, which the Atwia community practises with extraordinary skill. It is a monument, moreover, to the insight of one woman, Efua Sutherland, and the cultural heritage of Ghana generally. The 'House of Stories', called *Kodzidan* in the Fante language, functions as a community meeting place, a forum for adults, a stage for performances of local indigenous dramas, storytelling and a venue where children gather to listen to the creatively distilled wisdom that adults eloquently transmit in their performances. An Akan proverb says:

It is through other people's wisdom that we learn wisdom ourselves; a single person's understanding does not amount to anything.

Efua's account of her motivation for building the 'House of Stories' was typical of her. She was not content, she said, to record the results of her research in papers to be shelved in academic libraries. No! Atwia would not become another statistic! Her research project would be a tangible contribution to improve the quality of village life and raise the level of 'cultural consciousness' for the sake of posterity. Indeed, she would leave Atwia all the better for her having been there. As an advocate for children, Efua's mission was to preserve Ghanaian culture in the oral tradition of storytelling and to help children come to appreciate that culture.

EFUA SUTHERLAND, PAN-AFRICAN CULTURAL NATIONALIST

Efua Sutherland, who loved Ghana, was a 'cultural nationalist' to the core. In the spirit of what Nkrumah called the 'African Personality', its cultural base was the heart, soul and psyche of Ghanaians: their languages, their traditional music, drama and folklore, arts and crafts, their poetry, their customary practices and even their dress. Chinua Achebe writes that 'Africa is not only a geographical landscape – it is in fact a view of the world, and of the whole cosmos perceived from a particular position.' This position, as Efua Sutherland saw it, is inscribed in the Ghanaian belief system, their way of viewing the world, made visible in the aesthetic expression of the Ghanaian's everyday life. This is a position that Efua spent her lifetime trying to preserve and pass on to posterity. She saw traditional theatre as LIFE in the oral tradition.

Efua Sutherland's Ghanaian cultural nationalism was expressed through the environment she created in her home as well as through her love for her country's natural environment. The interior of Araba Mansa was decorated with African artifacts: wall hangings, paintings, sculpture, Akuaba Dolls, many white Asante stools, and Ghanaian-made furniture. I told Efua T. that I was often surprised and disappointed that I saw little African art in Ghanaian homes. Her response was that it saddened her to see a lack of appreciation for things 'African', even in dress, for many young people who had adopted western-style attire. We are losing our cultural heritage. On one occasion when we were in Cape Coast, Efua T. said, 'There is a very special scene that I want you to see, my sister.' It was just at sunset as we headed for the ocean. She pointed out scores of fishermen singing and hauling in their nets filled with their catch to the rhythm of their songs. What a beautiful sight and Efua T, the artist, wanted me to see nature's painting!

Conscious of the importance of the Arts in society, she told me of the movement she initiated to preserve those Arts. In 1961 she founded the Ghana Drama Studio. It was in 1975 that I saw my first performance of *The Marriage of Anansewa*. I was impressed by the massive structure of an Asante Stool motif as I entered. The Studio was somewhat modern in design but the open courtyard reflected African architecture. At the entrance was an Akuaba Doll and an *Adinkra* design, *Mate, Masie* meaning 'What I hear, I contain'. The Drama Studio presented Efua's traditional dramas as well as plays written by contemporary African playwrights. Sitting in this open-air theatre I was reminded that here was a woman who was preserving and passing on Ghana's oral tradition to posterity.

But Efua Sutherland was not content. 'It is not enough to present traditional theatre in Accra. We had to find a way to bring traditional theatre to Ghanaians around the country,' Efua said. In fulfilment of this dream, Efua founded the Kusum Agoromba players in 1968, a tremendous undertaking. *Kusum* means 'the right cultural thing to do', *Agoromba* means 'players'. Efua had conceived the right cultural idea and these players were doing the right cultural thing. They travelled around the country performing traditional works in traditional languages thus preserving traditional Ghanaian culture. Kusum Agoromba was based at the Drama Studio. The Akuaba dolls which represent creativity were the symbols for the players.

Many years later, the Drama Studio was demolished to make way for the construction of a Chinese-built National Theatre on the site of *her* Drama

Studio. A version of the original Drama Studio was built at the University. When asked about her feelings about the demolition of the Drama Studio, which she founded in Accra, she said, 'My sister, remember the Bible verse, "And Mary kept all these things in her heart".' That was the introspective, private Efua Sutherland that I soon came to know.

I remember Efua T.'s visits with me in New York City. One of the very first places Efua T. suggested we go was the Abyssinian Baptist Church. She wanted to say hello to Rev. Calvin Butts and thank him and his parishioners for their contribution of books to her libraries. She loved to hear Spirituals, the soul-inspiring music of the Black church. She would close her eyes, sway to the music, and sometimes grasp and squeeze my hand. She once remarked that she was convinced that the soul-inspiring music of the Black Church evolved from an oral tradition in song, from the depths of the soul, as a result of the pain and suffering of the Black American slave experience. She would never miss an opportunity to buy books, tapes and CDs of the music of Marian Anderson, Roland Hayes, Paul Robeson, and Mahalia Jackson (a favourite). Similarly, she appreciated the harmonious music of the Black South Africans developed as a result of their Apartheid experience.

In 1991 the University of Ghana awarded Efua Sutherland an Honorary Doctorate in acknowledgement of her contributions to Ghana. The citation read:

To Efua Theodora Sutherland, for the inspiration provided to the development of the Dramatic Art, and in recognition of your efforts on behalf of children for whose benefit you have canvassed children's libraries and amusement parks, the University of Ghana is privileged to honour you with the degree of Doctor of Laws, *honoria causa*.

But Efua's response to this recognition was typical of her 'bigness of spirit'. She invited me and close friends to a special programme at Akuafo Hall Chapel that she planned for the dedication of the Honorary Degree of Doctor of Laws conferred by the University of Ghana.

The dedication read:

TO MY PROFESSIONAL COMMUNITY OF ARTISTS, SCHOLARS, DONORS, ADMINISTRATORS who, for 34 years (1958 to date) have shared with me in a spirit of GOODWILL, the aspirations and burdens of the tasks undertaken for the development and promotion of DRAMATIC ART as an essential Medium of Communication in GHANA. TO MY PERSONAL FAMILY AND FRIENDS at home and abroad whose love, trust and faith, whose beautiful concern and care have sustained me.

As an African-American woman, I am happy to share these cherished memories of Efua Sutherland, the cultural nationalist, the prolific playwright and poet, the dramatist, a professional colleague, my 'sister' AND an advocate for children. She viewed the world through the eyes of an artist. Her contributions were unique GIFTS to Ghana, Africa, and the world at large.

Femi Osofisan

'There's a Lot of Strength in Our People': Efua Sutherland's Last Interview

On October 10, 1995 exactly, that date made forever famous now by the fate of my dear compatriot, Ken Saro-Wiwa, I was in the living-room of Auntie Efua. With me was Kofi Anyidoho. I had come to talk to Auntie, as part of my field research for the play I was writing about Dr. Du Bois, specifically about the final days of that great man in Ghana. While we waited for Auntie to be woken up from her convalescent bed, the news suddenly came, a bolt of lightning, on the radio, telling of the hanging that morning of Saro-Wiwa and his fellow Ogoni activists. The news changed the atmosphere at once. Initial disbelief, then astonishment, then indignation, then grief, then despair – all these feelings rushed though us in rapid succession. [Later, I was to pass men and women weeping openly on the streets as we drove back.] But Auntie emerged, and after a brief moment, rallied us to surmount our crushing sense of hopelessness, of devastation.

Her laughter, her warm hospitality as she fed me her select dishes, and above all, her unwavering optimism gradually washed over me like a balm. And so we talked – to forget, to kill sorrow by the sharing of aspirations, to invite the process of consolation, of healing…

And the interview that followed, spiced so richly with her African sense of caring, and of generosity, is a testimony to the incredible resilience and courage of this great daughter of Africa, virtues which however she insisted belonged to all of us as members of the race.

Now Auntie Efua is no longer with us. By the time I returned to Accra a few months later, the following year, she had left. But because of her voice – oh so sparkling – on my tape, I shall not cry. Because it tells me that she has not really died, that she has only mounted the rafters like our other venerable ancestors, and so will always be with us.

I have edited the interview rather heavily, to hoard to myself those portions which rightly belong only to me. But the following words are a gift she left behind, preciously, and which I am proud to share with you…

FO – Dr. Du Bois wrote of you, when you were in China…

ES – I was never in China. Russia…I went to the Soviet Union for the 21st Afro-Asian Conference of Writers…I'd just started the Ghana Society of Writers in 1957, that year of Independence, and then up came the notice of this conference. So they asked me to go…

FO – Dr. Du Bois…

ES – There were people who were very close to him, like Col Deborah, and I'm happy you've spoken with her. It was…I was closer to him on the day he died. When we heard about his death, you know…I was with Maya Angelou[1].

And…er, there was a march on Washington that day, wasn't there?

FO – Yes.[2]

ES – Yes, that's right. And I remember going to the house immediately…And, er, the day of the funeral, I just wasn't at all…I was…That was the first day I heard about 'undertakers' in Ghana. It doesn't take… I mean, the whole idea of this man being taken care of by undertakers…I just – no,no,no,no! I went to where they were preparing his lying-in-state place, the pavilion where he's buried now…it used to be a summer hut…that's where they laid him in state. I just took all the…I ripped off those sheets and dressed him myself.

FO –Why? So it doesn't become an impersonal thing?

ES – Yes! A woman's hand had to touch it, you know. I was in a pretty spiritual state that day…I mean, if we have a Du Bois here, and we are laying him in state, we should still do the cultural…Look, I find that the nation-state of Africa is doing everything to make us lose weight as a people. There's no amplitude, you know, they keep dehydrating us… And that occasion was one occasion when I really felt that the personal touch…you know, this is his home, and the women of Ghana should be around that body. I get quite emotional about these things. Anyway I'm happy that we have put him in that place. And I just love it that my son was one of the designers of the tomb. My son Ralph and his friend, whose mother is also an Afro-American. That was very meaningful.

FO – Do you think Dr. Du Bois had any impact at all on Ghanaians? I mean, he was really old, when he came here…

ES – And he didn't circulate among the generality of Ghanaians, not even the academia…

FO – But he was given Legon's first honorary degree…

ES – Yes, he was. Of course. Like we should give honorary degrees to all these greats who cared about who we are and our historical past.

FO – Had you heard of him before he came here?

ES – Oh yes…

FO – But I don't suppose many Ghanaians did…

ES – No. In fact, the other day I was reading about this conference in Manchester[3] and I said – When is all this going to get into the books our young generations read in schools?...I wanted to see Ngugi when he came here but unfortunately I was travelling at the time. But I would like Ngugi, all these first-rank writers of the immediate post-Independence era, I'd like to see them demanding that all the literature that they have tried to develop for Africa, it should get into the school system. There should be this transmission line, we're very poor at it…The African nation-state is very poor about its transmission responsibilities…

FO – No sense of history…?

ES – Is that it? Is it no sense of history or what? What is it? What is it that makes us so negative?

FO – I was thinking that maybe it's because the generation which succeeded Nkrumah's just lacked this kind of vision … They had…they were soldiers, without his kind of training, his educational background, the experience...

ES – Well, we have to come to grips with the necessity of transmission…Somebody was here the other day, and we were talking about this issue. He is in the Commission for Culture. And I was saying to him that every year, still, the African society that has lived the cultural life, you know, all these years, despite all…every year they take care of their transmission, holding their festivals at least, transmitting history live. All the younger generations, from about the age of five, up to the youths, you know and so on, they see, they hear, they FEEL their history…every year, without fail. I didn't get around to asking – what do we do? – for example. I mean, I would say that very modern African state…every independence anniversary day should be so considered, as the occasion to enable us to do this kind of transmission. But what happens? You go there, and it's some parade, you know…

FO – A military parade...

ES – Just some parade, marching, you know…When it comes to the point where we feel about these national anniversaries the way we feel about our ethnic festivals, then we will be making progress. When somebody has reared a sheep, so that the whole group can come in togetherness and eat that sheep, that day… But now, they're not enabling us to feel this anniversary thing in our homes. And a Commission on Culture has a role in evolving that. But they're too busy fighting for positions...

FO – Well, I'd like to ask whether you think that the Afro-Americans could play any role in this kind of consciousness that is lacking now?

ES – They certainly can. But we've got to create a framework within which they can relate with us, in order to make that contribution. I was thinking of PANAFEST in those terms. For it's a very wonderful opportunity…we're getting together because we want to, because we have a sense of our history, and know that the greatest thing that happened to us was this interruption of our natural evolution, you understand? Once you understand what was the nature of the interruption, what it did for you; for instance, making you lose your self-confidence, a whole people losing their self-confidence…and it has to be regained, for us to go anywhere, you know. So we need to talk among ourselves, and feed our strengths. PANAFEST is about our strengths, our excellences. And when we get together, we say, 'Oh look at what they did', and despite all this suffering, 'Look at what we attained', you know. We need that achievement; we can use it to move forward, to move on. So it's reconnecting with our strength, our evolution. But people are not looking at these things. We are too busy looking at all sorts of things, talking about development which we have not really defined. Development in what? Roads and so on? My goodness, anything you can sign a cheque for is not development. We need to get together, think about it. And there are people who are ready for this kind of dialogue. But where's the framework for convening us? And that's what Du Bois and others were about all the time. They were looking at our strengths, you see what I mean?

FO – Quite a lot of them, of African-Americans, came during that time?

ES – Yes, a lot of them came over, because they could sense that we were building up some strength here. It was during that time that they were also able to move forward here. You understand? Because something strong was happening in Africa. And they need the strength here in order to build up the strength there. So I'm not surprised that they came. We were asserting ourselves.

FO – So what would you say they achieved, when they came?

ES – Well…they were not here long enough.

FO – Why did they leave?

ES – They left because, you know, we ourselves set ourselves back. You know, we overthrew our government and started the whole process of making people doubt… making people discomfited so they couldn't really stay.

FO – Those who took over, I hear they burnt down the Padmore library…

ES – They did…. Nkrumah himself had a library. They also burnt it down. It was a library that was painstakingly collected with the assistance of various people around the world, to assist development thinking…

FO – So, that disconnected…

ES –It's always discontinuities…There's this syndrome of discontinuity in our developmental efforts. We're not developing, I tell you. We're wasting developmental time and the human resources we have. It's the most tragic thing we're doing. So when we get around to this realisation in a manner that will make us sit up…look, you're getting me to talk…

FO – But it's good to hear you talk! And it's this kind of talk that we need, because we hear too much of the negative talk all the time…

ES – Oh everything is set to go. We have the people, there's been fantastic effort, you know. We're wasting it. There are a lot of people sitting around, even here in Ghana, who have all kinds of experience in different kinds of institutions. They're around, some of them now at an age where they are mature, really mature, and they're sitting around, nobody is using them…

FO – Is that because they're unknown?

ES – Oh they are known, they're known! But maybe because the focus is not there, on what they represent.

FO – This is why I'm really bothered, because it looks like the awareness of the need to do something is still very much in the Diaspora, and yet here, we seem to have gone into slumber. So I'm wondering if this is the kind of thing we ought to try to promote; that is, to try and get them more interested in us, and we more interested in them, so that through these connections, some kind of cross-fertilisation can…?

ES – It's a necessity...it's a necessity! Now when I was thinking of PANAFEST I said, we need some powerful symbolisms, new telling symbolisms... See, the castle, the fort, has always been there, and people don't know what to do with it, except clean it for tourists. But that's a powerful symbolism, you cannot just slumber around that edifice. It's done something to us, you know...and it occurred to me that the particular one in Cape Coast represents both the slave trading and the colonialism. It was there that the entity 'Ghana', the bond of 1884 and so on...all of that was signed there, in that castle... People lived there, in that castle. That used to be the headquarters of the colonial government. And I said, okay, the Afro-Americans will come and use the place better than we do. They'll bring a certain inspiriting approach which we need, you know, around that symbolism. Because we can't go to sleep on that nasty history. That amnesia is unacceptable. So if we can gather around, have a communication system that tells us – you know, say through the theatre – that helps to wake us up to the past, even if we reject that past. There are also people, creative minds, who can do the drama, wake all of us up, not just a few people. Waking us up for what? To get up and get on with continuing our natural evolution, you see. It won't do the way we are, it just won't do. All this talk about marginalisation and so on. They call us Third World; we say, 'Yes, we too call ourselves Third World.' Other people [are] always deciding our identity for us.' And the greats are not around to stop this nonsense. Du Bois and all, they are not around, those who understand.

FO – So what do you see, then, as a solution?

ES – The solution is you, me...we're to awake our people. Awake people, not just talk about the problems. Writers get up and make African governments transmit your writings through the school system, so that the sensibilities you try to deal with are transmitted to young people. We can make them sit down. Let's do it, let's get it together and do it! You see, this thing called Oral literature; boy, all that we...our intellectualism and so on is so embedded in it. Yet we're not using it in the schools. We will sit there, until generations come who don't even know what it's about. Yes, we allow a few scholars to sort of do it, you know, for scholarly reasons, but it's got to be an absolute programme, of a very serious nature, to get it collected, now. And the writers must take that responsibility, and package it for use in the schools. All sorts of things that we can do. And I think people, individuals, have become major writers, et cetera. They've built their career, but now, what can we do *as a body*? Er, can we bind together and participate in this other movement, this independence movement?

FO –You see any possibility of this?

ES –What's PAWA⁴ doing? For instance, if that body exists, shouldn't it be a channel?

FO – Oh, undoubtedly PAWA should be a very good way to do it. But in fact PAWA has no power! The problem is that, like with many such organisations, there's no backing, no cash, and no financial strength to pursue any of these projects we've mapped out. Our governments don't spend money on such things...

ES – But have we leaned too much perhaps on getting supported by governments?

FO – Well, the private sector doesn't support the Arts either. So where else can we turn?

ES – Maybe we all ought to get together and really think – what's it that we need? For instance, the business of collecting the oral literature; what kind of assistance do we need for it?

FO – Well, quite a lot of people seem to be doing that nowadays...

ES – And when they collect, what happens? All these collections, are they not just sitting around? So what's the next step? And what do we do for that?

FO – Don't we come back to the question of finance? I mean, to get them published and disseminated...

ES – You do...

FO – What you were doing with the Drama Studio, for instance, was very good, but it has stopped...

ES – Well, I call it...some foolish understanding of what we need to do. That kind of development venture, there's no such thing now in Ghana. The Drama Studio was there to help find out, and work with, and experiment towards new creations. But they didn't look at that. So we have a National Theatre there now that's just...I mean, that's not a place for experimentation, though I haven't really ever been inside it. But I can't do *The Marriage of Anansewa* in that theatre, as we could in the Drama Studio, very beautifully. Not there! I can't do *Edufa* there...But they didn't think of all that at all...Somebody came and said I'll give you a loan to build a big theatre... But I'm sure, when the artists want to do something again, they'll develop their own theatre. I can see that happening in the future. Because this one won't allow developmental thinking...it's a monument.

FO – But are you not worried, that you began something so good, so dynamic and creative, and that it just stopped like that?

ES – No, it won't get lost. You believe it's a good thing, and so many other people also think so. So it won't get lost. After the 25th anniversary of the Studio, I was using it as a transition, where you know, you go out to the district level and take all the experience of the Drama Studio work, and you lay it there. That was the next step. So I had a play producers' seminar within the anniversary programme, where those people who had been producing plays were being got ready to go and do this work.

FO – But they never went?

ES – No. Because it was during the time of the anniversary programme – I had a year long anniversary programme. It was during that time that they started to get going on that building...and the real story behind it all is so silly...

FO – Silly?

ES – It was just the flaunting of power. The site that they actually chose for the theatre is still there. But there were some people living in the buildings that had to be pulled down there. So they just got up and said, 'No, not here. Go and pull that one down.' And it happened all of a sudden, arbitrarily...!

FO – Even though your anniversary was on?

ES – No, they didn't do it until the anniversary was over. They did it in 1988 or 89. The anniversary was 86, 87. But they started talking about the project during the anniversary. And very arbitrarily, they just...They didn't discuss anything with the university...the studio! You could see, during the anniversary, that the whole Drama Studio thing had developed, with all different kinds of...All of these people, and people from the villages and so on, they were all together as one family in the Studio for the anniversary. Fantastic! On the night when we opened, you know, I had a programme called the Ceremony of Remembrance. Come and see the Drama Studio! It was as if the spirits themselves...At midnight or one o'clock when I said, 'Well, let us...' They said, 'Madam, go where?' They said, 'We came here to do the cultural thing, and we are going to go on till day-break.' Fantastic! So I said, 'Okay, now everybody is together, we can now do a programme to put them all to good work throughout the country.' You see. But none of that was on the minds of the people who wanted a big structure...Did you see Ama Ata Aidoo's poem on the Drama Studio?[5]

FO – No, I'm sorry. But then, as I said, nothing seems to be going on nowadays...

ES – Nothing. Everybody is sort of sitting around...Some routine lectures on theatre, you know, now and then. There's not a single major play going on. The playwrights are not being developed any more. So we have to wait. If people like Kofi [Anyidoho], Mohammed Abdallah – I was working with all of them, we were together – if they could be allowed, and encouraged, to go on. They carry the seeds in them; they can do the work. But they are being wasted. Which brings me back to the point I made earlier: that people who are the human resources for development work are being wasted? And not only in this field, it's in many other fields unfortunately...

FO – Well, I'm sure this question must have been asked many times before, but do you see any real usefulness for the artist? I mean...you don't control power, and you have all these programmes, and they're just erased, nobody listens. In that sense, isn't the artist's work superfluous?

ES – But hasn't it always been so, that humanity has demonstrated its need again and again for the artist, and for artistic creation? It's indispensable, it will go on...

FO – But is it having any impact in the way the country is moving along? You can dream all the dreams you want to dream, but the rulers will...

ES – It's a passing phase, I'm sure of it! I mean, the individual hasn't got time to wait, you know. But the society itself does. I go to the village where I work, where I've been working quietly all these years, thirty years. And I see what has happened there. I feel that the development effort has been invested in people. People who were children when I was there are now young fathers and mothers. And see what has happened to them, they are now taking leadership roles there. When I first went there, it was in the interest of theatre development. But I saw something there, and I knew they would lose it if you didn't do something else. And I devoted myself to that something else…There's a young man there, for instance, whose father used to be a major cantor there in the *asafo* oral musical tradition, a paramilitary organisation. His father is a wonderful cantor. This young man, he's in the Ghanaian Fire Service now, and I still use him as a performer. And he's also one of the major story-tellers now…So that's why my interest was keen…to send people out, let them find these enclaves, you know. For most Ghanaian villages have rich storehouses of things for us to work with. Send them…budget on that…that was the Drama Studio's plan, to use this extension work to transmit experience at these other bases, you see. It works, because it's working in this village…

FO – But have you thought of carrying this to other places?

ES – I can't do it alone…no. I've always sort of carried people along with me in my work and …It takes a lot of effort you know, and dedication. I mean, the village is 70-something miles away from Accra, and there was a time when I was going there every week, and sometimes twice a week! But it will go on…

FO – So you're quite optimistic then about…

ES –Yes, quite optimistic! Our people are very…There's a lot of strength in our people.

PART III
REMINISCENCES AND TRIBUTES

Michael McMullan

'Tommy'
(Efua Sutherland)

I first met Efua in 1950, in the language laboratory of the School of Oriental and African Studies in London, where I was trying to learn Twi with a dozen other Colonial Service cadets. The laboratory was a series of small rooms in the basement, each with recording machines and headphones. The rooms were stuffy and it was dull sitting alone, talking to a machine. It was agreeable to be joined one morning by a beautiful and lively young woman. She – who went from room to room along the corridor making us all laugh and correcting our pronunciations – she was Miss Theodora Morgue and everyone called her 'Tommy'.

She had been in England for some years, first at the (Anglican) Convent at Whitby, Yorkshire, then at the Homerton Teachers' Training College, Cambridge. She had just finished her course there when I met her and was in London for a few months before going home. Ronald Wraith, (later author of a biography of Guiggesberg) and Peter Canham, a Gold Coast Administrative Officer, who were in charge of our course, both knew Efua – I soon learned that Efua knew nearly everybody – and thought that it would cheer up the process of learning to let her loose in the basement. She was a great success, though I fear it misled some of us into thinking that the Gold Coast was full of girls like Efua which, sadly, was not quite true.

She was very tall, very slim, very lively, and very attractive. She wore clothes that were unemphatically but distinctively Ghanaian: head cloth, a bodice or blouse, slim skirt to her ankles and, unless the weather forbade it, sandals. Occasionally at dances or parties she would dress up, but I don't think I ever saw her in European clothes, apart from gloves, raincoats and overcoats of course – I seem to recall the weather was rather bad that winter.

After classes we sometimes went in a group to a pub or tea shop. She had a bed-sitting room in a University Hostel somewhere in Bloomsbury and there she sometimes cooked groundnut stew on the gas ring. I had never eaten the dish before but have been very fond of it ever since. I remember a trip to Cambridge and lunch at my sister's there. Efua delighted my six-year-old nephew who had never met an African lady before. In the afternoon, we all went on the river in punt. Efua was not a very good punter; neither was my sister, but they were both confident of their abilities and it was a wonder we were not all drowned.

Efua gave me advice about how to behave in Ghana, about social life there, meeting people and avoiding offence. She gave me blunt and sensible warnings about the dangers for inexperienced young Englishmen of drink, the climate and disease. She even lectured me severely on undesirable female acquaintances. She knew a good deal about the lives of Europeans in Ghana and had many friends among them. She made the country and the people sound enormous fun, as indeed it turned out. This was a help, as we were all a little apprehensive at the time.

When the course was over, I was posted to Kumasi. Whether Efua had already left England by then, or whether she came on later I am not sure but I know that the next time I saw her was when she bounded into the District Commissioner's Office in Kumasi to see me. Part of her personality in those days was her physical and mental energy, her high spirits and her self-confidence. Her eyes were always shining, her talk animated and smiles and laughter accompanied her everywhere. She was, by then, on the staff of St. Monica's Teachers' Training College, Asante-Mampong. This was fitting, as most of the Twi I had learned at the SOAS was about going to or coming from Mampong, announcing that the Mampong people greeted you and enquiring if the Mamponghene was at home.

Efua was an old student of St. Monica's. It was a pleasant place. Numbers were small, many of the buildings were quite new and the grounds were pleasantly laid out with trees and gardens. I used to go over there for tea or supper and meet members of the staff and other friends of Efua. Father Martin, the chaplain, was often in her room. There was an alliance between him and Efua. I think he may have moderated the views of some of the older Sisters who found the newly returned Efua a bit of a handful. Efua in return was protective towards his rather other-worldly attitudes – such attitudes could get you into quite a bit of trouble in Mampong, or elsewhere.

I remember a party for *Homowo*, the Ga festival. We sat on her veranda and ate the special dish of baked corn with palmnut soup. This was not as good as groundnut stew but I was finding it all right till I asked about the pieces of meat in the stew, which were extraordinarily tough. She revealed they were snails...the great, black, forest snails. This, I am sorry to say, was too much for me, so she kindly gave me bread and cheese instead.

She introduced me to the Mamponghene. He greatly admired her. Indeed I suspected him of a plan to incorporate her into the stool property in some way. She was also on friendly terms with the District Commissioner, Arthur Elliot, and a favourite of his wife, Dorcas, who did some teaching at St. Monica's. Again, Efua was known and valued by all sorts of people.

She used to visit me in Kumasi and I remember driving with her down to Lake Bosumtwi for lunch at the Rest House there which, in those days, was the nearest thing to a tourist attraction in Ashanti, though there were, happily, no tourists. Kit Watling, an Australian Assistant DC at the Kumasi office, was with us. We ate groundnut stew. Efua loved singing particularly calypsos and we sang 'Brown Skin Girl', 'My Girl Left Me in November', 'Devaluation Gave Me a Pain' and others all the way back in the car. We also sang, then at other times, the soldiers' songs, 'When shall I See my Home' and 'Kumasi Bantama'. And another song I never heard from anyone but Efua, part of which went, though the words might not be quite right:

On the road to Lumley,
I met a bus conductor
He said I was a drunkard,
Drunkard! I am a free born and Freetown is my colony,
Everywhere I go, baby, palm wine they bring for me,
And other suitable and improving pieces.

The sequence of events is uncertain to me after this – I did not keep a proper diary. I was posted away from Kumasi and Efua did not remain very long at Mampong. I think she was still there when she visited me at Juaso, where I was stationed for sometime. She arrived by train at the little station and I recall it was the first time I saw her wearing sun-glasses, which was rather a sophisticated thing for a Ghanaian lady to do in those days and caused a good deal of chatter among the crowds hanging about the station. She admired the charming view from the bungalow, then we drove up to Agogo to see the view from the rest-house there, which was even better. I was reading for the Bar at the time and was due to go to Accra to take the paper in Roman Law. She seized the textbook and questioned me severely about the subject, bursting into laughter every now and again when something struck her as funny. It was a great help and gave me an idea of what she must have been like as a teacher.

Not long after she married Bill. I did not get to know him properly until I was posted to Accra but I met him first when I took local leave on the coast. I spent the day on the beach and in the evening had supper with Efua, Bill and friends of theirs. I cannot remember very much about it as, like so many foolish white men, I had been deceived by the cooling trade winds into exposing myself too long to the sun. By half-way through the meal, after a drink or two, I was feeling very strange indeed – and had to leave the party early to go to bed, where I was rather ill. Never say that skin colour doesn't matter. It was on this visit I first met Ralph, then only a few months old.

I saw them from time to time on visits to Accra or going to and from England. She was now very busy with the children and her many projects for the University, the theatre and for schools. It was not until I was posted to Accra, not long after independence, that I saw much of her again.

I was in the Ministry of Finance and Bill was Personal Assistant to the Minister, Kobla Gbedemah, so I got to know him well. They were living in a small house a little way out of Accra; friends of theirs were living in a caravan in the garden and the whole place had the air of an agreeable little camp. Efua was now in demand everywhere. One of her many inventions was the writers' circle, which usually met somewhere down on the seafront but sometimes at the University. Several Ghanaian writers started their careers there. The meeting I remember best was addressed by Camara Laye. He was a great figure at that time, internationally praised for his autobiography, *The Dark Child*, very much *le maitre* in the French style and magisterial towards his audience. After he had spoken through a translator there was a time for questions. No one spoke. Efua expected me to get the ball rolling on such occasions, so I asked him if he ever used *African French* in his writing – French as it was spoken in the French colonies. Writers in Nigeria and Ghana had been using their own English and there was a long tradition of this in India and the West Indies. He was very chilly. To the best of my recollections his words were: 'There is no African French. There is only the French of Flaubert and that is the language in which I write. It is the only language in which it is possible to write.' That was that.

In 1960 I left Ghana and so saw Efua only infrequently, when she was in England. We wrote letters but she was too busy, writing, working, teaching, setting up groups and theatres, to write often. The Mmofra Foundation was, from her letters, her major pride.

Of course, events in Ghana were taking their toll. One summer she spent a day with us in London. Catherine Heath the novelist (now, sadly, dead) was there. Ghana had just suffered a coup, I cannot recall which. Efua gave us a marvellously funny, though rather bitter, dramatic monologue about sitting in her house in Ghana listening to the radio and distant shouts and shots. She said that if she heard one more voice on the radio urging her to keep calm, followed by martial music, she would scream, leap out of the window and run into the bush, never to return. She described a visit to the new head of state in a room full of men lounging uncouthly about carrying enormous rifles. It was a brilliant picture of the miseries of civil disorder. Catherine was fascinated and never forgot it.

In 1992, my son John went to work for a few weeks at the Korle Bu Teaching Hospital in Accra and, to my delight, met Efua and other old friends. He remembers her vivacity and wisdom.

In recent years, her letters were full of the children's and grandchildren's achievements of which she was enormously proud. When I saw her in London, often at the Clifts' house[1], she was still full of ideas and projects, but I sensed that she was, very sensibly, turning more towards the family and the private satisfactions of friendship and writing. Her last visit to England was, of course, shadowed by illness. Her energy was less but she was still during these short periods that I saw her, the same person, full of laughter and affection.

A human being is born at a certain place and a certain time. There is no choice about this but there are consequences. Efua was happy to be a Ghanaian, fortunate to be born in the south of that country among the schools and colleges there, to a family who valued education and who had the means to encourage her remarkable talents and ambitions. I know little about her parents, but she used to speak with particular affection and gratitude of her grandmother (maternal, I understood) with whom she spent much of her childhood. The beauty of the sea always held her in thrall and the coast where she played as a child.

As to the time she was born, this is a mixed story. She was fortunate to have spent her childhood in the comparative stability of pre-independence Ghana, fortunate to experience the excitement and optimism of the coming of independence and the stimulating first years of the new country when everything seemed possible, not only for Ghana but for Africa. After that things were not so good and Efua, like all Ghanaians, suffered the limitations and distortions of economic mismanagement, political instability and public disorder. Happily she steered her family through the difficulties and hardship without disaster but at a price we cannot know for the work she did and the work she might have done if she had not been burdened, distracted and constrained. But it was a time of great opportunities and she led an abundantly fruitful life in a country she loved. She worked wholeheartedly at splendid and transforming designs for education, for the theatre, for literature and for society and she achieved recognition and fulfilment. She was admired and praised not only in Ghana but in many other countries and had a world of friends, colleagues and admirers. Above all she had a beloved and loving family centred in her delightful home.

Florence Laast

My Mentor

It happens frequently that, when great events take place in our lives, we have no time to record them. I will try to give a picture, the conglomeration of the imagery that has been banking up before my inner eye, waiting and pushing for expression.

Stronger than any other image in my life about Auntie Efua Sutherland is one in my early adulthood of Auntie saying softly to me (in Fante), 'You've got to do something to correct the unpleasant situations.' I hear her soft voice in my ear, repeating those words. That has remained the strongest sensation within me.

Mrs. Efua Theodora Sutherland had known me from my childhood. She was my teacher in the primary school and then again in the training college. Her life had so profoundly positive an impact on the direction of my life, that she was my foster mother through these years.

As a teacher, I realise now that Mrs. Sutherland led you to an awareness through observation and reasoning. With this awareness would follow acceptance, and then the truth and values gradually would unfold themselves and deepen your faith in them until the whole process raptured into completion and glowed into harmony and fulfilment, the ingredient being an intellectual and spiritual blend. Thinking of these things now, I can see wonders in the past that I had not realised at the time.

Auntie Efua drew me to herself, in person and in spirit. She was not aware of it, but I am. I became part of her like a lover. I like the confidence she built in me, encouraging me to take the challenge every now and then. My admiration of her was so great she became my role model. She aroused my interest in the study of child psychology.

I see Mrs. Sutherland as one of the greatest thinkers of our time. She devoted herself to the study of the child, and with great energy and singularity of purpose, would direct the child to find fulfilment in life by analysing deep-lying processes of human personality.

Mrs. Sutherland believed in creative education, and so gave practical demonstration of the effective method of teaching. She had the patience and wisdom to wait and watch, until the child's line of thought became apparent. In the seventh decade of life, she was still actively engaged with drawing programmes for children and writing poems and plays for both children and adults.

Seeking ways and means of leading people to achieve success in life, Mrs. Sutherland delved into early childhood processes and development, and came out with useful solutions to children's problems. She liberally shared her findings with others in order to affect and help those who needed it.

She laid emphasis on the importance of good and responsible family life in the development of human character. She believed that letting the child know of his/her roots and appreciate his/her indigenous and traditional way of life was of crucial importance in the rearing of high achieving individuals. 'The home is our first classroom, and our parents the first teachers,' Auntie Efua maintained.

She cared deeply about the future of this nation, Ghana, and showed concern about certain societal conditions that must change to secure our future. It was her belief that the strength and vitality of Ghana rested upon the leadership qualities, the will and the character of our people. Therefore, strong, positive, effective, and intelligent leadership would be paramount if a high quality of education in this country was going to promote the quality of life of our people.

Jung's view of personality is prospective, in the sense that it looks ahead to the person's future line of development, and retrospective since it takes account of the past. It is in this light that Mrs. Sutherland translated her ideas and aspirations into realities through active programmes or through corrective actions. She brought into perspective the importance of early intervention to prevent school failure. Through hard work and perseverance, she was able to accomplish what many believed to be impossible.

Mrs. Sutherland had many admirers in this country, and may well be considered as the most outstanding playwright of Ghana. She had a wonderful gift of the narrative and her approach to teaching was always sociological rather than pedagogical treatise.

With this projection of this illustrious daughter of our great nation in mind, I now give testimony of my experiences in connection with one of her legacies to Ghana – the 'Children's Drama Development Programme'. Under the instrumentality of Auntie Efua, St. Martin de Porres School was used as a centre for a children's art and drama workshop for the residents in Dansoman by the students of the Institute of African Studies, University of Ghana, Legon. Children from all walks of life – that is, both school-going and non-school going alike – participated in the programme twice a week from 4:00 pm to 6:00 pm. The programme covered story-telling and other traditional performing arts, drama, and art.

The children's interest was raised and their appetite for learning and doing things for themselves was whetted to the point that when it was time for closing, they simultaneously groaned in disappointment and disapproval.

This craving for more was partially satisfied when a three-day camping and seminar were organised for them during the school holidays in August, 1980, featuring playwrights and the children's drama workshop. While their cravings were satisfied they also learnt to share, to give and take, and accept other children's views. For some of them that camping experience remains unique up to this day because they had had no exposure before nor after. They enjoyed doing things for themselves and others, and had fun together while they let themselves go.

The children were encouraged to express themselves through art and dramatisation, and through that they built their vocabulary. I realise now that this system helps the child to listen or watch attentively, and is able to record faithfully what he or she has heard and/or seen. The emotional content of such drawings is enormous because of the satisfaction the child gets from being able to express himself naturally and much more so when such expression wins the admiration of others. The confidence of the child is thus immediately built up. The child then experiences pride and has success through his own creativity. It is exhilarating to notice the exuberance on the face of a child for this great achievement.

Later, I became a member of the Ghana Commission on Children, one of Auntie Efua's creations of which she was the chairperson. This took me to a village where a lot of school drop-outs were organised and persuaded to return to the classroom by activities very similar to the programme at St. Martin de Porres School at Dansoman. The school and library were built for them and were sufficiently equipped. I was among a few others who visited them quarterly to help with the teaching and to encourage them. I was given the assignment of preparing a reader for beginners for children along the coast, using their local experiences. This was to serve them as their prime reader to help achieve the desired result. That was a high-point in working with the Ghana Commission on children.

There, the little children were left at the mercy of the harsh realities of life. I formed a number of impressions regarding infant mortality. One was that the attachment between parents and their children was almost nil or lived very briefly. Childhood seemed almost non-existent, because it was treated as a period of transition, which was short-lived and quickly forgotten. Teenage pregnancy was alarming and the children born out of this became liabilities to the society and a big burden on old people who were saddled with the caring for these children without funds.

The children were timid and prematurely assumed adult behaviour, their somber demeanour reflecting the fact that life was hard. They entered early into the world of work and many of them gravitated towards the cities in the classic rural-urban drift, because they had to find any means for their survival as they grew up. Children's arts and drama clearly portrayed much about local culture and the values and style of their community.

Participating in such a programme through the help of, and my fortunate relationship with, Auntie Efua made me more observant, understanding, and deferential. It influenced my interpretation of other people's behaviour. It made me aware of how the physical world can, in large measure, influence the way we perceive things and to notice a child in difficulty and try to identify his or her problem.

This country would have been an envy of many if we could get a dozen of Auntie Efua's kind sprinkled all over, so that her personality would have a profound influence on society, and season a great number of people like the biblical salt that would prepare potential leaders. It would serve the country for the better in no small way, especially at this time when there is a desperate need to raise future leaders, when there is a compelling need to improve education and direction and shape the lives of youth upon whom the country's strength rests.

William Branch

Efua Theodora Sutherland: A Personal Reflection

The telephone call was most unwelcome. Well, not the call itself, which came from my good friend Dr. Vivian Windley in New York City, but the disastrous message it conveyed. Efua Sutherland was dead. 'What? Not Efua…!' 'Yes, Bill, Efua. Efua in Ghana has died.'

How does one begin to reflect upon the life and career of so special a person as Efua Sutherland? I don't know. I just don't know. I've been stymied for days now in getting underway with this testimonial. The words won't flow. There's a barrier blocking expression. Somehow there's still a resistance to the very idea that Efua is no longer the living, vital, busy, creative force I've known ever since that day in mid-summer, 1963, when it was my good fortune to step from a plane, kiss the tarmac spread over Mother Africa, and be whisked up to Legon to the University of Ghana, there to meet a tall, slim, strikingly handsome woman who bid me welcome to a six-week sojourn as a visiting scholar at the University's Institute of African Studies.

The visit had come as a result of meeting and helping to host her colleague, Joe de Graft, who had been to the United States on a study grant. While in New York, he and I exchanged information and views on various aspects of African and African-American culture – drama and theatre in particular, since that was our mutual career interest. Before leaving, Joe volunteered that if an opportunity arose to bring me to Ghana, he'd certainly lend his support. It did, and he did; hence my presence in Legon.

During my all-too-brief stay, I had the welcome opportunity to engage in classes, discourse, trips, and social events, with professors and students at the University, Joe and Efua being my attentive hosts and guides. They saw to it as well that I had a chance to meet and interact with members of the populace, from government officials to artists to ordinary citizens. On one occasion, they took me with them to a local festival in a fishing village up the coast from Accra, where, despite my inability to speak or understand the language, I was greeted and fêted as a long-lost brother who, after many years, had returned from a far-distant journey across the water!

Our special focus, of course, had to do with the work of the Ghana Drama Studio, which Efua had founded and which she and Joe ran together as an increasingly important contribution to the Ghanaian cultural scene. There I observed and worked with actors, dancers, budding playwrights and directors (producers, they called themselves). It was a rich and rewarding experience.

While I was there, an unexpected but notable event of international significance occurred in Legon. Dr. William Edward Burghardt Du Bois, the African-American pioneer sociologist, civil rights activist and political dissident, who three years before had left the U.S. and become a Ghanaian citizen, died at the age of 95. His death, seemingly a last great protest against racism and injustice, came on the eve of the now legendary August 28th, 1963, 'March on Washington' back in the US by African-Americans and their allies, which proved to be a seminal event in the great civil rights movement of that time, eventually leading to reforms abolishing legal racial discrimination in the 'land of the free and the home of the brave'.

Befitting her involvement nature, Efua at once contacted Shirley Graham Du Bois, Du Bois' distinguished widow, and worked with her and others in planning for the state funeral decreed by the President of Ghana, Dr. Kwame Nkrumah. The morning of the funeral itself, Efua took me with her to the Du Bois residence, where she helped with the last-minute arrangements before a solemn account of the day's festivities.[1] After that fateful summer in Ghana, I made it a point to keep in touch with both Efua and Joe DeGraft, until his untimely death in East Africa some years later. Upon Efua's occasional visits to the U.S., we reunited, and it was my great pleasure one year to host a special gathering of artists, writers and academics in her honour at my home in New Rochelle, N.Y. In my introduction to *Crosswinds: An Anthology of Black Dramatists in the Diaspora* (Bloomington: Indiana University Press, 1993), I mentioned that gathering and Efua's curious (to us) interest in the male chef preparing the festive repast. When queried, Efua replied, with a seeming hint of disdain, 'In my country, men don't cook!' She took great delight in my telling of this story on subsequent occasions, throwing back her head and giving out a peal of laughter.

In *Crosswinds*, too, appears Efua's fine play, *Edufa*, which, at my request, she personally selected from among her works to be included in the collection. Thus, *Edufa* continues to be read and studied by people around the globe as an important offering from the dramatic literature of the African continent.

While others are far more qualified than I to assess Efua's work and influence during her whirlwind of activity in her lifetime, perhaps I may be permitted to submit that Efua Theodora Sutherland and her work will certainly live through the years – in her legacy of published words, in the institutions she created, nurtured and advanced; in the memories of those who, like me, were indelibly touched by knowing her; but most especially in the legions of those, most yet unborn, who, though perhaps unknowingly, will yet profit from Efua's endeavours, because she cared enough to get involved.

Again, how does one begin…? I still don't know. But I do know how to end. And that is to say, simply: 'Thank you, Efua.'

Margaret Busby

Reaching Out to Your Africa: Obituary of Efua Sutherland[1]

EFUA SUTHERLAND, who has died, aged 71, has been described as Black Africa's most famous woman writer. She was actively creative long before many of today's younger stars were born, as a pioneering playwright-director, community activist and patron of the arts; her stories, plays and poems have been much anthologised and translated since the sixties, winning international critical attention. In the Ghanaian cultural landscape she held a special place having been the dominant presence in theatre there for more than three decades.

Born in Cape Coast, in what was then the Gold Coast, she came to England to take the BA at Homerton College in Cambridge and studied linguistics at London University's School of Oriental and African Studies. Back home in 1951, she worked as a secondary-school teacher and three years later married an African-American, William Sutherland, with whom she had three children.

In 1958 she founded her Experimental Theatre, which drew on local folklore, performing in both the Akan language and English; she was concerned with the development of a bilingual society in Ghana, so some of her children's writing is also in both languages. She established Accra's Ghana Drama Studio and in 1960 built a courtyard theatre using traditional performance areas. Her writing was bound up with her mission to make theatre more pertinent, particularly to young people. 'I started writing seriously in 1951,' said Sutherland. 'I can even remember the precise time. It was at Easter. I had been thinking about the problem of literature in my country for a very long time. I was on teaching practice with my students once in a village and I got positively angry about the kind of literature that the children were being forced into. It had nothing to do with their environment, their social circumstances or anything. And so I started writing.' Her first book, in 1961, was a pictorial essay for children, *The Roadmakers*, and the next year she collaborated with photographer Willis E. Bell on another, *Playtime in Africa*.

As an educationist she lectured at the University of Ghana and elsewhere, and was also a popular broadcaster. She is best remembered, however, for her innovative and accessible dramatic work. *Foriwa* and *Edufa* – both focusing on women's roles – were first performed at the Drama Studio in 1962, and her works for children include *Vulture! Vulture!* and *Tahinta* (1968), which she called 'rhythm plays'. With the aim of involving villagers in both the production and consumption of drama, she developed *Anansegoro*, dramatised extensions of the storytelling tradition featuring Ananse, the 'spider man' trickster figure.

In the preface to her 1975 play *The Marriage of Anansewa*, Sutherland writes: 'That Ananse is, artistically, a medium for society to criticise itself can be seen in the expression, "Exterminate Ananse, and society will be ruined".' Her accommodation of traditional values and dramatic forms to cultural change has been particularly praised by Ama Ata Aidoo, Ghana's other well-known woman writer.

Sutherland was involved with establishing the Ghanaian literary magazine *Okyeame* in the post-independence era, the publishing company Afram, and the Ghana Society of Writers. She held many key official posts and exerted immeasurable influence. Her 1980 paper aimed at bringing life and relevance to the former slave castle in Cape Coast inspired Panafest – a Pan-African cultural and historical festival, launched in 1991 and with a 1994 sequel headlined by Stevie Wonder.

'Auntie Efua' was a supreme facilitator with a talent for organisation, maintaining Pan-African links and lasting bonds of friendship with people around the world, formidable in her enthusiasm for developing new projects, dedicated in her determination to safeguard a legacy of motivation for young generations. In her most anthologised short story, 'New Life At Kyerefaso', the Queen Mother, embodiment of Akan matrilineal power, recognises the need for change and breaks with tradition by letting her daughter marry a stranger, a worker, whose example has a beneficial effect on the people:

A new pride possessed them. They were no longer just grabbing from the land what they desired for their stomachs' present hunger and for their present comfort. They were looking at the land with new eyes, feeling it in their blood, and thoughtfully building a permanent and beautiful place for themselves and their children ...

'See!' rang the cry of the Asafo leader. 'See how the best in all the world stands. See how she stands waiting, our Queen Mother. Waiting to wash the dust from our brow in the coolness of her peaceful stream. Spread the yield of the land before her. Spread the craft of your hands before her, gently, gently. Lightly, lightly walks our Queen Mother, for she is peace.'

Efua Theodora Sutherland, writer, community activist, born June 27th, 1924; died January 21st, 1996.

Maya Angelou

Tribute to a Sister

This tribute, this declaration of love and sisterhood is most onerous to write. I always imagined, but did not envy, Efua with this burdensome task. Years ago, I pictured her being asked to write about me after I had made transition to another stage. I saw her sitting at Araba Mansa, dressed in white with a gay head tie on her noble head, remembering our laughter. Never! I never dreamed that I would have to sit at a table in North Carolina, and as the tears slipped down my cheeks and my writing hand growing weak with misery, be forced to recall the love and tears and laughter we shared.

During my first week in Ghana, over 30 years ago, my only child was involved in an automobile accident, and his neck was broken. After hovering dry-eyed around his bed at the Korle Bu Hospital for four days, a friend took me to meet Efua Sutherland. She welcomed me, gave me a glass of Club beer, then said, 'Sister Maya, you need to cry. And you need a sister to watch you cry. I am that sister.' I looked into that beautiful face, her large, black eyes steady and calm, and for the first time since the accident I relaxed and wept.

Efua knew a lot about being a sister. Wise, always ready to give advice, and wise enough to withhold it if not wanted.

A lover of education, the world will never know how far and wide her influence reached in the preparation of young minds. A lover of Ghana, wherever she was, in fact, wherever she is right now, she dazzles everyone with her pride in Ghana and her love of Ghanaians.

A lover of literature, she wrote the best, and taught the best, and shared the best always informing readers and students that their lives could be, had been, and would be told in prose, poetry, and plays.

A lover of family, she took such pride in her beautiful children and their children that a visitor had to take pride in the glow of her pride.

I know she knew how to be a sister; for much of who I am, who I might be and who I hope to be, can be credited to the truth that Efua and I knew each other and called each other 'Sister'.

Maya Angelou
February 1996

Kofi Anyidoho

Mother Courage: A Tribute to Auntie Efua From All Her Children in the Arts

There is a boil in the throat of your children's joy. Maame Efua, there is a raging boil at the centre of your children's hope. We were busy carving new praise-songs for your next birthday. We did not know you must choose the peace of death to cease the pain of life.

We cannot sing our joy. We could have cried at least. We could have stretched our voice to touch your soul in flight. But there is this boil in the throat of your children's hope. Your *Children of the Man-Made Lake* say they are set adrift upon the floods you so often spoke about.

Yesterday our joy was young and green, with the sharp freshness of the lemon grove. Today, our sorrow ripens into a burst of sun flowers. And there is no voice to sing your praise.

Someone, perhaps, will broadcast our Sorrow on Joy Radio. Let them recall how you gathered the best among our dreams, transformed them all into a vision of a New Life, with the Stage as the medical lab where you diagnosed our nation's diseased condition, the Theatre where you performed corrective surgery on our anaemic self-esteem.

Once there was a Ceremony of Remembrance at the Old Drama Studio, your original miracle house. Those to whom you gave birth in the arts, we all gathered for a harvest of your dreams: Uncle Bob Cole in a solo re-enactment of an original masterpiece of life as Ananse's web; Uncle Kwamena Ampah with Kusum Agoromba in *Odasani* and his tragic choice of fleeting Joy. All the Studio Players, old and young, they came to recall the dreams we lost to those years the infant men took away from us. In the midst of all sorrows, you stood tall, and proud and firm against the force of hostile winds.

The poets said it once so well: 'You were Mother Courage with a Heart the size of Love, large enough for your children's tears for your nation's fears. You were Foriwa the young gazelle who tip-toed into our dawn, rearranged the world you found, gave life a new meaning, disappeared before we could think of saying "Thanks".'

Auntie Efua, when you go, please tell them, tell Uncle Joe de Graft and Tata Amu that the National Theatre is ready at last. We are doing our best to put back on stage the festival drama you all composed at the dawn of our nation's birth. We are doing our very best. But there are technical problems with our grand design: Your vision created so many parts for Giants. All the original cast is gone. And we are stuck with a Dwarf Brigade.

They say you said our grief must be brief. That we cannot mourn your loss longer than a day. They also say you said we must be modest with our farewell piece. We are doing our best to honour your wish. We are doing our very best. But really, Auntie Efua, how can we offer an antelope's burial to an elephant?

Margaret Busby

The Pathfinder (For Auntie Efua at Araba Mansa)

Your shadow falls ahead of us
So the sun does not dazzle our eyes.
You have taught us the right thing to do.

Your footprints lead the way
So our steps will not falter.
You have shown us the direction.

I am learning the words,
I am practising the dance.

I know it can be done
Because of your example,
Because of your example.

I turn back and you are there,
Pointing ahead.
I look forward and you are there,
Beckoning me on.

I am still shaping the words
And my tongue has been loosened
Because you spoke them first.

So the sun will not blind my eyes
Your shadow falls ahead of me.
Your footprints lead the way;
Though my steps cannot fill them

The path is clear
Where you have trodden
As we follow your footsteps
The river will not engulf us…

One way, the forest;
Another, the ocean —
How many hopeful roads
Dappled with shadow!
Now the choice is ours.
The stronghold of the castle —
Does it confine?
Does it protect?

The mystery of creation leaves us
Sacred responsibilities.
When we were starving
Such rituals were performed
For us all to eat in peace.

The map is not uncharted where you have gone.
The page is not blank where you have written
We hear you
Telling our story
To the rhythm of a heartbeat,
To the rhythm of a heartbeat...

Sankofa. Let the elders teach the children.
The gracious strength of your creation
Others will build upon:
Our future history,
More precious than gold.

See! The endless roads are many now
Over the horizon.
Listen! The story starts again.
Can you hear it?

Your shadow falls ahead of me
So that light will guide my way,
So your light will guide my way.

Margaret (Peggy) Watts

Spirit of the Red Earth: Remembering Efua

I.
Spirit of the red earth
Reveal the wonder of our worth

I did not know hibiscus
when Aunty Efua showed me
the singular bush at her Home
rooted in tradition and red earth.

The blossom was pink and perfect.
Otherworldly, she knew
it was unique in Ghana.
I had that to learn.

Spirit of the red earth
Teach us the secrets of rebirth.

Efua in head tie appeared
at life's celebrations and griefs
with a gift of tongues that married
gods of home to gods of the world.

Hold your family together.

New Year's around the fire, under the guava tree.
'Champagne is foreign to me.'
A wine glass thrown and shattered.
Yam and palm oil with eggs for celebration.

Spirit of the red earth,
Teach us the art of elation.

The children must respect their father.
A woman's body is always clean.
Palm soup restores strength after birth.

Reveal the edicts of the hearth
Spirit of the red earth.

My aunt, my teacher, my sister
brought Nana Atwia from her storytelling village
with its flag dancer's inexorable gyration
and the deep throated songs of the asafo company
to outdoor and name our daughter, Gyasiwa*.

Do not scold her in public.
Keep the ancient glass bead / and the gold nugget always.
Cope and rejoice.

She called me sister,
laughed at my naïveté;
she knew the world would not allow it,
though the Afram River flowed
through her mind and heart.

She prepared my daughter
to accept village origins.
Respect mother earth, the ancestors,
the rootedness of ritual and relation.
Reject the ignorant world's perceptions,
learn the language of her spirit,
ground herself in red earth.

Teach us about relation
Spirit of the red earth.
*Rachel Gyasiwa Watts, daughter of the author, who performed the poem, with
Chandra Adjoa Eaton, at A Thanksgiving Celebration for Efua Theodora
Sutherland at the Schomburg Centre for Research in Black Culture, New York
City, 28 April 1996.

Ama Ata Aidoo

An Interrogation of an Academic Kind: An Essay

Dear Auntie Efua,

'Auntie' Efua?!

In lieu of
Dramatist Extraordinaire,
Teacher, Enabler, Inspirer,
Impresario Supremo?

So,
how come you could be thus addressed
not just by the youth – near and far –
not just by family – close or extended –
but your peers too:
academic, intellectual, and sundry other learned ones?

Some industrial,
others mercantile,
but all reverential?

- and not to mention those who politically and otherwise
could, and may have tried, to burn you in a latter day
auto-da-fé.

Now this is a confession of sorts:
some – not all – of us
wondered every now and then
-not loudly or in any unquiet way mind you
but perhaps irrelevantly and irreverently–

what in the Creator's name this kind of domestication was all about?

'It's a sign of our respect,' we said.
'And? …'
'…and wanting to own up to those

wondrous nurture-filled Fridays
– mid-morning, late afternoon, details indifferent –
and the sterling honour of such an appellation.

And seeing too that you had
more than earned that right
from mothering a nation across its
right reaches, left banks, northernmost posts and southern shores…
Ow-w-w,
how you had mothered us:
with that [maddening] formidable [self-] assurance,
those humorously luminous and luminously humorous eyes that
sought out
our inner weaknesses
in hopes of setting us straight
not just some day
but right away,

plus that indulgently mocking laughter
so charming and often tinkling with
the sheer wonder at the wonder that you knew
was this earth, us humans, and our lives…

You walked for us too.
And girl, how you walked!

Purposeful steps
down, inside, and along
cold castle and other walls
clutching carefully crafted
weighty-with-wisdom bits of paper
forty hours a day
ten days a week

to plead and cajole
in the [vain] hope that
someone, but anyone up there –
and they always were up there –
through you
could might would
hear our cries
feel our pain and

see the neglect of us and
all that held our life's health,
our almost-complete destitution
and if only for a while,
taste the bitterness of our
despair.

Dear Gold-Nuggets-Giver and Precious Beads Distributor,
Our true Lady Silk of the Slender Arms,

we remember you so sharply
swinging those arms and cutting the breezes with
the grace and the power of a woodland goddess
striding and gliding
your way to sundry sites of creative construction:
— the classrooms
— the theatres
— the lecture and other halls where meetings were held of great national
import…

All in your effort to build and have 'something built'.

Me na Oye-Adee-Yie,
you knew us
didn't you?

the incompetence-with-an-attitude
the envies
the jealousies
the boastful lack of confidence
the glaring ignorance that sought to hide a knowledge of itself
in negativity, greed and mindless cruelty.

And not to counting out that puzzling viciousness which gloried
only in the ability to deny others any entry through
doors that should have stayed open for
achievements,
or provided exits from
frustrations and
humiliations…

But then,

You never gave up on us:
not for a minute.
Knowing as you did
that given half the chance,
we could, and still can, soar
high above our normal human frailties and
make a glowing glittering something of ourselves and our world.

No wonder then that with such knowledge,
You did
Ananse and his daughter
the only way
they should be done today.

Yet you tiptoed through it all
disregarding the no[n]-sense
forgiving the foolish-ness

Encouraging
Supporting
Affirming.

So what did You think we were going to do without you,
Dear Dr. Mrs. Efua Theodora Sutherland?
Not much:
unless you counted our best under the circumstance.

But,
and this is the other confession of sorts,
since we knew
You brooked no spinelessness,
we hope you had some way to know
we called you 'Auntie'
only
in lieu of…
…'Mother', 'Teacher',…

APPENDIX

Efua Theodora Sutherland: A Life in Brief

Kofi Anyidoho

Dr. Efua Sutherland
(A Biographical Sketch)

On 21 January 1996, the African world lost one of its most remarkable daughters of the twentieth century: Dr. Efua Theodora Sutherland. 'Auntie Efua' is best known for her pioneering work as a cultural visionary and activist, her impact on society at once comprehensive and enduring. Teacher, research scholar, poet, dramatist, and social worker, she devoted her life to the building of models of excellence in culture and education, and to the training of young people who would carry her vision into the far future.

Born in Cape Coast on 27 June 1924, she was named after her maternal great-grandmother Nana Ama Nyankoma. Her father, Harry Peter Morgue from the family of Chief Moore of Nsona Paado, Cape Coast, was a well-known teacher of English who once taught at Accra Academy. Her mother, Harriet Efua Maria Parker, was from the royal families of Gomua Brofo and Anomabu, particularly the branch founded by Barima Ansaful at Gyegyano, Cape Coast. Despite her royal birth, Efua had a very humble and difficult early life; her eventual greatness may be more of a personal achievement than an inherited family fortune. Her young mother died in a lorry accident at age 18, leaving a 5-month-old Efua in the care of her grandmother Araba Mansa, whose personal sacrifice and example of hard work as a baker ensured Efua's survival and provided the single most important impact on her later development into a most resourceful personality.

Theodora Olivia Morgue, as Efua became known, began her primary education at the Government Girls' School and later moved to St. Monica's, both in Cape Coast. She took the Standard Seven examination while she was still in Standard Six, and did so well she won a scholarship to the St. Monica's Training College at Asante Mampong. St. Monica's was founded and run by Anglican Sisters of the Order of the Holy Paraclete, based in Yorkshire, England. The nuns in both Cape Coast and Mampong had such significant influence on the young Efua that she seriously considered becoming a nun and would have gone to England for convent training had her grandmother not intervened.

At 18, she began teaching at senior primary level but soon joined the staff of St. Monica's Training College. In 1947, after five-and-a-half years of teaching, she went to England, where she studied for a B.A. degree at Homerton College, Cambridge University. She spent another year at the School of Oriental and

African Studies, London, specialising in English linguistics, African languages, and drama. Back in Ghana in 1950, she returned to St. Monica's but later transferred to Fijai Secondary School and then to Achimota School. In 1954, Efua married William Sutherland, an African-American who had been living in Ghana and worked from 1951 to 1957 to help found what is now Tsito Secondary School in the Volta Region. Efua spent part of the period in Tsito helping with the foundation work. Efua and Bill had three children, Esi Reiter, Ralph Gyan, and Muriel Amowi, who have since become a university research fellow, an architect, and a lawyer, respectively.

It is against this family and educational background that we must assess the unusual impact of Efua Sutherland's public life as educator, creative artist, and activist social visionary. She is best known as a dramatist, but her work in this area was always informed by a compelling vision of a better society, and she chose appropriate cultural education as the best foundation on which such a society could be established. Like many others, she could have used her considerable talents and skills in the promotion of a spectacular individual career. Instead, she chose to share her gifts with society at large by investing her energies in the building of model programmes and institutions, and in the training of future generations. Efua Sutherland's reputation as the founder and mother figure behind the National Theatre Movement may best be measured by the many key institutions and programmes she was instrumental in bringing into being. She was the prime mover in the founding of the Ghana Society of Writers (1957). A year later, the Ghana Experimental Theatre company was launched under her direction. She helped to found *Okyeame* literary magazine in 1961. Through her pioneering research into Ghanaian oral traditions, she introduced onto the stage the unique dramatic form of *Anansegoro*, deriving its creative model from traditional storytelling drama. To provide an ideal rehearsal and performance space for the emerging National Theatre Movement, she mobilised funds and supervised the building of the Ghana Drama Studio, ensuring that its design was in harmony with performance demands of African theatre practice. She founded Kusum Agoromba, a full-time drama company based at the Drama Studio and dedicated to performing quality plays in Akan, in towns and villages all over the country. She provided creative leadership to the Workers' Brigade Drama Group and to the Drama Studio Players.

In May 1963, Efua Sutherland became a Research Associate of the Institute of African Studies. As a part of the move, she handed over the Drama Studio to the University of Ghana to be used as 'an extension division of the School of Music, Dance and Drama'. Through the Drama Studio Programme and the Drama Research Unit of the Institute, Efua Sutherland worked with the late Joe de Graft and others to build the foundations of what was soon to become a model programme in drama and theatre studies and practice in Africa. One of her most frequently cited projects, the Atwia Experimental Community Theatre Project, is recognised world-wide as a pioneering model for the now popular Theatre for Development. *Araba: The Village Story* is a major documentary film done in 1967 by the American television network ABC to record the success of this unique experimental project.

A particularly significant aspect of Efua Sutherland's work was the Children's Drama Development Project. This multi-year project, focused on research into the cultural life of children in society, used the information gathered as a basis for writing, producing and publishing appropriate plays for children. Conferences, workshops and test productions organised as part of this project have left us with an important collection of plays for children, among them R. A. Cantey's *Ghana Motion*, Togbe Kwamuar's *The Perpetual Stone Mill*, Kwamena Ampah's *Hwe No Yie*, Koku Amuzu's *The New Born Child* and *The Maid Servant*, Joe Manu-Amponsah's *Gates to Mother*, Kofi Hiheta's *A Bench of Chances*, and Kofi Anyidoho's *Akpokplo* (Ewe & English). Regrettably, the preparation of these plays for formal publication in a major anthology is one of the many vital projects which Auntie Efua's death has left unfinished.

The 25th Anniversary Programme of the Drama Studio, the final phase of Efua Sutherland's distinguished career in the National Theatre Movement, coincided with her retirement from the University of Ghana in 1984. The programme opened with an impressive and symbolic Ceremony of Remembrance and moved into a major documentation project covering various forms of drama that have evolved as part of the National Theatre Movement. The 25th Anniversary Programme, ironically, suffered a serious setback when the Drama Studio was demolished to make way for the construction of the National Theatre. Although Auntie Efua was deeply hurt by the demolition of the studio, she continued to work over the next two years to bring the documentation programme to a reasonable completion. It was also in this final phase of her work that she gave to Ghana and the African world probably her grandest artistic vision for uplifting and reuniting African peoples through the arts – an original proposal for the Pan-African Historical Theatre Festival, the Panafest Movement. This final gift underscores the significance she attached to connections between Africa and the diaspora. She played a very critical role in the establishment of the W. E. B. Du Bois Memorial Centre for Pan-African Culture. She belonged to an extensive global network of friends, many of them eminent creative minds.

Efua Sutherland's long and distinguished career has also left an impressive corpus of creative works, making her one of Africa's best-known writers. In addition to a number of essays, articles, short stories and poems, her published works include a short biography of Bob Johnson, 'the father of the concert party tradition', as well as several other books – *Playtime in Africa*, *The Roadmakers*, *Edufa*, *Foriwa*, *Odasani*, *Anansegoro: Story-Telling Drama in Ghana*, *The Marriage of Anansewa*,

You Swore an Oath, Vulture! Vulture! [and *Tahinta*]: *Two Rhythm Plays*, and *The Voice in the Forest*, and *Children of the Man-Made Lake* . Her unpublished plays for children include *The Pineapple Child, Nyamekye, Tweedledum and Tweedledee, Ananse and the Dwarf Brigade, Wohyee Me Bo*. As a major literary voice, she was concerned about the need for making works by African writers available through local publishing. To this end, she played a key role as founder of Afram Publications Ghana Limited in the early 1970s and until her death maintained an active role in the editorial work of Afram. It is to her credit and to that of all who have worked with her that three of the winners of the 1995 Valco Fund Literary Awards were works published by Afram.

A concern for children was central to all of Efua Sutherland's life and work. Even after her retirement from the University of Ghana, she was to devote the final phase of her public life to foundation work in the establishment of the Ghana National Commission on Children. She was a foundation member (1979-1983) and later chairperson of the Commission (1983-1990). The work of this commission, especially through the impact of child education programmes designed around a national network of children's park-library complexes, the documentation of the situation of the Ghanaian child, and the influencing of state policy on child life, shall remain one of Efua Sutherland's most significant gifts to her nation. Efua Sutherland served on several other national and international boards and committees, including the Education Commission, the Valco Fund Board of Trustees, and the Ghana National Commission for UNESCO. Her work received recognition and sponsorship from both the state and such major agencies as the Valco Trust Fund, the Rockefeller Foundation, the Ford Foundation, UNICEF, and UNESCO.

On the occasion of the 30th anniversary of the achievement of full university status, the University of Ghana selected Efua Sutherland as one of a small group of eminent individuals whose contribution has had a profound impact on the development of the university and of the society at large:

> Efua Theodora Sutherland, for the inspiration provided to the development of the Dramatic Art, and in recognition of your efforts on behalf of children for whose benefit you have canvassed children's libraries and amusement parks, the University of Ghana is privileged to honour you with the degree of Doctor of Laws, *honoris causa*.

We recall this citation in this moment of her passing away, words that reassure us that Efua Sutherland's legacy remains with us through her words, her works, her many models of excellence, and above all, through the many children she has given birth to in and through the arts.

Auntie Efua, may your soul rest in lasting peace.

Amowi Sutherland Phillips

Chronology

1924, June 27th	Born Theodora Olivia Morgue aka Efua Nyankoma, after her maternal grandmother Nana Ama Nyankoma (aka Araba Mansa), in Cape Coast, Ghana, only child of Harriet Efua Maria Parker and Harry Peter Morgue.
	She loses her mother in the same year through a lorry accident and is cared for by her grandmother and extended family.
1930s	Attends St. Monica's School, Cape Coast, established by nuns of the Order of the Holy Paraclete.
1939	Wins scholarship to St. Monica's Teacher Training College in Asante-Mampong. During this period, begins to direct theatrical productions including *The Medea*, *Antigone*, and *Alcestis*.
1940	Teaching practice posts at the Presbyterian School, Mampong Town and at St. Monica's School, Cape Coast.
1942	At age 18, commences teaching at Senior Primary level in Cape Coast.
1946	Transfers to Asante-Mampong to teach in new St. Monica's Secondary School.
1947-1949	Attends Homerton College, Cambridge, England, to study for a B.A. degree.
1950	Assists with Twi proficiency for Colonial Service cadets in the language laboratory of the School of Oriental and African Studies, London.
	Returns to Ghana in September, taking up teaching post at St. Monica's Secondary School, Asante-Mampong. Begins to express dissatisfaction with content and scope of educational material.
1951	Begins creative writing (poetry).
1952	Submits poem for publication in the April issue of the Royal African Society's magazine *African Affairs*.
	Resigns teaching position at St. Monica's in December.
	Teaches at Fijai Secondary School, Sekondi.
	Marries William H. Sutherland, an African-American, in Accra. They move to Tsito-Awudome in the Volta Region,

	where she supports his work in establishing a school. Birth of first child, Esi Reiter, in Sekondi. Birth of second child, Ralph Ekow Gyan, in Cape Coast.
1957	Founds the Ghana Society of Writers, with the encouragement of Michael Dei-Anang, Dr. J. B. Danquah, and Dr. Kofi Abrefa Busia. Birth of third child Muriel Amowi, in Accra.
1958	Leads the Ghana delegation to the Afro-Asian Writers' Conference in Tashkent, USSR.
1959-60	Initiates the Ghana Experimental Theatre, ultimately acquiring land to build the Ghana Drama Studio.
1960	Founds *Okyeame* literary journal. Publishes *Playtime in Africa*, in collaboration with photographer Willis E. Bell.
1961	Publishes *The Roadmakers*, in collaboration with photographer Willis E. Bell.
1961-63	Opening of the Ghana Drama Studio in Accra with *Odasani* (based on *Everyman*), followed by period of active development of theatre practice centred in the Drama Studio.
1962	Production of plays *Foriwa* and *Edufa*.
1963	Joins Institute of African Studies at the University of Ghana, Legon, as Research Associate. Drama Studio absorbed into the Institute of African Studies and its theatre programmes adopted by the new School of Music and Drama at the University of Ghana. Builds and moves into home and work studio named 'Araba Mansa' in honour of her grandmother.
1964	Begins Ekumfi Atwia Experimental Community Theatre Project. Conceptualises and builds the *Kodzidan*, or 'story house', which becomes a second locus of theatre development in a rural community.
1967	Publishes *Edufa*. Produces *Araba, The Village Story*, a documentary film for ABC-TV (USA), which records the success of the Atwia Experimental Community Theatre Project.
1968	Publishes *Vulture! Vulture!* and *Tahinta*, Two Rhythm Plays for children. Forms *Kusum Agoromba* theatre group.
1973	Founds indigenous publishing house, Afram Publications, with the Ghana State Insurance Corporation as major shareholder.
1975	Publishes *The Marriage of Anansewa*.

1977	Production of *The Marriage of Anansewa* at the Festival of African Arts and Cultures (FESTAC) in Lagos, Nigeria.
1979-1983	Foundation member, Ghana National Commission on Children.
1980	Writes 'Proposal for Historical Drama Festival at Cape Coast', to become the inspirational document for the establishment of the Pan-African Theatre Festival PANAFEST.
1983-1990	Chair, Ghana National Commission on Children.
1984	Retires from the University of Ghana.
1985	Du Bois Memorial Centre is commissioned. Special Honour for Drama awarded by the Entertainment Critics and Reviewers' Association of Ghana (ECRAG).
1991	Receives honorary doctorate degree from University of Ghana. Demolition of the Ghana Drama Studio to make way for National Theatre.
1992	First Pan-African Historical Theatre Festival (PANAFEST) under the theme 'Re-emergence of African Civilisation' held in Cape Coast, Elmina, and Accra, Ghana, 12-19 December. Registers charitable organisation, Mmofra Foundation to support creative work particularly in the arts and audio-visual media for the benefit of children in Ghana.
1993	Second Pan-African Historical Theatre Festival under the theme 'Uniting the African Family for Development'.
1995	Receives the Entertainment Critics and Reviewers' Association of Ghana (ECRAG) Flag Star Award.
1996, January 21st	Passes away in Accra after an illness.
1997	Park adjacent to the National Theatre is renamed the Efua Sutherland Children's Park.
1998	Replica of Drama Studio built at University of Ghana named the 'Efua Sutherland Drama Studio'.

NOTES & REFERENCES

Notes to Introduction

1 Letter from W. E. B. Du Bois to Kwame Nkrumah, on the occasion of Ghana's Independence, which Du Bois was prevented from attending because his passport had been revoked.
2 Notes of Sutherland on the vision for Mmofra (Children's) Foundation.
3 Highly Indebted Poor Country: Programme of International Monetary Fund/World Bank sponsors for economic re-structuring of developing countries. Public toilets purchased by funds from this programme are the subject of ironic jokes, as symbols of the level of Ghana's Development.
4 Gilroy, Paul. *The Black Atlantic: Modernity and Double Consciousness*: Cambridge: Harvard University Press, 1992; Appiah, Kwame Anthony. *Cosmopolitanism: Ethics in a World of Strangers*. New York: W.W.Norton, 2006; Wilson-Tagoe, Nana. "Reading Towards a Theorization of African Women's Writing: African Women Writers Within Feminist Gynocriticism." In Stephanie Newell ed. *Writing African Women, Gender, Popular Culture and Literature in West Africa*. New Jersey: Zed Books, 1997:11–27; Hall, Stuart and Paul Du Gay. *Questions of Cultural Identity*. London; Thousand Oaks, Calif.: Sage Publications, 1996.
5 Kwame Nkrumah. Speech delivered at Formal Inauguration of the Institute of African Studies, Legon. Mimeograph, 1963. Quoted in Kofi Anyidoho, *The Pan-African Ideal in Literatures of the Black World*. Accra: Ghana Universities Press, 1989.
6 Marilyn Slutzky Zucker uses this expression in her discussion of the Senegalese writer Ken Bugul in her article, "On Teaching *The Abandoned Baobab: A Senegalese Woman's Autobiography*"in *Women's Studies Quarterly* XXV No. 3-4.
7 On the occasion of the tenth anniversary of the passing away of Sutherland, the Central Region Centre for National Culture has announced the establishment of an annual storytelling festival for the region to be located at the Atwia *Kodzidan*. Beyond the *Kodzidan* project, Sutherland collected stories from skilled tale tellers from many other communities throughout the country. These have been transcribed and translated and are available in the archives of the Ghana Drama Studio and the Institute of African Studies, University of Ghana.

Notes to Rotimi: "The Attainment of Discovery: Efua Sutherland and the Evolution of Modern African Drama"

1 *Cultural Events in Africa* 42 1968: p. II.
2 *Ibid.*

References

Banham, M and Wake C. *African Theatre Today*. London: Pitman, 1976.

Brown, Lloyd I. *Women Writers in Black Africa*. Westport, Connecticut; London Greenwood Press, 1981.

Jones, Eldred D., ed. *African Literature Today*, No. 8 Drama in Africa: London: Heinemann; New York: Africana, 1976.

Ogunba, Oyin and Irele, Abiola, eds. *Theatre in Africa*. Ibadan: Ibadan University Press: 1978.

Sutherland, Efua. *Edufa*, London: Longman, 1967.

—. *Foriwa: A Play*. Accra: State Publishing Corporation, Accra: 1967.

—. *The Marriage of Anansewa*. London: Longman: 1975.

Notes to Jeyifo: "When Anansegoro Begins to Grow: Re-reading Efua Sutherland Three Decades On"

1　Efua Sutherland's Ghana Drama Studio in Accra, and the University of Ibadan School of Drama and its Theatre-On-Wheels project both emerged at roughly the same time in the late 1950s. The developments in Nigerian drama and theatre that followed on the heels of the creation of the School of Drama are much better known worldwide than work in Ghana influenced by the Ghana Drama Studio and the range of theatrical experimentalism for which it became quite famous in West Africa. But as to Efua Sutherland's personal contribution at the time, it is comparable in significance to the contribution of any other figure active in the period, people like Geoffrey Axworthy and Wole Soyinka included.

2　Regrettably, Sutherland did not pay much attention to committing to essayistic or metacritical writings, thoughts and reflections she might have had on her work as a playwright, director and institution builder. Thus, what I write of her as a theorist in this essay derives from extrapolations I have made from the short Preface to the volume *The Marriage of Anansewa and Edufa*. Whatever errors of interpretation and attribution I have made in the distinction I am making between *anansesem* and *anansegoro* are mine, not Sutherland's.

3　On the institution and practice of *sati* in postcolonial India, see, among others, Susan Abraham, 1977.

4　Gayle Rubin, 1975.

5　Biodun Jeyifo, 2004, Chapter One.

6　On the 'occult economy' in Africa in the wake of the neoliberal Structural Adjustments Programme of the World Bank and the International Monetary Fund, see among others, Jean and John Comaroff, 1999.

7　Biodun Jeyifo, 2002.

References

Abraham, Susan. "The Deorala Judgement Glorifying Sati." *The Lawyers Collective* 12 (6) 1977: 4–12.

Comaroff, Jean and John. "Occult Economies and the Violence of Abstraction: Notes from the South African Postcolony." *American Ethnologist* 26(2) 1999: 279–303.

Euripides. "Alcestis." In *Alcestis, Hippolytus, Iphigenia in Tauris*. (Translated by Phillip Vellacott). Penguin Classics, 1974.

Jeyifo, Biodun ed. *Modern African Drama: Norton Critical Editions* (NCE). New York: W.W. Norton, 2002.

—. Wole Soyinka. *Politics, Poetics and Postcolonialism*. Cambridge: Cambridge University Press, 2004.

Rubin, Gayle. "The Traffic in Women: Notes on the Political Economy of Sex." In Rayna Reiter ed. *Toward an Anthropology of Women* 1975: 157–210.

Soyinka, Wole. *Death and the King's Horseman*, London: Methuen, 1975.

Sutherland, Efua. *Foriwa: A Play*. Accra: State Publishing Corporation, 1967.

—. *Two Plays: The Marriage of Anansewa and Edufa*. London: Longman, 1975.

Notes to Donkor: "Kodzidan Mboguw: Supplanted Acts, Displaced Narratives and the Social Logic of a Trickster in the 'House of Stories'"

1　Nana Baah Okuampah VI was among the small number of women chiefs in the Akan society of Ghana. Even though accession to office is through the maternal line, very few women are made chiefs.

2   In considering the story of how the Kodzidan came to be, I have combined my own recollections of the anecdotes I heard at the University of Ghana with accounts by E. O. Akyea (82–84) and R. W. July (78–80).

3   Tepketey writes that in one narrative Ananse is referred to as 'the child of Nsiah, the Mother of Nyame the Sky god'. This reference, however, is exactly the way it appears in Rattray's translation of the story 'How Kwaku Ananse Got Aso in Marriage' (135).

4   This notion is used here in its Fante dialect of the Akan Language because the people of Atwia are Fante. The notion is often referred to in the literature as *Mmguo* which is in the majority Twi dialect.

5   Among Akan, one has no legal existence or status until one acquires a name.

References

Appiah, Peggy. *Ananse the Spider: Tales From an Ashanti Village*. New York: Pantheon, 1966.

—. *Tales of an Ashanti Father*. London: Deutsch, 1967.

—. *The Pineapple Child and Other Tales from Ashanti*. London: Deutsch, 1969.

Akrofi, C. A. "Preface." E. O. Ayeh. *Mmrebua*. Tema: Ghana Publishing Corporation, 1978.

Akyea, E. Ofori. "The Atwia Ekumfi Kodzidan – An Experimental African Theatre." *Okyeame* Vol. 4 1968: 82–84.

Barker, W. H. and C. Sinclair. *West African Folktales*, Northbrook: Metro, 1972,.

Brown, E. J. P. *Gold Coast and Ashanti Reader Book 2*. London: Crown Agents, 1929.

Courlander, Harold. *The Hat-Shaking Dance and Other Tales from the Gold Coast*. New York: Harcourt Brace Jovanovich, 1957.

Drewal, Margaret Thompson. "Performance Studies and African Foklore Research." In *African Folklore: An Encyclopedia*. Philip M. Peek and Kwesi Yankah eds. New York: Routledge, 2004: 334–339.

July, Robert W. *An African Voice: The Role of the Humanities in African Independence*. Durham: Duke University Press, 1987.

Pelton, Robert D. *The Trickster in West Africa: A Study of Mythic Irony and Sacred Delight*. Berkeley: Univeristy of California Press, 1980..

Rattray, R. S. *Akan-Ashanti Folk-Tales*. Oxford: Clarendon Press, 1930.

Sutherland, Efua. *The Marriage of Anansewa*, London: Longman, 1975.

Tekpetey, Kwawisi. "The Trickster in Akan-Asante Oral Literature." *Asemka* 1979 5: 78–82.

van Dyck, Charles. "An Analytic Study of the Folktales of Selected Peoples of West Africa." Ph.D Dissertation: Oxford University, 1967.

Vecsey, Christopher. "The Exception Who Proves the Rules: Ananse the Akan Trickster." In *Mythical Trickster Figures: Contours, Contexts and Criticisms*. William J. Hynes and William G. Doty eds. Tuscaloosa: University of Alabama Press , 1993: 106–121

Yankah, Kwesi. "The Question of Ananse in Akan Mythology." In *Perspectives on* Mythology. Esi Sutherland Addy ed. Accra: Woeli Publishers, 1999.

Notes to John Collins: "The Entrance of Ghanaian Women into Popular Entertainment"

1   Also see an interview by Esi Sutherland-Addy with Ama Buabeng published in the journal *African Theatre* and the Volume entitled "Women," edited by Jane Plastow, in 2002.

2   This is probably a misspelling of the Akan name Akosua.

References

Adih, Senanu. "Article on Miatta Fahnbulleh." *Uhuru* Magazine 1985 : Ghana, June, 5.

Asante-Darko, Nimrod and Sjank Van Der Geest. "Male Chauvinism: Men and Women in Ghanaian Highlife Songs." In *Female and Male in West Africa*, Christine Oppong ed. George, Allen and Unwin: 1983 chapter 17.

Bender, Wolfgang. *Sweet Mother, Modern African Music*, Chicago: University of Chicago Press, 1991.

Brun, Kwame and Catherine Cole. Lecture on the History of the Concert Party Entitled *Ebia Ma Adwennen* USIS Library, Accra, June 25, 1995.

Clark, Ebun. *Hubert Ogunde: The Making of Nigerian Theatre*. Oxford: Oxford University Press, 1979.

Collins John, E. T. *Mensah the King of Highlife*. Off the Record Press: UK, 1986,

—. *West African Pop Roots*. Philadelphia: Temple University Press, 1992,.

—. "The Ghanaian Concert Party: African Popular Entertainment at the Crossroads." Ph.D Thesis: Faculty of the Graduate School of the State University of New York (SUNY) at Buffalo, 1994.

Coplan, David. *In Township Tonight: South Africa's Black City Music and Theatre*, Johannesburg: Ravan Press, 1985.

Crass, Randall. Shnachie Records publicity sheet on the Lijadu Sisters: USA, 1988.

Duran, Lucy. "Djely Mousso." In *Folk Roots* 11 (3) September 1989: 68–74.

Drinker, Sophie. *Music and Women*. Washington, D.C.: Zerger Publishing Company Inc, 1948.

Finnegan, Ruth. *Oral Literature in Africa*. Oxford: Oxford University Press, 1970: 500–517.

Frisbie, Charlotte. "The Anthropological and Ethnological Implications of a Comparative Analysis of Bushmen and Pygmy Music." In *Ethnology* 10(3) July 1971 .

Ghanaba, Kofi (Guy Warren). Unpublished Autobiography Sent to Dr. John Collins for Editing by James Moxon in 1975.

Hampton, Barbara. "Music of the Ga People of Ghana." In *Sleevenotes for Folkways Records Album* No. FE 429. New York, 1978.

Harrev, Flemmin. "Francophone West Africa and the Jali Experience." In *West African Pop Roots*. John Collins ed Philadelphia: Temple University Press, 1992: Chapter 22.

Kazadi, Pierre. "Trends in 19th and 20th Century Music in Zaire-Congo." In von Robert Gunther ed. *.Musikulturen Asians Afrikas Und Oceaniens*. Gustav Bosse Verlag Regensburg, No. 9 1973: 267–288.

Makeba, Miriam and James Hall, *Makeba-My Story*. New York, New African Library, 1987.

Makwenda, Cecilia Joyce. "Zimbabwean Contemporary Music in the 1940s to the 1960s." In a Paper Read at the Audio-Visual Archives Conference, Fayum Sweden, 1st -15th July, 1990.

Nketia J. H. K. "African Music: An Evaluation of Concepts and Processes." In *Music in Ghana*, Vol. 2 May 1961: 1–35.

—. "The Instrumental Resources of African Music." In *Papers in African Studies*. Institute of African Studies: University of Ghana, Legon No. 3 1968: 1–23.

Oakley, Giles. *The Devil's Music: A History of the Blues*. London: Ariel Books, BBC, 1983.

Oliver, Paul, Max Harrison, and William Basson eds. *The New Grove Gospel, Blues and Jazz*. New York: W. W. Norton and Company, 1986,.

Omibiye-Obidike, M. A. "Women on Popular Music in Nigeria." In a Paper at the 4th International Conference of IASPM (International Association for the Study of Popular Music), Accra between 12th – 19th of August, 1987.

Ottenberg, Simon. "The Analysis of an African Play." In *Institute of African Studies Research Review* 7 (5) 1971.

Roberts, John Storm. *Black Music of Two Worlds*. New York: William Morrow and Company, 1974.

Sutherland, Efua. *The Original Bob: The Story of Bob Johnson, Ghana's Ace Comedian*. Accra: Anowuo Educational Publications, 1970.

Turnbull, Colin M. *The Forest People*. New York: Touchstone Books; Simon and Schuster, 1962.

Van Oven, Coetje. *An Introduction to the Music of Sierra Leone*. Published by the Ministry of Development Cooperation of the Netherlands, 1981.

Waterman, Christopher. "Juju: The Historical Development, Socio-Economic Organisation and Communicative Function of a West African Popular Music." Ph.D Thesis, Department of Anthropology, University of Illinois, 1966.

Yankah, Kwesi. "The Akan Highlife Song: A Medium for Cultural Reflection or Deflection?" In *Research in African Literatures* 15 (4) 1984: 29–42.

Zuesee, Evan M. *Ritual Cosmos: The Sanctification of Life in African Religions*. Ohio: University Athens Press, 1979.

References for Mlama: "Empowerment for Gender Equality Through Theatre: The case of Tuseme"

1997 – 2003. *Tuseme* Project. *Tuseme* Workshop Reports. Department of Fine and Performing Arts, University of Dar es Salaam, Dar es Salaam.

1999 – Materego, G. An Impact Assessment of the *Tuseme* Project 1997/98. Department of Fine and Performing Arts, University of Dar es Salaam, Dar es Salaam.

2001– FAWE, FAWE Centre of Excellence. *Case Studies from Kenya, Rwanda, Senegal and Tanzania*, FAWE, Nairobi.

2001 – *Tuseme* Project – School Visits. Bagamoyo Secondary School, Department of Fine and Performing Arts, University of Dar es salaam, Dar es Salaam.

2002 – Bakari, J. and Flodin C. *Evaluation of the Children's Theatre Project and the Education for Democracy Theatre Project in Secondary Schools*. Tuseme, SIDA, Stockholm.

2002 – FAWE, Quest for Quality Education: Transforming an Ordinary School into a FAWE Centre of Excellence: FAWE, Nairobi.

2002 – FAWE, Workshop on Girls' Education. FAWE Girls' School, Kigali, Rwanda, FAWE, Nairobi.

2004 – FAWE, FAWE Centres of Excellence – "Creating a Conducive School Environment: Kenya, Rwanda, Senegal, Tanzania." In *Best Practices in Girls' Education in Africa*, FAWE, Nairobi.

2004 – Makoye, H. *"Tuseme Let Us Speak Out."* In *Best Practices in Girls' Education in Africa*, FAWE, Nairobi.

2004 – Miali Centre. Report on Empowerment Workshop for Mgugu Centre for Excellence. Miali, Dar es Salaam.

Notes to Komasi: "Efua Theodora Sutherland: Visionary Pioneer of Ghanaian Children's Literature"

1   The July 1976 and September 1984 Seminars for Playwrights.

2   It should be noted, however, that Ghanaian children are familiar with nursery rhymes in their own languages.

3   Ghanaian children are already familiar with nursery rhymes in their own languages. These L1 rhymes have parallel benefits for children since they provide them with the requisite foundation upon which Sutherland's poems build.

References

Achebe, Chinua. "The Novelist as Teacher." In *Morning Yet on Creation Day*. London: Heinemann, 1975: 45.

Angmor, Charles. *Contemporary Literature in Ghana – 1911–1978: A Critical Evaluation*. Accra: Woeli Publishing Services, 1996: 39–43.

Anyidoho, Kofi. "National Identity and the Language of Metaphor." In *Fontomfrom: Contemporary Ghanaian Literature, Theatre and Film*. Kofi Anyidoho and James Gibbs eds. Amsterdam-Atlanta GA: Rodopi, 2000: 79

Casely Hayford, J. E. *Ethiopia Unbound*. London: Frank Cass, 1969 : 17.

de Graft Hanson, J. O. *Children's Literature: The Ghanaian Experience*. Accra: Ghana Academy of Arts and Sciences, 1993: 17.

Khorana, Meena ed. *Critical Perspectives on Postcolonial African Children's and Young Adult Literature*. Westport, Connecticut: Greenwood Press, 1998: 2.

Nichols, Lee. *Conversations with African Writers*. Washington D.C.: VOA, 1981 279.

Sekyi, Kobina. *The Blinkards*. London, Rex Collings 1974: xxii.

Sutherland, Efua. *Playtime in Africa*. London: Brown, Knight & Truscott, 1960.

—. *The Roadmaker*, London: Neame Ltd,1961.

—. *Vulture! Vulture!* and *Tahinta*. Accra: Ghana Publishing Corporation, 1968.

—. "Textbooks for the Study of Ghanaian Languages." In Brinie, J. R. and Ansre G eds. *Proceedings of the Conference on the Study of Ghanaian Languages. University of Ghana, Legon*. Tema: Ghana Publishing Corporation, 1969: 30. (http://ctreview.southernct.edu/essays/spring98essays/bailey.html) Site Visited 20.09.04.

Notes to Sutherland-Addy: "Creating for and with Children: Efua Sutherland's Children's Plays"

1   *Playtime in Africa* was illustrated with photographs of Ghanaian children at play taken by veteran photographer, Willis Bell (1924 – 2000).

2   VALCO is an aluminium smelting plant set up by Kaiser Engineering Company in the early 1960s.This enterprise established an independent trust fund which has established a reputation for supporting educational causes.

3   These studies have been documented in the form of field reports and a compendium of photographs. Reports include "Child Rearing in Nzema" (1975) by Egya-Blay, "Lobi Gonja/Vagla/Safalba and Frafra Games" (1975) collected by Abubakar Von Salifu.

4   The Ghana Drama Studio was established by Sutherland in down-town Accra in 1958. The building was constructed with funding from the Sloan, Ford and Rockefeller Foundations and inaugurated in 1960. It served for many years as the hub and the cutting edge for drama in Ghana. It was demolished at the beginning of the 1990s to give way to the National Theatre. It was subsequently rebuilt on the Campus of the University of Ghana and was named The Efua Sutherland Drama Studio in 1999 .

5   Among plays written are *The Perpetual Stone Mill* by Sebastian Kwamuar, *Ghana Motion* by R. A. Cantey, *Akpokplo* by Kofi Anyidoho, *Hwe No Yie* by Kwamena Ampah,*The New Born Child* and *The Maid Servant* by Koku Amuzu, *A Bench of Chances* By Kofi Hiheta and *Gates to Mothe'* by Joe Manu-Amponsah.

6   Abu Abarry discusses the structure of play songs by Ghanaian children in his article, "The Role of Playsongs in the Moral Social and Emotional Development of African Children," published in *Mapping Intersections: African Literature and Africa's Development*, edited by Anne V. Adams and Janis A. Mayes. African World Press: Trenton New Jersey, 1998.

7   This terminology is taken from a set of bullet points in notes discovered among Sutherland's papers on Children's Education of the Drama Composer.

8   Isidore Okpewho describes these techniques in his book , *African Oral Literature*, 1992; see pp.78–83.

References

Abarry, A. "The Role of Playsongs in the Moral, Social and Emotional Development of African Children." In Anne V. Adams and Janis A. Mayes ,eds, *Mapping Intersections: African Literature and Africa's Development*. Trenton, New Jersey: Africa World Press, 1998.

Anyidoho, K. and Gibbs, James eds. *Fontomfrom, Contemporary Ghanaian, Literature, Theatre and Film: Matatu 21–22.* Amsterdam-Atlanta GA: Rodopi::2000:

Okpewho, Isidore. *African Oral Literature*, Bloomington, Indiana University Press, 1992.

Sunderland, E. T. (with Willis Bell, Photographer). *Playtime in Africa*. London. Brown, Knight and Truscott, 1960.

—. *Ananse and The Dwarf Brigade*. Unpublished Manuscript, Accra, *c*.1975.

—. "The Playwright's Opportunity in Drama For Our Children." Unpublished Paper. Seminar on Writing and Production of Literature for Children's Institute of African Studies, University of Ghana, Legon, 1976.

—. *Tweedledum and Tweedledee*. Unpublished Manuscript. Accra, *c.* 1976.

—. *Children of the Man-Made Lake*. In Anyidoho, K. & Gibbs, J. eds. *Fontomfrom: Contemporary Ghanaian Literature, Theatre and Film*, Amsterdam-Atlanta GA: Rodopi, 2000.

Note to Martini: "Meshack Asare: Transforming Folklore into Children's Literature"

1   Meshack Asare, 'Oral Tradition and Reality: The Place of History and Mythology in African Children's Literature'; lecture given in Oslo at the Centre for Afrikansk Kulturformidling, 23rd September, 1997, p.5 of MS.

Interview with Meshack Asare 29 January 2005

References

Asare, Meschack. *Tawia Goes to Sea*. Accra: Ghana Publishing Corporation, 1970.

—. *I Am Kofi*, Accra, Ghana Publishing Corporation, 1971.

—. *Mansa Helps at Home*, Accra, Ghana Publishing Corporation, 1971.

—. *The Brassman's Secret*. Accra: Educational Press 1981; Full Colour Edition, Legon, Accra: Sub-Saharan Publishers, 2002.

—. *The Canoe's Story*. Accra, Miracle Bookhouse Ltd, 1982.

—. *Chipo and the Bird on the Hill*. Harare: Zimbabwe Publishing House, 1984.

—. *Die Katze sucht sich einen Freund*. Wien: Jungbrunnen, 1984.

—. *Cat in Search of a Friend*. New York: Kane/Miller Bookpublishers, 1986.

—. *Seeing the World*. Tema, Ghana Publishing Corporation, 1989.

—. *Children of the Omumborombonga Tree*. German edition Göttingen: Lamuv; African edition published simultaneously in Windhoek, 1990.

—. *Halima*. London and Basingstoke: Macmillan, 1992.

—. *The Magic Goat*. Legon, Accra: Sub-Saharan Publishers, 1997.

—. *Sosu's Call*. Legon, Accra: Sub-Saharan Publishers, 1997.

—. *Cat in Search of a Friend*, Legon, Accra, Sub-Saharan Publishers, 2000.

—. *Meliga's Day*, Legon, Accra: Sub-Saharan Publishers, 2000.

—. *Nana's Son*. Legon, Accra: Sub-Saharan Publishers, 2000.

—. *Noma's Sand*. Legon, Accra: Sub-Saharan Publishers, 2002.

—. *Ighewi's Return*. Oxford: Macmillan Education, 2004.

Illustrations by Meschack Asare

Fairman, Tony. (Reteller). *Bury My Bones but Keep My Words*. New York: Holt and Company, 1991.

(Cover for) Granqvist, Raoul and Jürgen Martini eds. *Preserving the Landscape of Imagination: Children's Literature in Africa*, Amsterdam: Rodopi, 1997.

Mawngi, Meja. *The Hunter's Dream*. London and Basingstoke: Macmillan, 1993.

Research in African Literatures Vol. 17 1986. University of Texas Press.

Essays by Meshack Asare

Asare, Meshack. "Kinderliteratur in Afrika: Ursprünge and Gegenwart." IJB Report, 1984: 3–8.

—. "The African Writer in the Child's World." Sierra Leone Library Board, ed. *Proceedings of the Seminar on Creative Writing and Publishing for Children in Africa Today*, Freetown, 1983: 13–19.

—. "The Oral Tradition and Children's Literature in Ghana." Deutsche UNESCO-Kommission ed. *African Youth Literature Today and Tomorrow*. Bonn, 1986: 42–49 [German Version In: Der Überblick 3 1986:72–75]

—. "Writing for Children in Africa." In James Gibbs ed. *A Handbook for African Writers*. Oxford London; Munchen: K.G. Saur, 1986: 80–85.

References

de Graft Hanson, J. O. *Children's Literature: The Ghanaian Experience*, Accra: 1993.

Martini, Jürgen. "Der Autor als sankofa-Vogel." *Fundevogel* 24 1986: 14–17.

—. "Meshack Asare." *Beitrage zur Kinder-und Jugendliteratur* 85 1987: 42–49.

—. "The African Literary Community – A View from Outside." In Deutsche UNESCO-Kommission, Hg. *African Youth Literature Today and Tomorrow*. Bonn, 1988: 111–120.

—. "The Author as Sankofa-Bird: History in African Books for Children and Young People." *Matatu* 1 1987: 35–52.

Schmidt, Nancy. "Award-Winning Children's Books." In Meena Khorana ed. *Critical Perspectives on Postcolonial African Children's and Young Adult Literature*, Westport, Connecticut: Greenwood Press, 1998: 27–44.

Notes to Adams: "Revis(it)ing Ritual: The Challenge to the Virility of Tradition in Works by Efua Sutherland and 'Fellow' African Women Writers"

1 Werewere Liking, *Elle Sere de Jaspe et de Corai. Journal d'une Misovire*. Paris: L'Harmattan, 1983.
2 Aminata Sow Fall. *Le Jujubier du Patriarche*. Dakar: Editions Khoudia, 1993.
3 Efua Sutherland, "New Life at Kyerefaso." In *An African Treasury*. Langston Hughes ed. London: Victor Gollancz, 1961.
4 Efua Sutherland. *Foriwa*, Accra: State Publishing Corporation, 1967: 23. Further page references are in the text.

References

Aidoo, Christina Ama Ata. *The Dilemma of a Ghost*. New York: Collier Books, 1965.

—. *Anowa*, London: Longman, 1970.

Ajayi, Omofolabo. "Who Can Silence Her Drums? An Analysis of the Plays of Tess Onwueme." In Jane Plastow ed. *African Theatre Women*. Bloomington: Indiana University Press, 2002: 109–121.

Amuta, Chidi. "The Nigerian Woman as Dramatist: The Instance of Tess Onwueme." In Henrietta C. Otokunefor and Obiageli C. Nwodo eds. *Nigerian Female Writer: A Critical Perspective*. Lagos: Malthouse Press, 1989.

Bascom, William R. *African Dilemma Tale*. The Hague: Mouton, 1975.

Berrian, Brenda. "The Afro-American-West African Marriage Question: Its Literary and Historical Contexts." In *Women in African Literature Today* (*African Literature Today* Vol.15) Trenton: Africa World Press, 1987: 152–159.

Dunton, Chris. "Nigeria and the Diaspora, Solidarities and Discords: The Drama of Osonye Tess Onwueme." In Toyin Falola ed. *Nigeria in the Twentieth Century*. Durham: Carolina Academic Press, 2002: 791–797.

Eke, Maureen. "Diasporic Ruptures and (Re)Membering History: Africa as Home and Exile in *Anowa* and *The Dilemma of a Ghost*." In Ada Uzoamaka Azodo and Gay Wilentz eds. *Emerging Perspectives on Ama Ata Aidoo*. Trenton, NJ, Africa World Press, 1999: 61–78.

Gilroy, Paul. *The Black Atlantic: Modernity and Double Consciousness*. Cambridge: Harvard University Press, 1993.

Gourdine, Angeletta K. M. *The Difference Place Makes: Gender, Sexuality, and Diaspora Identit.* Columbus: Ohio State University Press, 2002.

James, Adeola. "Ama Ata Aidoo." In Adeola James ed. *In Their Own Words: African Women Writers' Talk*. London: James Currey, 1990: 8–27.

Odamtten, Vincent. *The Art of Ama Ata Aidoo: Polylectics and Reading Against Neocolonialism*, Gainesville, University of Florida Press, 1994.

Onwueme, Tess. *The Missing Face: Black Drama* [an Electronic Resource]. Alexander Street Press, L.L.C, 1997.

—. *The Missing Face: Musical Drama for the Voices of Colour*, New York: Africana Legacy Press, 1997.

Richards, Sandra L. "Writing the Absent Potential: Drama, Performance, and the Canon of African-American Literature." In Andrew Parker and Eve Kosofsky Sedgwick eds. *Performance and Performativity*. New York: Routledge, 1995: 64–88.

Sutherland, Efua Theodora. "The Second Phase of the National Theatre Movement in Ghana." In Anyidoho, K. and Gibbs J. eds. *Fontomfrom: Contemporary Ghanaian Literature, Theatre and Film*. Amsterdam & Atlanta GA: Rodopi, 2000: 45–57.

Notes to Richards: "Dramatising the Diaspora's Return: Tess Onwueme's The Missing Face and Ama Ata Aidoo's The Dilemma of a Ghost"

1   (http://www.postcolonialweb.org/africa/ghana/aidoo/aidoobio.html), accessed 30 July 2004.

2   Note that *A Raisin in the Sun* had been produced in Ghana by 1963, though I don't know whether Aidoo had seen this production.

3   In a 1986 interview with Adeola James, Aidoo said of her drama experiences: "I am happiest with drama. Given some other circumstances I would have liked to write more plays....I stopped writing plays deliberately because somehow I had not managed to get *Anowa* produced before it was published....I told myself, I would write plays again only when there was a chance of getting the play produced before publication."

4   http://www.ex.ac.uk/~ajsimoes/aflit/AidooEN.html, accessed 30 July 2004.

5   http://www.bbc.co.uk/worldservice/arts/features/womenwriters/aidoo_next.shtml, accessed 30 July 2004.

6   http://www.writertess.com/education.htm, accessed 30 July 2004.

7   http://www.writertess.com/professional_appointments.htm, accessed 30 July 2004.

8   The page numbers cited here are approximate and correspond to, I believe, from where this electronic version has been produced.

9   On the iconic quality of Onwueme's plays, see Dunton; Chidi Amuta, who terms her a "symbolist dramatist"; or in a similar vein, Ajayi, who begins her essay by characterising

Onwueme as "a talented, socially committed and serious political writer" and asserts that Onwueme's plays "ask individuals, nations and international communities to turn a searchlight on themselves and conduct a critical self-appraisal" 109.

10 One should note, however, that marriage in many instances simply marginalises women in a different way, for the woman may go from being a daughter in her father's male-privileged house to a wife in her husband's male-dominated home/family. See Maureen Eke who cites Chikwenye Ogunyemi on this point.

11 I should note that not only do many Diasporans hope to find a home, but locals oftentimes seem eager to satisfy that longing through naming ceremonies that are part of many tourist packages.

12 Though diasporic audiences obviously have different perspectives from that of Aidoo's local spectators, it is important to note multiple positions within a Ghanaian audience itself: some of them, like the Ashanti and Fanti, in the south were deeply involved in the slave trade, and, through sustained interactions with Westerners, positioned to become an emerging elite at the time of independence, while others in the northern and more interior areas are the descendants of victims of the trade.

Notes to Lemly: "Hesitant Homecomings in Hansberry's and Aidoo's First Plays"

1 Ama Ata Aidoo. "Ghana: To Be a Woman." In *Sisterhood is Global*. Robin Morgan ed. New York: Anchor Doubleday, 1985: 262.

2 Edward Said. "Mind of Winter: Reflections on Life in Exile." *Harpers Magazine*. September 1984: 54.

3 Efua Sutherland. "The Second Phase of the National Theatre Movement in Ghana." Rpt. In *FonTomFrom: Contemporary Ghanaian Literature, Theater and Film*. Kofi Anyidoho and James Gibbs eds. Amsterdam: Rodopi 2000: 55. In Sutherland's list of Arts Programmes, 1956–65, Hansberry's is one of very few plays from America.

4 Hansberry tells of her own family's "fighting white supremacy in America" in *To Be Young, Gifted and Black: Lorraine Hansberry in Her Own Words*, adapted by Robert Nemiroff. Englewood Cliffs: Prentice-Hall, 1969: 20–21. Hereafter cited as YGB.

5 Nelson Algren, quoted in Julius Lester's Introduction to *Les Blancs: The Collected Last Plays of Lorraine Hansberry*. New York; Random House, 1972: 5. Hereafter cited as L. B. Lester recalls that weeks before his murder even Malcolm X himself was purchasing a house in the suburbs, "bourgeois aspirations" notwithstanding (9). Cf. Harold Cruse's claim that *Raisin* is a "cleverly written piece of glorified soap opera," in *The Crisis of the Negro Intellectual*. New York: William Morrow, 1967: 278.

6 "Make New Sounds: Studs Terkel Interviews Lorraine Hansberry." *American Theatre*. November 1984: 41.

7 *A Raisin in the Sun*. New York: Random House, 1994: 134. All references to this edition, by act and page.

8 "The Negro Writer and His Roots: Toward a New Romanticism." *Black Scholar* 12.2 1981:, 6; quoted in Steven Carter. *Hansberry's Drama: Commitment amid Complexity*. Urbana: U. of Illinois Press, 1991: 36. Cf. her "oneness with the African peoples and their struggle for liberation" in John Killens "Lorraine Hansberry: On Time!" *Freedomways* 19.4 1979: 273.

9 See also "An Author's Reflections: Walter Lee Younger, Willy Loman and He Who Must Live." *Village Voice* 4. 42 August 23, 1959: 7–8.

10 *The Dilemma of a Ghost and Anowa*. Harlow, U.K.: Longman, 1987. Cited hereafter by act and page number.

11 *The Art of Ama Ata Aidoo: Polylectics and Reading Against Neocolonialism*. Gainesville: University Press of Florida, 1994: 41.

12 Cf. Walter's difficulty until the end; e.g. *"He can say nothing,"* when confronted with Ruth's intended abortion at the end of Act 1 (75). Ato and Eulalie's ambivalence about having a child constitutes their most baffling affront to his family throughout Aidoo's play.

13 *The Souls of Black Folk.* In *Three Negro Classics.* New York: Avon Books, 1965: 361.

14 "Ama Ata Aidoo's Orphan Ghosts: African Literature and Aesthetic Postmodernity." *Research in African Literatures* 34.4 Winter 2003: 86.

15 Brenda Berrian, "The Afro-American-West African Marriage Question: Its Literary and Historical Contexts." *African Literature Today* 15 1987: 152–59, earlier noted the parallels between the two plays, but focused largely on the prospects of such marriages. See also Anne Adams. "Literary Pan-Africanism." *Thamyris/Intersection: Place, Sex & Race* 11.12003: 137–51.

16 *Our Sister Killjoy.* Harlow, U.K.: Longman, 1977. *No Sweetness Here and Other Stories.* New York: Feminist Press, 1995: 7. In Anuradha Dingwaney Needham, "An Interview with Ama Ata Aidoo," *Massachusets Review* 36.1 Spring 95: 123–33, Aidoo considers her own dilemma between "living in economic exile, even political exile, and the compromises those who live at home have to make in order to survive" 127.

17 Needham 127.

18 Letter to an American Studies Professor 3 Feb. 1959. In Carter. *Hansberry's Drama* 60. Cf. Walter Lee's ironically premature triumph, "Let the future begin!"II.iii;125.

19 *In Their Own Voices.* Adeola James ed. London: James Currey, 1990: 20–21.

20 Interview 6 March 1994; Accra.

21 *An Angry Letter in January and Other Poems.* Sydney: Dangaroo Press, 1992: 18–20.

22 Quoted in Robert July, *An African Voice: The Role of the Humanities in African Independence.* Durham: Duke University Press, 1987, 76. See also *Okyeame,* 4:1 December 1968 82. Cf. Bill Marshall's criticism of the new National Theatre: people "feel cowed by the very mass of the building .. . Me, too . . . I feel awed, like a dwarf . . . Going here, I become conscious I can't just walk in like that – you must give reverence to the place. Put on something nice, you're likely to meet the Minister for Information, and she shouldn't see you in a T-shirt." Interview10 February 1994, Accra.

23 Telephone interview 17 November 1994. See also James, *In Their Own Voices,* 22.

Notes to Busby: "Introduction" adapted from Daughters of Africa

1 Alice Walker, "Saving the Life That Is Your Own." *In Search of Our Mothers' Gardens: Womanist Prose.* New York: Harcourt Brace, 1983; London: Women's Press, 1984: 13.

2 Filomina Chioma Steady ed. *The Black Woman Cross-Culturally.* Cambridge, Mass.: Schenkman, 1981: 7.

3 Lauretta Ngcobo ed. *Let It Be Told: Black Women Writers in Britain.* London: Pluto Press, 1987: 2.

4 Edward Kamau Brathwaite. *History of the Voice: The Development of Nation Language in Anglophone Caribbean Poetry.* London: New Beacon Books, 1984: 7.

5 Ibid: 13.

6 Claudia Tate ed. *Black Women Writers at Work.* New York: Continuum, 1983; Harpenden, Herts: Oldcastle, 1985: 163.

7 Ibid: 164.

8 June Jordan. "White English/Black English: The Politics of Translation." *Moving Towards Home: Political Essay.* London: Virago, 1988: 34.

9 Ibid: 40.

10 John Newton. *The Journal of a Slave Trader 1759–1754.* Bernard Martin and Mark Spurrell ed. London: Epworth Press, 1962: 104.

11 W. J. Cash. *The Mind of the South*: New York, 194: 87.

12 H. Mattison. *Louisa Picquet, the Octorron: or Inside Views of Southern Domestic Life*, 1861: 18; New York/Oxford University Press, Schomburg Library of Nineteenth-Century Black Women Writers, 1988 (facsimile).

13 Ibid: xxxiv.

14 Peter Fryer. *Staying Power: The History of Black People in Britain*. London: Pluto, 1984: 373.

15 Beverly Bryan, Stella Dadzie, Suzanne Scafe. *Heart of the Race: Black Women's Lives in Britain*, London: Virago, 1985: 25.

16 *The Gentleman's Magazine* 34 1794: 483.

17 "Double Jeopardy: To Be Black and Female." In Toni Cade Bambara ed. *The Black Woman: An Anthology*. New York: Signet/NAL, 1970: 92.

18 "Multiple Jeopardy, Multiple Consciousness: The Context of a Black Feminist Ideology. In Micheline R. Malson., Elisabeth Mudimbe-Boyi, Jean F. O'Barr and Mary Wyer eds. *Black Women in America: Social Science Perspectives*, Chicago/London: University of Chicago Press, 1990: 277.

19 Ibid: 295.

20 Walker. *In Search of Our Mother's Gardens*: xi–xii.

21 Jeanne Noble. *Beautiful, Also, Are the Souls of My Black Sisters: A History of the Black Woman in America*. Englewood Cliffs, NJ: Prentice-Hall, 1978: 76.

22 Introduction to Mary Helen Washington. *Black-Eyed Susans: Classic Stories By and About Black Women*. Garden City, NY: Anchor/Doubleday, 1975: ix.

23 *Invented Lives: Narratives of Black Women 1860–1960*. Garden City, NY: Anchor/Doubleday, 1987, Introduction: xxi.

24 Adeola James ed.*In Their Own Voices: African Women Writers' Talk*. London: James Currey;Portsmouth, NH: Heinemann, 1990: 2.

25 Audre Lorde. "Scratching the Surface: Some Notes on Barriers to Women and Loving." In *Sister Outsider: Essays and Speeches*. Freedom, CA: The Crossing Press, 1984.

Editors' note to Gibbs: "Efua Theodora Sutherland: A Bibliographyof Primary Materials"

1 Prof. Gibbs' extensive bibliography has been augmented by the editors, primarily with the addition of posthumously produced publications and recordings of productions of some of Efua Sutherland's works for children.

Editors' note to Caulley Hanson: "The Ghana National Commission on Children"

1 That school is today known as Adisadel College.

Notes to Wellington: "Architecture: Spatial Deployment for Community Experience"

1 Literature review on the subject of 'Social Architecture' shows that by and large, most of the available material is terse and seemingly remote to the African socio-cultural realities. Nonetheless, my interest in the subject has led me on to some exploratory research activities from which papers have been published to add to the growing literature. Refer e.g. "The Ashanti Black Ikons and Architecture in Ghana-Means to responsive African Architecture," published in the Horizon, maiden volume, July, 1996, Nairobi, Kenya; "Don't Take Them for Granted: A Plea to Cogitate upon the Child Factor in Urban Housing Design and Development in Ghana," presented for publication in "Children's Environments," New York, 1995.

2   A Design Colloquium was set up under the auspices of the Ghana National Commission on Children during the period Efua Sutherland was in office as Chairperson. One of the objectives for setting up of this colloquium was to convene scholars and professionals, who had indicated remarkable levels of consciousness of the inbuilt capacity of architecture to impact a positive development of society as manifested in their respective architectural thought and practice. They were brought together to harness their intellectual synergy to bring to bear on the development of child-related physical facilities in the country, especially, the Park-Library Complexes being undertaken by the Commission during Mrs. Efua T. Sutherland's tenure as the Chairperson.

3   Refer Cornelius Van de Ven's essay on "The theory of space in architecture," published in Ben Farmer and Hentie Louw: 357–360.

4   Refer Labelle Prussin's discussion on architecture as a bridge between culture and environment in her book *African Nomadic Architecture: Space, Place and Gender.* 1995: 22–24.

5   Rene Dubos alludes to this fact in his essay on "Our Buildings Shape Us," in the 2nd Edition of *Housing Perspectives: Individuals and Families* by Carol S. Wedin and L. Gertrude Nygren, 1979: 13. Furthermore, insightful discussion is made on this observation by Barrie B. Greenbie in his essay on "Harmonizing the Human Habitat" in Ben Farmer and Hentie Louw: 82–83.

6   For an exhaustive discussion of the significance of space in architectural design, refer to Ben Farmer and Hentie Louw: Chapters 15, 56, 57 and 59. For further reading on the subject with special reference to African architecture, the following sources can be consulted:

   i.   Bourdier, Jean-Paul/Minh-Ha, Trinh, *African Spaces:Designs for Living in Upper Volta.* Africana Publishing Company: New York, 1985.

   ii.   Oliver, Paul ed. *Shelter in Africa.* London: Barrie and Jenkins, 1978.

   iii. Sutherland, Ralph. "The Outdoor Room: A Study of the Use of Outdoor Space in Ghanaian Architecture." Unpublished M.Sc. Architecture Thesis, UST, Kumasi, 1981.

   iv.   Wellington, H. Nii-Adziri. "Fidua Architecture: An Ashanti Spatial Expression of Communality and Cosmology." A lecture delivered at the School of Fine Arts, Miami University, Oxford, Ohio, 1996.

   v.   Wilkes, Ivor. *Asante in the Nineteenth Century.* Cambridge: Cambridge University Press, 1975.

7   Although she never executed any known architectural design project in her lifetime, not having had any formal training in architecture, Efua Sutherland's intellectual and creative energies penetrated some notable architectural works in Ghana, discernible e.g. in her own house built at Dzorwulu, Accra; the razed Drama Studio in Accra; National Children's Park (named after her as a posthumous national honour); the Park Library Complex at Gomoa Brofoyedru and the Asanteman Children's Park, Kumasi.

8   The Position of Efua Sutherland vis-à-vis use of space is succinctly presented in a Memorandum titled, "The Official Condition for Permitting the Drama Studio Development on the Site it Occupies," Dated July, 1986 and addressed to the Acting Vice Chancellor of the University of Ghana. Writing of the Memo was occasioned by the PNDC Government's decision to demolish the old Drama Studio for the purpose of using the site to develop the National Theatre.

9   Describing the triumphant feeling of Foruwa in "New Life at Kyerefaso" in Charlotte Brunner ed. *Unwinding Thread: Writing by Women in Africa,* Efua Sutherland characteristically stated: "She burst through the *courtyard* gate; and there she stood in the *courtyard,* joy all over. And a stranger walked in after her and stood in the courtyard beside her, stood tall and strong as a *pillar*" 1983: 21; emphasis added. The importance of her allusion to an

architectural value of a space in the traditional house in this stated piece, cannot be lost on any one, who knows the mind of Efua Sutherland on architecture.

10 I was enchanted to hear Efua Sutherland reflect on the Ghanaian traditional courtyard at a workshop convened at the premises of the Ghana National Commission on Children in 1987. While brainstorming together with her and some professionals to evolve design guidelines for the Park Library Complex, she made us feel the poetics of architecture as she tried to explain some of the functions of the traditional courtyard in the moral, social and cultural upbringing of the child. By this effort, she endeavoured to challenge us as architects, to apply the Sankofa principle of going back to borrow ideas from some of the Ghanaian traditional architectural concepts.

11 The author is the architect for the Asanteman Children's Park. Besides Dr. (Mrs.) Efua Sutherland, as the then Chairperson of the Ghana National Commission on Children, he also collaborated with the Commission's Regional Co-ordinator, Ms. Juliana Kwatemah, who provided all the details regarding the objectives and programmes of the Commission for the Ashanti Region.

References

Appleyard, D. *Planning a Pluralist City*. Cambridge, Mass: MIT Press, 1976.

Farmer, Ben and Hentie Louw eds. *Companion to Contemporary Architectural Thought*. London, Routledge, 1993.

Ghana National Commission on Children. Project Design Brief. Accra, 1987.

Glover, Ablade. E. *Adinkra Symbolism Chart*. Accra, Artists Alliance, 1993.

Majodina, M. Z. *Kyekyewere Study Vol. 2* – "Growing up in Kyekyewere." Accra: Ghana National Commission on Children, 1998.

Mumford, Lewis. *The City in History*. New York: Harcourt, Brace and World, 1961.

Muschamp, Herbert. *File Under Architecture*. Cambridge, Mass: MIT Press, 1974.

Nuttgens, Patrick. "The Nature of Architecture." In Farmer, Ben and Hentie Lou eds.

Prussin, Labelle. *African Nomadic Architecture: Space, Place and Gender*. Washington and London: Smithsonian Institute Press and The National Museum of African Art, 1993.

Shepheard, Paul. *What is Architecture?: An Essay on Landscapes, Buildings, and Machines*. Cambridge, Mass: MIT Press, 1995.

Sutherland, Efua T. "The Playwright's Opportunity in Drama for our Children."

Unpublished Paper. Seminar on Writing and Production of Literature for Children's Institute of African Studies, University of Ghana, Legon, 1976.

Wellington, N. N. A. Significance of the Architectural Space in the Development Process of the African Child, Benin City: OMEP Congress, 1988.

Notes to Osofisan interview: "There's a Lot of Strength in Our People"

1 Maya Angelou, in her famous book about her stay in Ghana entitled *All God's Children Need Travelling Shoes*. New York Vintage Books: 11, gives the following description of Efua Sutherland at their first meeting: "Efua Sutherland could have passed for the original bust of Nefertiti. She was long, lean, Black and lovely (and) wore an impervious air as obvious as a strong perfume…"

2 This is the famous march on Washington led by Rev. Dr. Martin Luther King Jr. on August 27, 1963.

3 The 5th Pan-African Congress in Manchester in 1945, over which Dr. W. E. B. Du Bois was invited to preside. Dr. Du Bois had been instrumental in organising the previous Congresses, right from the very first one in Paris in 1919.

4 The Pan-African Writers' Association, with headquarters in Accra, of which Atukwei

Okai is the Secretary General and Osofisan the Vice-President, West Africa.

5   Ama Ata Aidoo's poem is entitled, "In Memoriam: The Ghana Drama Studio."

Editors' note to McMullan: "Tommy":

1   The Clifts are the family which adopted Efua as a brilliant young student through Sister Dorothy, a member of the family, who had been sent by the Order of the Holy Paraclete to the Gold Coast to engage in missionary work.

Note to Branch: "Efua Theodora Sutherland: A Personal Reflection"

1   A record of Dr. Du Bois' state funeral was published in the New York *Amsterdam News*, Sept. 7, 1963: 1, and later recounted in Chapter One of Dr. David Levering Lewis' book, *W. E .B. Du Bois: Biography of a Race*. N.Y., Holt, 1963, which was awarded the 1964 Pulitzer Prize for Biography.

Note to Busby: "Obituary"

1   27th January 1996: *The Guardian*, London: 28.

INDEX

ACKNOWLEDGEMENTS

The following essays appear previously in *Fontomfrom: Contemporary Ghanaian Literature, Theatre and Film*. Kofi Anyidoho and James Gibbs eds. Amsterdam-Atlanta GA: Rodopi, 2000.

Adams, Anne V. "Revis(it)ing Ritual: The Challenge to the Virility of Tradition in Works by Efua Sutherland and 'Fellow' African Women Writers," appears with a slight change of title, as

Adams, Anne V. "Revis(it)ing Ritual: The Challenge to the Virility of Tradition in Works by Efua Sutherland and Other African Women Writers.": 85–94.

Anyidoho, Kofi. "Mother Courage (A Tribute to Auntie Efua From All Her Children in the Arts).": 83–84.

Anyidoho, Kofi. "Dr Efua Sutherland: A Biographical Sketch.": 77–81.

Gibbs, James. "Efua Theodora Sutherland: A Bibliography of Primary Materials, with a Checklist of Secondary Sources.": 117–23.

Sutherland-Addy, Esi. "Creating For and With Children: Efua Sutherland's Children's Plays," appeared earlier as

Sutherland-Addy, Esi. "Creating For and With Children In Ghana: Efua Sutherland, A Retrospective." In M. Etherton ed. *African Theatre 6*. Oxford: James Currey 2006: 1–15.